# PILOT OF FORTUNE

© 2009 Ted Beaudoin. All rights reserved. No part of this book may be scanned, copied, uploaded or reproduced in any form or by any means, photographically, electronically or mechanically, without written permission from the copyright holder.

Second Edition
September, 2016

ISBN 978-1-943492-17-6 (hard back)
ISBN 978-1-943492-19-0 (soft cover)

Book and cover design by **designpanache**

**Elm Grove Publishing**
San Antonio, Texas, USA
www.elmgrovepublishing.com

# Pilot of Fortune

**The extraordinary true-life adventures of aviation pioneer and trailblazer Sheldon Luck**

## Ted Beaudoin

### What readers said about the first edition of *Pilot of Fortune*

"...an amazing book...
I strongly recommend Pilot of Fortune to all Canadian schools and to anyone interested in Canadian Aviation."

*– Stan Taylor*
*Member, Editorial Committee*
*Science Teachers Association of Ontario*

"...a must read for anyone interested in flying...
Mr. Beaudoin successfully weaves the biography of a man who is truly a pilot of fortune into the fabric of Canadian history and the prominent role that aviation has played in it."

*– James Griffith*
*Retired 747 captain, Air Canada*

## Dedication

I dedicated the original book, first published in 1986 in Vernon, BC, Canada, as *Walking on Air*, to the memory of Sinclair Stanley McLean, my late father-in-law and Laura Rix-McLean, my late mother-in-law.

To this new second print edition, I add the following dedications:

Fernand Beaudoin and Gilberte Trottier-Beaudoin, my deceased parents, d. 2001 and d. 2003 respectively, and my youngest sister, Anne, d. 2002.

**This book would not be complete without a poem dedicated to every man, woman and child who aspires to flight ...**

## High Flight

by P/O John Gillespie Magee RCAF

Oh! I have slipped the surly bonds of Earth
And danced the skies on laughter-silvered wings;
Sunward I've climbed, and joined the tumbling mirth
Of sun-split clouds, - and done a hundred things
You have not dreamed of - wheeled and soared and swung
High in the sunlit silence. Hov'ring there,
I've chased the shouting wind along, and flung
My eager craft through footless halls of air....

Up, up the long, delirious, burning blue
I've topped the wind-swept heights with easy grace
Where never lark, nor even eagle flew -
And, while with silent, lifting mind I've trod
The high untrespassed sanctity of space,
Put out my hand, and touched the face of God.

# Contents

Dedication ................................................................. v

High Flight ................................................................ vi

Preface to Second Edition ............................................ 8

Introduction ............................................................... 9

1. A Fistful of Firsts ................................................. 13
2. Hopes and Headlines .......................................... 41
3. Search and Rescue and other Mercy Missions ........... 77
4. All for Laughs ..................................................... 93
5. Who Influenced Whom? ..................................... 117
6. Visions in Conflict ............................................. 149
7. Spooling up for Ferry Command ......................... 179
8. Ferry Command in Flight ................................... 199
9. 231 Telecommunications Squadron, Royal Air Force ................................................. 227
10. Pilot of Fortune ................................................ 237
11. Challenges Continue – from Freelancing to Flying Firefighter .......................................... 275
12. Father Dies on Take-off, Son Becomes Instant Solo Pilot ............................................. 285

Epilogue .................................................................. 295

Acknowledgements .................................................. 307

Select Bibliography ................................................. 309

## Preface to Second Edition

It's often said that it's a small world. Sometimes as small as a book page.

This happened to me when I was considering a second edition of *Pilot of Fortune*.

Out of the blue, while rereading the manuscript for the umpteenth time, Monte Engleson of Vancouver Island in British Columbia contacted me.

Monte, a fine writer in his own right, and possessing a wicked sense of humor, introduced himself by informing me that he had a cameo role in the original version of my book when it was first published as *Walking on Air*.

Since he had no way of knowing that I was in the process of preparing the book for reprinting as a second edition, he certainly got my attention. The coincidence was astounding. Stumped for a reply, as those who know me will testify that this is a rare occurrence, I eventually managed to ask him to explain himself.

It turns out that Monte had come across a copy of *Walking on Air* among his mother's possessions. He read it, said that he enjoyed it and wanted to let me know of his connection, via his mother, to one of the anecdotes.

So how did he find me? Any why?

He mentioned Sheldon Luck to another well-known Canadian author and friend of his, Leslie Kopas. It turned out that Kopas also interviewed Sheldon Luck later in his life. Sheldon told him about me. Another remarkable coincidence!

As to why Monte tracked me down: without giving away too much of the story, Monte was the as yet unborn child of Mrs. Anna Engleson who Sheldon was attempting to fly to hospital in time for Monte's arrival (see page 111 in this new edition: *Two women, one man, one sleeping bag and a few mice do not comfort make*).

That was in 1939.

Actually, it's a good job Monte's appearance was just a small cameo. Had it been more of a "walk-on" part it could have caused even more problems for Sheldon - and turned into a whole chapter of its own!

Hearing from Monte was one of those wonderful moments when you just know you're doing the right thing. If there had ever been any doubts in my mind about reprinting *Pilot of Fortune*, hearing from Monte dispelled them.

I hope you will enjoy these stories as much as I have enjoyed visiting and revisiting them over the years.

*– Ted Beaudoin*
*Welland, Ontario, Canada*
*September, 2016*

## Introduction

This book stems from one previously written and first published with the title, *Walking on Air*.

It is now, as it was then, a biography, an aviation adventure, and a civilian and military aviation history book which came together in 1986 in Vernon, BC, Canada.

It is a compilation of vignettes and highlights woven around the fabric put together over a 50-year aviation career of one of the world's finest pilots ever – Sheldon Luck, who was the first chief pilot of a now gone international airline of Canada, Canadian Pacific Air Lines.

The first edition came out as a 300-page high-quality paperback book with but one illustration, sold more than 4,800 copies - most of them west of Winnipeg, Manitoba, Canada. At that time, it fell just short of being a Canadian best-seller by 200 copies.

But, that is history. Water under the bridge.

Interestingly, the first edition is still for sale through some internet pages in different countries. I had no idea that a book such as this one was would have such a long shelf life.

This second edition came together where I now live, in Welland, Ontario, Canada, throughout September and October, 2008 as I completed research for the sequels.

*Pilot of Fortune* is a collage of men, women, accidents and incidents spinning about the life of the first chief pilot of Canadian Pacific Air Lines.

He was the late Sheldon Luck, inducted into Canada's Aviation Hall of Fame in 1982. It is a collection of anecdotes and memories of men, women and companies who influenced him, and those he may have influenced.

It's often said that the stereotype "macho" guy as portrayed by the Hollywood view of things is not really representative of the heroes of the world in which we live, especially where adventure is concerned.

At times, Hollywood is bang-on.

Imagine the central characters in *Raiders of the Lost Ark,* and in *Romancing the Stone,* for example; or go back some years to the kind of pilot John Wayne played in *The High and the Mighty.* As unreal as they may seem on the silver screen, these dauntless fictional heroes of the air are based on real life characters.

Most often, these adventurous airborne swash-bucklers are composite personalities - molded under creative licence by writers who study their biographies, review headlines made by barnstormers, and who review the articles and books spawned by their derring-do exploits ever since humanity first flew heavier-than-air machines at Kill Devil Hill in North Carolina in 1903.

Canadians can consider themselves fortunate to have had, and still have, some of the men and women of the type highlighted in such movies.

Many sturdy, interesting and adventurous Canadian aviation pioneers have come and gone - folded their wings - since Canada first took to the air in Baddeck, Nova Scotia, on February 23rd in 1909, with the Aerial Experiment Association's *Silver Dart* - a group of intrepid pioneers led by Dr. Alexander Graham Bell.

Some of Canada's aviation pioneers are still living and many are commemorated in Canada's Hall of Fame, which is located near Edmonton, Alberta,

Two of these pioneers helped lay the foundation for an international airline.

One is Sheldon Luck, born in Kingston, Ontario, Canada, on January 26th, 1911, when Canadian aviation was still in its infancy. He folded his wings 93 years later, on May 9th,

*William Floyd Sheldon Luck.*
© *Copyright, reproduced with permission from the late Ms Irma Coucill, from a drawing of members of Canada's Aviation Hall of Fame*

2004. The sketch pictured on the previous page is the official artist's rendering from a photograph which hangs in Canada's Aviation Hall of Fame.

The second Canadian aviation pioneer is Grant McConachie, who created the foundations for what became Canadian Pacific Air Lines. Grant died in California, in 1965.

In March 1942 the *Saturday Evening Post* ran a photograph of Sheldon and Grant stating that they built Canadian Pacific Air Lines out of baling wire.

Grant has frequently been mislabelled the founder of CPAL, when in actuality he was the founder of one of the 10 regional air services which went into the fabric of CPAL.

Nevertheless, he became CPAL's first fiery, hard bargain-driving and outspoken president.

In 1949, a Canadian magazine, *Maclean's*, also featured Sheldon and Grant, under seemingly less friendly and more strained circumstances.

Nearly forty years later, in December 1982, Sheldon Luck made headlines again - this time in a *Reader's Digest* article written by Ly Schuyler, under the heading: "Sheldon Luck - Pilot for All Seasons." The brief descriptive paragraph by the editors before story reads:

> *"In half a century's flying over bush, ocean and Arctic tundra, his extraordinary skill and good fortune have made him a living legend."*

In their careers, both men made headlines with remarkable regularity, although Grant McConachie did receive far more attention than did Sheldon from the public media and aviation publications.

As the Saturday Evening Post article stated, Sheldon and Grant truly did help build Canadian Pacific Air Lines out of baling wire in its critical formative years, even before it got its name.

They had a lot of help in the process and this book brings to life the identities and characteristics of some of the many men and women who gave them the necessary boost to create a money-making international airline.

Without a doubt, Grant McConachie was an aviation giant, but in his shadow was his sometimes unheralded buddy, and first Chief pilot, Sheldon Luck.

Men and women don't make the roster in Canada's Aviation Hall Fame just by being nice people. They get there because their peers and colleagues judge them worthy of admission, and come to conclusions that their contributions have been of national significance to both the nation and aviation at large.

Grant dedicated his life, energy, resources and ample wits to building a global class airline in the face of stiff competition and little government support, such as was provided his corporate nemesis: Trans-Canada Air Lines.

Once Grant set his goals, he stuck to them with fierce tenacity and with all the dynamism he could muster.

Sheldon was the classic stereotype *Pilot of Fortune*, a tall, rugged, handsome, top-notch, smooth-talking, easy-walking professional and commercial pilot.

And when things did not quite suit his spirited style, he sought adventure elsewhere.

Adventure is what he got – plenty of it which the reader is invited to share in these pages.

Sheldon and Grant were steadfast in their outlooks on life.

They were card-carrying visionaries, sometimes operating on the same wavelengths, at times missing each other's perspective by a mile. They were men driven to pursue their objectives. Fortunately for many within the international aviation community, most of their goals were common to one another's.

Destiny and their own vibrant personalities liberally sprinkled with a burden of mixed blessings and curses characterized their relationship over the years.

These included agonizing times, frustrations, use and abuse of each other's strong points and weaknesses and a profound admiration for their respective skills - everything needed to create, generate and sustain a uniquely rich set of memories for each, until McConachie's death in California in 1965.

Grant chose the corporate route in the late 1930s, knowing full well that he had entered a world dominated by powerful and influential politics, a world of high finance, one with its own different and well-defined set of rules and code of behaviour.

Sheldon's world was in a completely different environment, high above the ground, *walking on air*.

These two different worlds rarely met peacefully.

But as often as their personalities clashed, they kept a large space in their hearts for each other, from their first meeting in the mid-1930s.

Neither Canada nor the world may never see another Grant McConachie, and, almost certainly the world is not likely ever to see another Sheldon Luck.

That they came together during the critical, foundation-laying days of what became Canadian Pacific Air Lines is a testament to the memorable part they played in the, sometimes, convoluted history of commercial aviation in Canada.

## 1. A Fistful of Firsts

Should a flying career always begin with a bang?

Yes, often with a crash - but it should be survivable, preferably without any damage to the pilot, aircraft or passengers.

This recommendation, at first glance, is not as naive as it may appear.

Flying has been defined within the aviation community, with tongue in cheek, as the art of avoiding ongoing disaster ... while at the same time making money.

Taking a heavier-than-air machine of any size into the air puts it into an environment in which the law of gravity unrelentingly keeps pulling at it.

There isn't any place up there to pull over and make on the spot repairs.

Since the Wright brothers first took to the air, every attempt has been made to bypass this immutable law of gravity, keep the planes flying and return them safely to the ground.

Almost all those involved in aviation have designed creative and ingenious techniques to try and overcome the famous Murphy dictate that whatever can go wrong will go wrong. Multiple redundancy, or bypass systems offer pilots alternate means of controlling an aircraft under certain emergency conditions in flight. Remarkable improvements in safety systems have been made over the years, wrought at the expense of many prangs, crack-ups, lives and valuable equipment.

No one in a right frame of mind wants anyone on an aircraft to experience that ultimate sinking feeling, unless the experience can be simulated, without risking one's life, so realistically that it's almost the real thing.

Today's computer-directed flight simulators allow novice and professional pilots alike to make minor and major errors without once leaving the ground. These flight simulators are so good at the job that many seasoned pros have been seen scrambling, white-knuckled, from flight simulator doors, sweat cascading from their blanched faces and nerves frayed to the limit.

It is a far, far better thing to prang a plane in a flight simulator than to have the real thing take place. *Prang*, for those unfamiliar with aviation buzzwords, is aerogeek-speak meaning a survivable airplane crash.

For one thing, it does not hurt as much as the real thing.

And it is far cheaper for the airline operator.

Also a simulator prang is a perfect proving ground for pilots in training, undergoing refresher or upgrading courses, or simply maintaining proficiency levels.

Difficult flights, especially those carried out in a simulator, help pilots accumulate vast batches of aviation wisdom - most often all at once.

Knowledge and emergency procedures learned in this manner are critical to a long and successful career in flying.

Literary excursions into the highs and lows of aviation clearly show what can go wrong at the best and at the worst of times. Under the stress of an airborne emergency, pilots rely on proven and tested procedures and their own experience ... and, at times with a dash of help from on High.

That fewer fatal accidents take place in today's modern airline systems is a solid testament as to what has been learned, and applied to aviation safety over the years in the unrelenting drive to provide as much security in the air as is humanly possible.

Sheldon went through a number of incidents and accidents in his long and colourful career, and only two of his accidents were major ones ...yet no man or woman in his charge was ever seriously hurt.

The first of Sheldon's two major accidents took place while he was competing directly against Grant McConachie. It took place late in the winter of 1935-36 at Peerless Lake, in northwestern Alberta. The second accident occurred three years later a little bit south of the British Columbia - Yukon Territory boundary.

### Alberta fish flown to American dinner plates

Circumstances which led to his first crash go back to the early 1930s when Sheldon had been flying throughout southern Alberta. He had come across Grant McConachie a number of times since 1932.

Grant's reputation had already travelled some distance, and Sheldon admitted having heard great and wonderful things about him. He never gave up trying to join Grant's company, United Air Transport (UAT) which was headquartered in Edmonton, 180 miles (290 km) north of Calgary.

Each time he asked Grant for a job, Grant would give him the standard reply, "no work," but always promised that he'd keep Sheldon in mind at the first opportunity – a refrain often heard to this day by fledgling pilots looking to land flying jobs from prospective employers.

UAT enjoyed lucrative fish-hauling contracts from the frozen lakes of northwestern Alberta, flying loads of whitefish from fishing camps directly to the railhead at Faust, 175 air miles (282 km) due north and slightly west of Edmonton, on the southern shores of Lesser Slave Lake.

Many primitive air services made good money on these fish-hauling contracts. Sheldon reckoned since he couldn't join Grant, he'd go one better with the fishermen in the process.

At the time Sheldon flew with Advanced Air Services (AAS), recently taken over by Vancouver entrepreneur Robert Pike and renamed Columbia Air Services (CAS).

Pike had noticed the many headlines Sheldon had made in his early flying days over and around Calgary. AAS wasn't making a go of things and Pike had planned to take the company into the black by building a large-scale airline out of it. He wanted Sheldon and his mechanic friend, Ron Campbell, to join him... to bring them in on the ground floor.

The new company had but one aircraft and a few wrecks on which its aeronautical students practiced their developing repair and maintenance skills. In the process of taking over the company, Pike got his hands on two Boeing 40H4s which had been found on board a New Zealand-bound ship in Vancouver, BC.

The previous owners were unable to pay for the planes and Pike is reputed to have purchased them for a song.

Pike wanted Sheldon to fly them into Calgary and help develop the business potential north of Edmonton. Ron was to service the aircraft in Calgary. Pike had retained the services of the previous owners of Advanced Air Services, members of the Muncaster family, to administer the company for him.

During the late summer of 1935, Sheldon and Ron had taken a flying sales trip for AAS through the north-central interior of British Columbia.

To their dismay, they discovered that Grant had been there first, leaving them bottom-of-the-barrel scrapings.

A beneficial side-effect of the trip overcame the initial humiliation of coming in second on a sales venture ... the jaunt proved to Sheldon that if CAS was going to make any money out of flying in the north in the winter of 1936, then the planes had better be equipped for water and for snow operations.

He convinced Pike that one of planes should be equipped with floats for summer water operations and the other rigged with snow skis for winter flying.

In January 1936, both Sheldon and Ron were putting in heavy-duty hours with this still financially-deprived company. Pike had little more than grandiose dreams to offer them. Tired of promises, Sheldon wanted cash assurances before flying-for-hire for Pike.

Sensing this attitude on Sheldon's part, Pike went hunting for him with a telegram, which he sent to him on Sunday, Jan. 19:

> *Boeing test flown today, second Thursday next. Skis delivered Calgary seventh. Want Luck in Vancouver shortly. Wire us his whereabouts, plans and work ready for machines and approximate date and how. Will fix Muncaster agreement when Boeings arrive Calgary next.*

Anticipating such assurances from Pike, Sheldon had been trying to line up work for the two Boeings that he would be flying into Calgary. In the process he again asked Grant for work, but without luck. In this case, his breadwinning capabilities did not live up to the potential suggested by his family name of Luck.

He stuck with Pike and he wired back:

> *I can take delivery of the Boeing. Otherwise I must look elsewhere to support all these companies ... have work starting at same time and I do not care to lose it. Wire me ticket and expense money at Edmonton or Calgary.*

Sheldon got his expense money, went to Vancouver and made more headlines ferrying the Boeing 40H4 to Calgary.

He went Grant one better by setting up his own fish-hauling business into Faust, AB, charging nothing at all for deadhead flights.

Deadhead flights are those which are flown empty on a back-haul. Deadhead in Sheldon's case meant flying from Faust another 90 miles (145 km) north to Peerless Lake. Somebody had to pay the flight bill and Grant had been charging the fishermen special deadhead rates between Faust and the lakes out of which he was operating.

### Fish-hauling by air thrilled newspaper editors of the day

Unlike today, where such an operation wouldn't even be noticed, hauling fish loads by air in the 1930s was a novelty, a very big thing... and, as such, it enthralled newspaper editors of the day. Little wonder they ran many stories on Sheldon's operation.

Whitefish were popular restaurant items in Chicago and other major cities in the United States. Airplanes made it possible for fishermen to save time in bringing their catches from remote northwestern Alberta lakes to the railhead. From there, they were frozen and put on board specially-routed trains for speedy trips to distant markets.

Grant couldn't be blamed if he was less than enthusiastic about competition from this big brash newcomer.

The Friday morning of March 6, 1936, at Peerless Lake began crisp and clear... truly a promising day for the fish haul. Sheldon had made a routine take-off, with nearly a ton of fish on board.

Nicely airborne, Sheldon experienced a loss of power. A glance ahead confirmed the Boeing was just NOT going to make it to the next lake in sight. He brought it back to Peerless Lake, hoping to make an emergency landing.

He was not the only one who thought he was going to crash... so did the fishermen below. They usually stood by, watching the planes take-off. The puzzled look on their faces rapidly deteriorated to fear as they saw Sheldon's plane suddenly go obviously out of control.

Another 20 feet (6 m) higher and the Boeing might have missed the tree tops.

As it happened, a lot of trees got a fast clipping as his plane rapidly lost altitude.

Sheldon tried to maintain control, but didn't remember how he managed it. The Boeing continued its descent, crashed and flipped onto its back.

The awestruck fishermen had been about a mile away from where the plane went down. They collected their dog sleds and raced to the site.

Nothing moved around the burning plane.

As far as they were concerned, Sheldon couldn't have survived the crash; and if he did, there was the fire, and Sheldon was still in the cockpit.

Had the cockpit been closer to the front of the aircraft, Sheldon would have been crushed to death.

However, the cockpit was set quite some distance above and to the rear of the passenger cabin. The impact pushed the engine through to the passenger cabin, which doubled as a cargo hold in freighting operations. The fish however didn't do so well... they were pulped in the process.

Sheldon regained consciousness, aware that his face was buried in the snow. He heard a crackling noise, much like that made by dry leaves being crunched underfoot.

That crackling meant only one thing: the plane was on fire.

He squirmed his way out of the cockpit, and stood, dazed, beside his burning plane, dimly aware of what sounded like men hollering.

He began to amble from the wreck. Slowly at first, until he heard: "The airplane's burning! Get the hell out of there!"

He looked back to see that his only source of income, a crumpled heap on the ice, was now in flames. Wondering what to do next, he started to check his body for injuries.

Just then the fuel tank exploded, lifting the fuselage into the air, knocking him flat on his face.

As he lay in the snow, stunned by the initial hit from the blast, the fishermen grabbed his clothing and dragged him from the inferno.

Soon after, his head cleared, and he returned to the burned, twisted skeletal remains of the Boeing, curious about the big black splotch adjacent to the wreckage. On closer inspection, he realized it was the blood of the mashed fish cargo, mixed with a mangled engine, unburned oil and miscellaneous aircraft parts.

His rescuers took him to their base camp about a mile-and-a-half from the crash and sent word to the telegraph station at Wabasca whose operator then notified authorities… in Edmonton… then at Columbia Aviation's head office in Vancouver and Sheldon's wife, Isabel.

No formal investigation took place, but the aviation community did learn a valuable lesson from this crash, one which was applied to every aircraft engine from then on.

Carburetor icing was the culprit and carburetor heating quickly came into use. To date, pilots still encounter this problem, but with the advent of carburetor heating, it can be prevented.

Inspectors from the then Department of National Defense Civil Aviation Branch (DNDCAB), equivalent to today's Canadian Transportation Safety Board, would have investigated the accident had there been a fatality.

But, these were the Dirty Thirties, and things were tough all the way around and budgets were tight not only in business, but in government departments as well.

To investigate this accident would have meant chartering an aircraft, on skis, and the DNDCAB didn't have any such equipped aircraft on hand, nor did it have the money to look into a survivable accident.

When Grant got word of the crash, he flew to the site from his own fish hauling operation at Wabasca.

He wanted a firsthand look. Sheldon later overheard remarks attributing the following quote to Grant: "*The pilot who flew that plane was born to fly.*"

No doubt but the deal between Pike and Columbia/Advanced didn't fly - it fell through.

Grant remembered his earlier promise to Sheldon and kept his word about promising him a job at the first opportunity – he hired Sheldon on August 11th, 1936.

Grant had changed the name of his company from Independent Airways (IA) to United Air Transport (UAT), and went after all the business he could get throughout the northwest region.

Grant, Ted Field, Sheldon and all the others in the company who busted their butts to generate business did so well that their competitors reacted by belittling them, in one case calling UAT an insignificant little operation whose pilots and mechanics went around with dirty faces.

By 1938, UAT's air and ground support crews were among the tops in the nation, and were also well-known throughout much of the United States.

Until this status had been attained, pilots who were with Canadian Airways (CA) or Mackenzie Air Service (MAS) usually got all the applause within the aviation community, and naturally, most of the business that went with this recognition.

"We were the poor brothers", Grant used to tell Sheldon during better days, whenever they opened hangar doors to rehash the "good old days".

However, they weren't "poor" for long.

UAT became the first large airline in Canada to have all of its pilots qualified on Instrument Flight Rules (IFR). At that time the current Commercial License limited commercial pilots to flying only under conditions known as daytime Visual Flight Rules (VFR).

The new Public Transport License, or PTL, meant that pilots were endorsed on Instrument Flight rules, or IFR. Flying blind had become a matter of routine;

Grant's pilots were admittedly proud of their upgraded stature and Grant had made it worthwhile for any of his pilots to take the PTL by sweetening the pot with a generous salary boost.

As great a technical advance as the PTL represented for bush lines then, not everybody was ready to jump onto the bandwagon. A limited number of pilots went after the PTL despite the fact that the Canadian Government provided Tiger Moths, each equipped for teaching full IFR operations, to many flying organizations throughout Canada.

UAT pilots had become so proficient that when it and nine other companies were later brought into Canadian Pacific Air Lines (CPAL), Grant took great pride in pointing out that his company was the only one absorbed into the new company whose entire pilot roster held current PTLs.

Most competitors' pilots flew on their commercial pilots' licenses.

Sheldon, North Sawle and Ralph Oakes took their PTL upgrading during the winter of 1936-37; Sheldon under the direction of Major Harold Sandgate at the Calgary Aero Club.

Proficiency notwithstanding, UAT still faced a pile of problems. First, it had to mature from being a primitive bush operation to actually being an ironically-sound, but regional airline... offering reliable service on a scheduled basis over a large chunk of wilderness geography.

Big business in the more heavily populated centres of the nation had to recognize UAT as a valid, regular, reliable and safe method of transportation.

Tourism wouldn't become a major industry for years.

Passenger traffic was still in the embryonic stage.

More and more, many were pushing past the outer limits of known civilization... trappers, miners, prospectors and handfuls of geographers seeking the unknown potential resources of the northern sub-Arctic and Arctic which were yet to be discovered and exploited.

UAT also faced fairly stiff competition from previously well-established air services such as Canadian Airways and Mackenzie Air Services, whose founders had pioneered and developed much of the business in the far north. The growth of a new air service in northwestern Canada meant little or nothing to the outside world of the mid-to-late 1930s.

The aviation community had come a long way since February 23$^{rd}$, 1909, the date of the first accredited heavier-than-air flight in Canada and in what was known as the British Empire.

A man named Samuel Franklin Cody is credited with having actually made the first powered flight in the British Empire in 1908 – in England – but his flight ended in a crash of his aircraft, and according to international aviation standards it did not count as an official flight – hair-picking maybe, but a reality nonetheless.

The first official and accredited Canadian and British Empire flight was, in fact, made by members of Alexander Graham Bell's Aerial Experiment Association (AEA) with the Silver Dart – piloted by Canadian J.A.D. McCurdy, who went on to become a Lieutenant-Governor of the Province of Nova Scotia.

By the mid 1930s, long-distance air records were being made and broken. Major airlines were rapidly taking wing across the United States and just about everywhere else in the world.

A year before Sheldon joined UAT, Pan-Am launched its famous globe-hopping Clipper Service, and in the summer of 1936, Douglas Aircraft introduced its first commercial version of the now famous DC-3.

The DC-3 set the standard for fast, reliable and above all, comfortable passenger travel.

UAT's accomplishment in its corner of the world merited little attention elsewhere compared to the phenomenal growth of inter-continental air travel.

About the only thing which would improve UAT's cash picture would be if Grant were to be bought out, or the company were to be taken over by a larger, more financially sound corporation.

A huge financial boost would inevitably spin off from the war clouds which were forming over Europe and the Eastern Pacific. Hitler's plans for global domination were rapidly taking root, menacing all of Europe, Russia, much of Africa and the Middle East. It's soon-to-be ally in the Axis, Japan – oil-starved by the United States of America - had already started tromping over China as early as 1931... both countries being frightening precursors of the global war that they would spawn just a few years down the road.

However, domestically, a lot of financial hope lay on the horizon from Grant's point of view.

He knew that aviation could only grow, soon, and at an unprecedented rate.

Some of the factors to influence this growth rate, and to prove him right, were increasing the need for raw material in the coming war ... which seemed to be unavoidable by the mid-1930s.

Much of what the Allies would need in the way of resources then lay in Canada's vast and still unexplored and untapped northwestern regions.

Grant also knew there would be a push for protected airspace across the top of the world. He would be the one to make the major thrust in that direction - flying to the Orient over the top of the globe. His dream generated considerable media attention in the process.

Visionary forecasting aside, bills still had to be paid, as salaries and other operating expenses continued to escalate.

### Canada was one tough country to develop

Other factors which led to rapidly growing aviation community included the constant need for more growth as a nation. Men and women in ever-increasing numbers wanted adventure away from the crowded cities. They wanted to do their pioneering thing way up there... in the distant wilderness.

Canada then was little more than a BIG chunk of real estate – a country of enormous size, but with a narrow, 5,000-mile long by 300-mile (8,046 km by 482 km) wide ribbon of population, with nearly 2,000 miles (3,218 km) of raw, untamed and undeveloped wilderness to the north of that ribbon. This was, and in many cases still is, a vast amount of real estate with hardly a soul in it by comparison to the heavily-populated ribbon of cities and towns that border the United States of America.

Remote communities and settlements depended heavily on regular freight shipments as their only contact with the outside world. Mining companies demanded regular freight and charter services. Government officials who served these regions needed reliable and regular air transportation to and from distant pockets of humanity.

Extended flights over desolate terrain such as the far North entailed special financial risks including development costs to establish fuel caches and maintenance services very long distances away from major cities.

This book is focused on Sheldon Luck, and those who influenced his life and whose lives he may have influenced. I have chosen to focus tightly on events surrounding his life and his role in the development of early Western Canadian aviation.

Massive problems stood in the way of rapid growth of British Columbia and the Yukon Territory – caused mainly by a series of 1,100-mile long strings of south-to-north mountain chains, starting with the Rockies on the east and through to the Coastal Mountain range on the Pacific Coast of B.C. and Alaska.

These mountains needed taming if Canada was to benefit from the immense resources which lay on top of, under and inside those mountains.

Mountains are spectacular to look at - from the comfort and luxury of a jetliner seven miles (11 km) above the ground. They are even more breathtaking when seen from a single engine aircraft, a few thousand feet above their perennially snow-capped peaks, or as viewed laterally from the beautiful valleys.

Mountain flying however, can be dangerous to the inexperienced and unprepared, and mountain regions could only be systematically developed rapidly by air, with seasoned pilots.

The aircraft used by UAT and its contemporaries were the right kind of machines needed to tame these mountains: bush aircraft to be precise... airplanes with short take-off and landing capabilities, able to operate year-round, under all types of weather conditions, with long-range, flexible handling characteristics, safe reliable performance and good load capacities.

It seemed that nobody else but UAT was up to the challenge of pioneering and developing mountain flying techniques or laying bases along routes which didn't appear to offer much promise.

Mountain settlements, communities, mining camps, First Nations villages were forced by terrain to nestle between the mountains, in the lower slopes and valleys - literally hundreds of lonely miles from almost anywhere. The vast road system which exists today simply wasn't there in the 1930s, 1940s and even the 1950s.

Pilots had to cross over mountain tops to get to them, or find the right combination of mountain passes at lower altitudes to avoid the inclement and often unforgiving weather which comes with each spring, fall, winter, and sometimes, even summer.

Pioneering and development work on a basis never dreamed of before could only have been brought about by a remarkable combination of skilled pilots, aircraft on skis and floats, all to take advantage of the thousands of lakes and river systems in the area in winter and summer.

But this combination was almost prohibitively expensive and, in many cases bankrupted a number of smaller operators who gave pioneering largely unexplored territory their best shot.

More than hope and grand visions lay down the road, however, which would help UAT clear these and other hurdles. In addition to the relentless drive and enthusiasm of McConachie and his personnel, some courageous aspects of human nature would help the company.

They would also vindicate McConachie's visions.

One of these turned out to be humanity's insatiable curiosity to explore and develop the unknown. Pioneering homesteaders were heading into the same areas being heavily explored by prospectors, mining companies, and forestry firms... all were pushing deeper and deeper into the wilderness. These newcomers wanted to farm, trap, work in the woods and establish all sorts of businesses and companies to make things and create service industries for the consumers already there.

Above all, these new pioneers wanted s-p-a-c-e, far away from the crowded and congested cities, a chance to make it big, and if not make it BIG!, to simply make it.

### A presence by mail if not by flesh

As the northwest began to show positive signs of growth yet another demand surfaced - that of regular human contact with the outside world, by mail if not in the flesh.

The only way to get letters into the remote regions regularly and quickly was, and is still today, by air.

Before Sheldon joined the company, its crews had already carried out extensive pioneering work as a natural extension of their routes spreading north and west from Edmonton.

Ted Field, Sheldon's first boss, and UAT's first chief pilot, spent hundreds of hours locating and consolidating pioneer air routes. He flew proposed and recommended routes, established fuel caches in such locations as Prospector's Bar on the Liard River, then west and north at Teslin, including points between Lower Post in BC and Whitehorse in the Yukon, to list but a few.

Among others who flew these early highways in the sky were Ernie Kubicek, Ralph Oakes, Charlie Tweed and Don Patry. Most of the northbound flights terminated at Whitehorse, and if the registry at the Whitehorse Inn could be located, it would contain a treasure trove for aviation buffs of the names of pilots and mechanics who overnighted there in the late 1930s and early 1940s.

The advent of air mail into the wilds meant a partial end to isolation. Contact with the civilized world promised to be measured in terms of bi-weekly or monthly air mail flights instead of the sporadic flights which came in about every two or three months apart. Pilots often brought a touch of "civilization" into the remote area of Canada's northwest, including at times such goodies as what became known as the "40-pounder," a 40-ounce bottle of over-proof

Jamaican rum.

During the winter of 1936-37, Grant together with Post Office Inspector Walter Hale made a number of exploratory flights from Edmonton into British Columbia to set up an experimental air mail service, paving the way for the first regular air mail service between Edmonton and Whitehorse over the next six months.

The Canadian post office system paid nothing more than basic air mail rates for these early 1937 air mail flights, in spite of the extra development costs to UAT.

And in its own way, this helped Sheldon make a small niche for himself in postal history.

He flew the first United Air Transport air mail flights on January 11, 13 and 15 in 1937 – to settlements which no longer exist. They now lie under the waters of the huge man-made Lake Williston which backs up behind the W.A.C. Bennett Dam on the Peace River.

Grant and Inspector Hale recommended the flight head north from Fort St. John to Fort Nelson and return. The plane would depart the next day for a flight west to Gold Bar, along to Finlay Forks, up to Fort Grahame – all now underwater history - and return to Fort St. John.

Scheduled to fly the first air mail for his own airline, Grant asked Sheldon to take over the historic run because his wife had taken ill. And he did, in temperatures as low as –50 ° F, in company with mechanic Red Rose.

Residents of these communities, barely dots on the maps, greeted them with considerable enthusiasm. Red and Sheldon often took along a camera to record these flights, and the reactions of the mail recipients to finally being able to rely on regular mail.

## First two UAT air mail flights overlooked by historians while Canadian government trumps McConachie

These two first UAT air mail flights weren't any big deal by Canadian air mail standards… and they were somehow overlooked by historians.

Six months would elapse before UAT could latch on to the first of two more lucrative air mail contracts, each with a much higher profile and greater publicity value, and thus more potential revenue than Sheldon's first air mail flight for the company.

These were the lucrative Edmonton-to-Whitehorse and Vancouver-to-Whitehorse links.

However, a corporate thorn poked its tip into Grant's hide on April 10th, 1937, and stayed there for the rest of his life.

This was but a few months before he would make that vital July 1st, 1937 flight for UAT from Edmonton to Whitehorse and it clouded his horizon. It also dimmed the hopes of other small unconnected airline operators in Canada who perhaps shared a common vision of incorporating to form a national airline.

The Canadian Government beat them all to it on April 10th, 1937, by creating Trans-Canada Airlines (TCAL), today's Air Canada.

The new airline enjoyed almost total government support and protection, and it began raiding the many small operators from coast to coast of their trained pilots and mechanics, and polishing their skills. TCAL's air crews, ground maintenance and service personnel spent the better part of 1937 gearing up. TCAL also introduced to the nation something new: the flight stewardess (known today as a flight attendant, or simply, a member of the cabin crew).

Canada's first national airline had to be good, reliable, safe and proficient, and the men and women from the regional airlines that were brought into the TCAL fold were the right kind of people to "make it so." And all of this was long before the fictional *USS Enterprise* Captain Jean-Luc Picard would even utter the phrase on international television in the Star Trek series.

Yet, UAT possessed some of North America's longest air routes for a company of its size. Most of its route structure was over terrain which pilots today consider to be the most difficult and potentially dangerous in the world. UAT needed to be counted in the natural scheme of things, and could only hope to score highly enough by its development work in the northwest.

In the mid-to-late 1930s and into the early 1940s, most airports across much of Alberta, British Columbia, the Yukon Territory (YT) and the Northwest Territories (NT) were simply aerodromes, or cleared patches of land. In the mid-1930s, the Whitehorse "airport", for example, was nothing more than a strip made of natural soil, with maintenance and service facilities located in a T-shape hangar built by another regional carrier, the White Pass and Yukon (WPY). Elsewhere such as at Mayo and Dawson City, airports were nothing more than short, rough strips of cleared forest or tundra

Most UAT operations throughout the 1930s and early 1940s were carried out on float planes in the spring, summer and autumn, then on skis in winter. It remained that way until the long string of airports were installed in a line heading north from Kamloops, BC, through to Williams Lake, Quesnel, Prince George, Dawson Creek, Fort St. John, Fort Nelson, Watson Lake and on into Whitehorse – what had become the *Northwest Staging Route*, to serve common North American and Allied Armed Forces needs during World War II.

In between and to the east toward Edmonton, Alberta, the communities of Grande Prairie, Valleyview, Peace River and Whitecourt had gotten used to frequent air services.

And they wanted more.

Population growth was pushing further and further north from the Canadian National Railway (CNR) line between Jasper in western Alberta, and the west coast city of Prince Rupert in BC. The heavily-populated provinces of Québec and Ontario needed more and more the minerals and resources of the west to satisfy the ever-increasing appetites of their manufacturing and distribution facilities.

In addition to the impetus naturally provided by the above factors, air mail indeed would be the icing on the cake and a key to survival for developing regional airlines. The company which copped key air mail contracts in the north-western regions would emerge as a financial winner. It would also tap the vast potential in freight and passenger traffic which would help accelerate this growth rate.

So what if TCAL was formed and operating in a narrow corridor across the width of Canada? As noted earlier, Canada was not much more than a large, unexplored and undeveloped chunk of land over much of which UAT and what became Canadian Pacific Air Lines flew ... effectively an area almost as large, if not larger than TCAL's turf in lineal mileage: it lay there begging for development and regular air mail service.

United Air Transport had successfully penetrated much of this new terrain, ever since Grant first began his one-airplane operation out of Fort St. James, BC, in the first three years of the decade. Closing the 1930s, UAT appeared to be in the driver's seat, with Grant behind the corporate desk, Ted Field managing the operations and Sheldon as senior pilot.

Grant personally generated a lot of press coverage when he piloted an air mail flight from Edmonton to Whitehorse on July 1st, 1937. Its importance lay in the fact that this inaugural flight set, once and for all, established, regularly scheduled air services between these two points, cutting ground transit time down from days to a matter of hours.

And the flight generated extremely valuable publicity for United Air Transport.

The thinking being, of course, the more publicity, the more contracts would come its way. Grant had become an expert at exploiting any kind of publicity to his advantage.

To carry out these flights, Grant chose UAT's large Ford Tri-Motor, registered as BEP. It boasted a large radio equipment rack installed by its previous owner, the predecessor to what became the Royal Canadian Air Force (RCAF). A radio operator always flew with the crew when the machine went on duty patrols for the air force. However, no similar provisions had been made for the inaugural Edmonton-Whitehorse flight, and during pre-flight ceremonies, Grant demonstrated the value of that all-important radio link.

He suspected that he could and would extract the full publicity value for UAT if he could use the radio en-route to Whitehorse and back.

Grant discovered to his consternation that the pilot could not do two things at once, fly and operate the radio at the same time... but not with those pioneer radios, so radically different from today's ultra-modern radio systems.

Crystals of a specified frequency had to be constantly changed in flight to match the crystals with the same frequency which had been assigned to each different ground station – usually an "airport". This also meant carrying an extra body, taking up weight and space intended for revenue-generating freight and passengers.

Grant was not a happy camper.

To top it off, there were only two stations that Grant could have picked up in flight, even if he had had a radio operator on board, besides Edmonton and Whitehorse. They were at Fort St. John and Lower Post, both in BC, and both employing expert radio operators - Jimmy Murdock at Fort St. John and Colin Reid at Lower Post.

They were familiar with Royal Canadian Corps of Signals operating procedures, and had the necessary frequency-matched crystals in their stations to correspond with those on board BEP.

To Grant's delight, UAT engineers remedied the problem in the summer of 1938 by removing the military radio equipment from BEP, replacing it with a smaller Lear 12E radio set which stayed with the aircraft until its retirement in Vancouver years later. The problem of carrying a radio operator had been solved.

Hans Broten, UAT radio expert, had also done his share of pioneering the evolution of a first-class air service by setting up something which was just as important as a stable string of ground fuel caches: air-to-ground communications. He did this with a series of 15-watt transmitters strategically placed between Edmonton and Whitehorse and at other locations in north central British Columbia.

This represented yet another first for the region and for aviation in remote areas: air-to-ground communications were almost unheard of in northwestern Canada until United Air Transport came along, but were routine where the larger regional airlines operated throughout much of North America, especially in the United States.

### Pioneering airport approach plates told what pilot needed to know about an airport

Sheldon and his pilot friends were among the first, if not the first, in early Canadian regional airlines to design and develop their own landing and take-off approach plates. These are small and handy-to-read printed charts which gave pilots important information about each airport along their flight paths.

While early approach plates were primitive by today's modern airport approach plates, they nevertheless gave UAT's aircrews a large measure of confidence and security, which reflected the advanced thinking shown by Grant and his dedicated and loyal employees.

UAT plates depicted landing and take-off patterns, indicating obstacles within a certain distance of each destination point and provided information about radio signals from each of the stops along their routes, yet another important first in flying the remote regions of the far northwest.

Canadian Department of Transport (DOT) officials in Vancouver monitored Instrument Flight Rules for most of Western Canada, and its inspectors knew Grant's aircrews were operating under what amounted to full-scale instrument approaches. They were doing quite well at landings and take offs from such places as Prince George in weather which, months earlier, would have grounded all air operations.

However, government departments operated on low budgets in the late 1930s where commercial air operations were concerned, all of which resulted in little governmental supervision of IFR routines.

### What's in a name? United will tell you

Little wonder no government official ever came around telling Grant how to operate his expanding airline, which soon had to change its name thanks to pressure from United Airlines (UA) in the United States.

According to Sheldon, by the time 1938 rolled around, UA had finally taken great umbrage at the word "United" in United Air Transport.

Grant knew better than to butt heads with this emerging American giant. Refusing to tackle this bull by its horns, he made a wise decision.

UAT quickly became YSAT - Yukon Southern Air Transport.

### Early airline pilots cut teeth on bush flying

Early airline pilots cut their teeth on bush flying, trusting their equipment, engines, instruments and especially ground maintenance and service crews. They had little trust in the weather staying the same from mountain chain to mountain chain. Weather reporting services in northwestern and western Canada weren't anywhere near today's standards. Commercial pilots knew very well that mountain weather could undergo sudden and drastic changes in between adjacent mountain ranges, an unpleasant characteristic which plagues pilots to this day when they fly in between mountain ranges at low altitudes.

Under the best of conditions, an engine failure in good weather can mean a long walk to safety. Under the worst of conditions, an engine failure can spell death for a pilot and passengers, stranded hundreds of miles from a base.

With the Edmonton-Whitehorse link secure, YSAT went for the brass ring, the even more promising Vancouver to Edmonton connection. To edge out competitors, YSAT's routes had to be proven better that its competitors' and its equipment had to be up to the constant challenges of such a routing.

### Before de Havilland introduced the Beaver, Bob Noorduyn's Norseman was considered best bush plane

One of the first acquisitions designed to upgrade the airline's fleet included a Norseman, which Grant got his hands on during one of his many jaunts back to eastern Canada.

Pilots considered it to be the best bush aircraft.

Bob Noorduyn designed, built and mass-produced 871 of these superb flying machines between 1936 and 1939 in a plant in St. Laurent, then a suburb of Montréal, Québec.

Whenever Sheldon bragged about the Norseman's cruising speed he constantly had to remind himself that he and his colleagues at UAT / YSAT did much more high-level flying than their competitors ever did.

UAT / YSAT personnel had also done much more challenging pioneering and exploration work than those operating strictly into and out of the tundra regions of the far north.

Sheldon and all other UAT / YSAT pilots were often at the mercy of their competitors, who constantly ridiculed them, their work and their growing company.

Despite the ill-intentioned jokes, no one today can dispute the fact that UAT / YSAT routes saw company aircraft routinely flying at 10,000 feet (3,048 m) or more above sea level - twice again the average altitude of comparative airline services across Canada - on their flights between Vancouver, Edmonton, Whitehorse and points in between.

Despite the promising growth potential throughout the company's territory, pickings were slim; almost everyone who owned an airplane for commercial hire was out for a share of the bush flying pie.

Operators learned every trick in the book, and wrote a few new ones, in cramming every ounce of freight they could into an airplane. If a private charter resulted in overloading, which it did more often than not, then, an overload it was.

Trappers and prospectors were notorious for wanting everything they had with them at the airport put into their aircraft. Although they were usually headed out on a one-way trip to their prospecting or trapping territory, they were paying for a two-way flight, and wanted to make every penny count.

Pilots caught overloading had their licenses suspended for a period of time, usually ninety days, without recourse to a formal hearing, something which exists to this day.

This was much like kicking the tire because it went flat: the penalties would have been far more effective if the companies had been penalized, rather than penalizing their overloading pilots. A penalized company could have taken its own necessary disciplinary measures against an offending pilot.

The immense value of the Norseman, aside from its speed, lay in the fact that it was licensed to carry 1,200 pounds (454 kg). Pilots quickly discovered it could take off quite easily with nearly 2,000 pounds (907 kg) on board. Under these conditions, it needed a longer take-off distance, and a shallower, flatter climb-out path.

**A pilot who did not fly over-loaded soon found himself looking for another job**

Other aircraft on the YSAT roster prior to going for broke on the Vancouver-Edmonton-Whitehorse competition for the air mail, included three Standard Universal Fokkers, three Custom Wacos, one Boeing 40H4, a Fairchild 72, a Fairchild CF2W2 and a Fairchild 71.

Initially the high-wing Fokker monoplane cockpit was open to the elements. By the time Sheldon began flying it for Grant, a hinged canopy had been installed, affording some measure of protection from the elements for its pilot. Its heating system turned out to be more of a promise than reality. Flying a Fokker in winter meant wearing a lot of good, warm clothing, usually heaps of fur.

Many bush pilots vividly recall how lonely it got in the far north in winter, hundreds of miles from a privy and thousands of feet in the air.

The Fokker, not exactly built to break speed records, left the ground at about 60 miles an hour (97 km/hr). Once airborne it would climb to altitude at about 65 miles an hour (104 km/hr) then cruise along at about 75 to 80 miles an hour (120 – 130 km/hr). Flapless, it had a flat glide angle, making it almost impossible to land in a short field surrounded by tall trees.

Nor was it an aircraft for a sissy.

But then, Sheldon and his peers weren't sissies … nor were they average pilots.

The Fokker worked quite well on skis, operating from lakes in winter.

However, emergency landings, compounded by a dead engine, resulted in nerve-tingling "dead-stick" landings in these short iced-over lakes, leaving many bush pilots with permanently etched memories.

The Waco, despite, the fact that it was underpowered, was considered a slick machine which could accommodate five persons and clip along at about 135 miles an hour (217 km/hr). Its flaps helped pilots pull into short strips when necessary.

But it left many pilots stranded on those short fields because it was underpowered; an embarrassing situation for pilots who forgot that, getting in did not necessarily mean getting out. Pilots are unrelenting in their teasing about such errors in judgment.

Other carriers had been extended the same opportunity as YSAT to carry out experimental air mail flights in the winter of 1936-37, but for reasons still unknown, hardly anyone ever tried to outbid Grant.

Competing for the Vancouver-Whitehorse link, by flying from Vancouver to Fort St. John, then on to Whitehorse, during the winter of 1937-1938, Grant did face one competitor however, George Simmons of Carcross, Yukon, owner of Northern Airways (NA). George had proposed a different routing.

He had insisted that the air mail should be flown along the coastal-inland route, from Vancouver, up to Squamish, inland towards Lillooet, then north to Burns Lake, and continuing north, right into Whitehorse, YT.

By 1938 Sheldon and his pilots knew coastal weather patterns intimately. They knew them to be worse in many respects than those encountered during their own charter flying throughout the southern and central interior. The company had systematically expanded operations and flew regularly around the Lower Mainland, along the coastal areas and over Vancouver Island, as well as into the north-central interior of the province and on into the Yukon.

YSAT provided reasoned arguments against NA's proposal for the coastal-inland route for yet another reason: mechanical problems would inevitably be compounded by unpredictable weather. Such circumstances often could and did force pilots to remain overnight at various bases, delaying the air mail schedules, and making a mockery of the supposed advantage of flying mail.

YSAT discovered later that, even with its superior routing, it too faced the difficult combination of mechanical problems and inclement weather, often forcing a second flight to overlap the first one.

Under these conditions, the Post Office refused to pick up the tab for the second flight, arguing that the flights had in effect merged into one.

Unfair to the operators perhaps but fair to the Post Office.

Such delays weren't too much of a problem in 1937, but had become a burden in the second year of operations. YSAT doubled its weekly flights to twice-weekly, but the development of more and better ground facilities failed to keep pace with accelerated flying schedules.

This imposed an increasing burden on pilots. When the schedules went to three flights a week, the company enjoyed better aircraft. Still, ground facilities lagged in their development, adding yet more pressure.

The actual competition trials took place over an eleven-week period starting on January 16, 1938. Whichever competitor made the greatest number of trips on time would win the contract. George Simmons had a lot of high-powered backing from the Vancouver Board of Trade, and he had a top-notch bush pilot in Bill Holland, who flew George's Waco.

Vancouver mail destined for Edmonton and Whitehorse went by Canadian Pacific Railway to Ashcroft where the YSAT plane took the mail and flew it in a series of hops through to Prince George, and on into Fort St. John. There, incoming mail from Edmonton went aboard the north-bound flight, while Edmonton-bound mail was transferred to the Edmonton aircraft for an immediate turn-around flight to Edmonton.

YSAT's aircrews completed the greatest number of trips on time and won the contract hands down.

With this first corner turned on the road to financial success, Sheldon and his colleagues eagerly awaited the next step - flying the mail directly from Vancouver to Ashcroft and points north. This was slated to take place during the summer of 1939.

Already endowed with a reputation for political acumen, Grant had acquired a bagful of smarts and had them on standby for other uses, such as promotion and publicity. As stated above, George Simmons had enjoyed great pre-trial backing, including the support of the Vancouver Board of Trade, for his trial runs.

Grant was thinking of longer terms, and began wooing a famous name which could be tied with YSAT, that of Ginger Coote, founder of Ginger Coote Airways (GCA), based in Vancouver. Ginger had earned a wide measure of respect on the Lower Mainland of British Columbia, and his name carried a lot of weight.

Meanwhile, Sheldon had moved his family a number of times, first from Calgary to Fort St. James in 1937 when he worked for Grant out of Fort St. James; then into Prince George for a while, and finally, into Vancouver in 1938 to head up flying operations in the now rapidly expanding airline.

Throughout much of 1938 and 1939 Grant was too busy scurrying across North America to do much flying. His hands-on flying days were just about over, thanks to the demands of flying a presidential desk. Keeping the company alive and financially sound took up so much effort that, by mid-1938, he had only flown to the Yukon six times. Grant's obvious passion for flying got displaced by a fiercer loyalty: building an airline with an international reputation. More and more he placed total reliance on Ted Field and Sheldon Luck as his two key men within the organization.

### First air-bound mail for Edmonton and Whitehorse – of 26,000 letters – made Vancouver headlines

A Fleet Freighter, one of three acquired by Grant, and a Norsemen became the hit of Vancouver on the morning of Thursday, August 3rd, 1939, when both airplanes took off, heading north with the first air mail destined for Edmonton and Whitehorse.

The media loved it and so did everybody else.

Grant's earlier move to bring Ginger Coote on board had paid off handsomely from a publicity and public relations point of view. For a while, spectators to these initial air mail flights at the south end only saw the name "Ginger Coote Airways" on aircraft taking off from Vancouver, destined for Ashcroft and points north.

These two planes carried 26,000 letters, to be distributed along the route. The original plan called for only one aircraft to make the first run with Grant as pilot and Ginger as his co-pilot in the Fleet.

But it alone could not carry the bulk of the letters as had been originally intended, nor could it carry as passengers the dignitaries and media who wanted to take part in the action. The dignitaries wanted to be seen making history and the reporters wanted to record history. Both won out, which resulted in the 26,000 letters being split between the Fleet and the Norseman at Vancouver.

In the Norseman, Sheldon's passengers were Vancouver Sun reporter Jack Meek, another reporter, and Vancouver Mayor Charles Miller and Mrs. Miller.

On reaching the base at Fort St. John, which had not yet been upgraded to a terminal status, Ginger decided to fly to Edmonton with Ted Field, who had met the incoming planes. Grant and Sheldon continued on through to Whitehorse with the Norseman.

This flight took longer than expected from Vancouver. Congratulatory telegrams were read and brief speeches made at every stop along the way.

Nearing Whitehorse, Grant told Sheldon: "If it weren't for the fact that you were coming with me, I wouldn't even try to get into Whitehorse tonight. You've been on this run for quite a while and you know the country better than I do."

Sheldon felt quite good on receiving this compliment as he knew full well how difficult a night-time landing on floats could be at Whitehorse, especially in the middle of summer with river traffic at its peak.

He felt better yet when Grant laid another on him: "You pilots have the toughest run in the world."

And he felt best when Grant wrapped it up with this promise: "Just as soon as we're able to afford it, I'm going to see to it that you guys get $1,000 a month salary."

That was a lot of money for a young pilot who was then only hauling down about $350 a month!

Nobody really asked Grant how he felt a little while later when, on Sheldon's fourth run from Vancouver to Whitehorse, the second Fleet nearly wiped him out, along with three passengers. However, the crash did cause the death of a loved pet.

That Fleet 50 Freighter had been billed as a daring concept, aimed specifically at the Canadian bush market. It never went far beyond the conceptual stage and planned production of the aircraft never took place.

Dubbed "Fat Albert" by most pilots, Grant wanted three of them anyway. The price was right, downright right – it was cheap.

His first Fleet caught fire at Chicago's O'Hare airport while he was showing it off to insurance officials. All on board scrambled to safety. Photographs of the blackened hulk show the wheel chucks still in place, as Grant had been warming it up for a demonstration flight.

The second Fleet, the one which unceremoniously dumped Sheldon, his passengers and the dog nose-first into lilac trees, determined the fate of the third.

It would be many months before YSAT mechanics and engineers discovered what had gone wrong with the second Fleet's Jacobs radial engine. It turned out that a sticky valve gave up the ghost, destroying a cylinder in the process.

After Grant had read Sheldon's written report on the accident and discussed it with him about it at some length, he called the manufacturer in Fort Erie, Ontario and simply said: "Contract or not, I don't want that third Fleet."

It wound up with the Royal Canadian Air Force for a thorough evaluation and additional testing, and then it was taken apart, bit by bit. Detailed inspections uncovered a number of deficiencies, vindicating Sheldon of any blame in the accident and confirming his initial suspicions of what could have gone wrong.

## Unceremonious departure from a cockpit – head-first, through the windshield

Just what had happened with that second Fleet?

Sheldon had taken off during the evening from Whitehorse late in August, planning to overnight at Lower Post where supper waited for him and his passengers, Danny Trousdell, his mechanic, and another mechanic and his wife, Danny and Eva Driscoll, along with their purebred Irish Setter which they were taking to a dog show.

Nearing Lower Post, Yukon, the Fleet's right engine began to lose power. Sheldon tried applying different power settings. He was unable get the engine to work properly. It continued to function well enough to take the plane into Lower Post, where Danny could have a look at it and repair it, if possible.

Danny and Eva accompanied Sheldon for supper while Danny Trousdell stayed with the plane. He showed up for supper a little later, grinning, saying the engine should behave normally on take-off the following morning.

It did.

For a bit.

Then, without warning, it quit. They had flown little more less than 10 miles (16 km) south of Lower Post, into British Columbia.

Moments earlier, Sheldon had noticed fog rapidly developing along the Liard River banks below, and he wouldn't risk a landing there. He had no choice but try a forced landing onto the terrain below.

Landforms straight ahead of him rose at an alarming rate, faster than the Fleet could climb on only one engine. Young aspen and pine trees covered the forest floor below. He knew however, that they would provide enough cover to cushion the impact of the emergency landing he had in mind.

He reckoned that, if he could just float the Fleet in, slowly, tail heavy, and let it settle among the tree tops, it could cushion its fall.

Similar "arrivals" had been done quite successfully over the years, and had become known as "walking into the tree-tops" type of landing.

This landing was no cakewalk, however.

The Fleet nose-dived towards the ground, leaving a legacy of wing parts along its path and smashing the right float in half.

As the Fleet plunged, Sheldon executed an emergency procedure with one of the plane's few redeeming features – a foot-operated trip switch which cut off the fuel flow between the tanks and engine. His left foot stomped onto that switch.

The impact forces did many things to those inside.

Momentarily pinned behind the control wheel column in his left hand seat, Sheldon looked up after a few seconds, shook his head to clear it, lifted it and looked straight outside.

A vision met his eyes.

Seconds before, Danny Trousdell had been sitting next to him in the cockpit.

Now Danny, with a glazed far-away look in his eyes, sat with his back against a tree, legs splayed, looking back right at Sheldon and at the Fleet. The impact had hurled him through the Plexiglas windscreen.

Danny and Eva Driscoll were jostled around in their seats, generally unhurt but quite shaken by the experience.

In extricating himself from the cockpit to see if Danny was all right, Sheldon noticed that his right shoe was missing. Once outside the cockpit, he found his shoe close to him. Danny seemed to be intact, suffering no internal injuries.

Sheldon walked over to the right side of the cabin section, calling for Danny and Eva to see if they were all right.

"We're fine," yelled Danny. Oddly, all of the passenger cabin windows remained intact. "However, something seems wrong with the dog. Can you smash one of those windows so we can get out?"

Entering delayed shock, Sheldon broke out in loud gales of laughter, and stood there shaking from head to toe. He thought the situation was absolutely ludicrous, almost hilarious.

Danny knew that Sheldon couldn't break the window from outside, not standing there laughing his guts out. He located an axe, standard emergency equipment, and broke a window. The sounds of shattering glass brought Sheldon back to reality, and next thing he knew, he was holding the Driscoll dog in his arms.

Dan and Eva had put the dog inside a special travelling cage before take-off, and in turn, secured the cage to the last row of the Fleet's ten seats. The impact must have sprung the latch, and propelled the dog forward to strike the bulkhead at the front of the passenger cabin, breaking its neck instantly.

The dog whimpered once in Sheldon's arms, then died.

Sheldon gently lowered it to the ground then helped Danny and Eva out of the plane. He went around to check on Danny one more time. He was still sitting there, blinking slowly, staring straight ahead.

Using his 9mm Luger automatic pistol, Sheldon fired off the standard international distress signal, three shots in succession. All hoped somebody nearby would hear them.

All YSAT pilots carried side arms on gold cargo flights; they were responsible for gold shipments until officially released at their terminals.

Gold shipments meant almost as much to YSAT as did the air mail. If any gold was lost, the company would incur financial disaster. Gold shipments on YSAT aircraft also meant nearly double payments in weight. If the air mail weighed more than five hundred pounds, dispatchers added a second section to the flight. Since gold shipped out under air mail, weights often exceeded the five hundred pound air mail limit, and YSAT would be paid for putting on a second aircraft.

Shipments ranged in value from as little as $30,000 to a high of $250,000.

However, no one was worried about the gold, at least not right away. While Sheldon knew they weren't far from Lower Post; he also knew that the Liard River was generally well-travelled at this time of year by trappers, prospectors, fishermen, natives, police and hunters.

Checking his watch to note the time, shortly after 6 a.m., Sheldon also calculated they were about half a mile from the Liard River.

Danny seemed to regain his composure.

He stood and in a normal voice offered to walk down to the river. From there, he could turn left, toward Lower Post, and walk to help. No one gave any thought to the fact that Lower Post was on the northeast or far side of the river. A loud clear shout would bring help.

Danny left and disappeared without a trace.

He wasn't seen for the rest of that day.

Sheldon, Danny and Eva waited at the crash site, their anxiety growing with every passing hour. Surely, something must have happened to Danny by now.

Sheldon had been scheduled to arrive at the next station, Fort Nelson, around eight o'clock. All three knew that there would be a lot of radio traffic up and down the route about his radio silence since leaving Lower Post, but that the airwaves wouldn't start being busy until about eight-thirty, half an hour after his estimated time of arrival (ETA).

They were certain a search and rescue effort would be launched for them before nine o'clock. They were right: Lower Post base radio operator Colin Reid alerted Fort St. John that although Sheldon hadn't radioed a *May Day* - an international radio distress call - there had been a report of three shots having been heard shortly after Sheldon had taken off.

Attempts made by radio to contact Sheldon in the Fleet proved futile, but that could have been for any number of reasons, including an unserviceable radio.

As luck would have it, someone heading up-river to Lower Post did hear Sheldon's three-group shots. But since sounds in the forests are deceptive at best, the listener couldn't tell BC Police Officer Clark exactly where the sounds came from, nor how far away from his position they might have been when he first heard them.

Since Sheldon had taken off a few minutes before six o'clock, base personnel thought something might have happened. Of course, it could always have been someone else in distress.

Officer Clark quickly rounded up a search party and headed downstream. Every now and then, he shut off the outboard engine, hoping to hear more shots, or sounds, or even sight someone on shore.

Sheldon worried that his repeating shots in groups of three in a row might not have been heard by passing motorized river traffic. Motorboats coasted quite some distance from the river bank, and those early outboard engines made quite a racket.

The trio made its way through to the river bank, figuring correctly that they had a better chance of being seen by passing river traffic, hoping that someone had launched a search and rescue mission for them. They also hoped they might find out which way Danny had turned, or learn something of his whereabouts.

After being sighted by a member of Officer Clark's search party soon after,

Sheldon, Danny and Eva all assumed that Danny had made his way to Lower Post after all.

Their hopes for Danny plummeted on learning that he hadn't made it there, at least not by the time Officer Clark had left them.

The search party helped Sheldon retrieve the gold shipment from the wreck, and in what seemed like no time flat, all were back at Lower Post. Colin radioed Fort St. John that pilot, passengers and gold shipment were safe, and was advised in return that pilot Charlie Tweed would take off the following day to return the group to Edmonton headquarters.

Naturally, the air mail in this case was delayed by an extra day, but it got there nevertheless.

What had happened to Danny?

He showed up later that evening.

Instead of turning left at the river bank, he went right, probably more confused than he or his colleagues would ever realize as a result of the trauma incurred during the accident.

Danny covered quite a few miles before a prospector, Angus McDonald, had spotted him.

Angus had been on the opposite shore at his camp and he looked up to see what his dog was barking at. He couldn't believe his eyes: an apparition, all dressed in immaculate white, was stumbling along on the far bank. Truly an amazing sight, given the time, locale and circumstances. All YSAT mechanics who flew the route wore white coveralls. This was a good public relations gesture which served the company well. Since Danny was the duty mechanic for this flight, he dressed accordingly.

He quickly got into his boat, fetched Danny over to his camp and warmed him by the campfire while Danny told him what had happened.

Grant, having been notified about the crash and having been given a report on the safety of the pilot and passengers, is reputed to have immediately quipped, in all seriousness: "What about the gold? Where is it?"

He also set up a recovery plan for Sheldon should Sheldon have been frightened of resuming his flying career by this, his second crash.

Grant had been the victim of a near-paralyzing accident himself before 1935, and knew quite well the terrifying chain of thoughts which can take place in a pilot's mind after recovering from an accident.

A Universal Fokker, registered as CAFU and affectionately dubbed "Old FOO-FOO," from its registration letters, waited for him in Fort St. John. Grant didn't want his best pilot to lose his nerve and thought that the best way to help was to put him back into the cockpit right away.

Sheldon never did have any qualms about returning to the air.

It was where he belonged.

As luck would have it a second time (who says lightning never strikes twice?) FOO-FOO's engine threatened to quit on him when but 40 miles (64 km) out of Edmonton.

Its World War I vintage engine had swallowed a valve, but Sheldon shrugged his shoulders and insisted that it keep on working on eight of its nine cylinders.

War clouds in the autumn of 1939 brought post office officials and YSAT together in close conference. Fears were high that coastal cities might come under attack; the Japanese were already moving into the Aleutian Islands. The company and the post office decided it would be a good safety measure to temporarily shunt the air mail service from Vancouver inland to Kamloops.

This suited YSAT to a "t". Its newest and most modern aircraft, a pair of two-engine Barkley Grows, BLV and BMG, were too poorly-equipped for icing conditions which prevail during winter over the mountains between Vancouver and the interior.

The BG was a good streamlined performer with a fixed landing gear. It cruised nicely at between 10,000 (3,048 m) and 12,000 feet (3,658 m), and was perfect for mountain work, carrying between eight and ten passengers along at about 160 miles an hour (257 km/hr).

However, it was not equipped with de-icing boots along the leading edges of its wings or tail assembly, although it did have conventional alcohol de-icing for its propellers.

Military and civilian authorities knew that Hitler was tightening his Axis belt, cozying-up to his Axis friend, Japan, thereby posing a distinct threat to many west coast cities in both Canada and the United States, alarmingly close to Alaska.

The post office moved the air mail flights into Kamloops on November 1, 1939, until March 1940. When Grant asked Sheldon to move to Kamloops to oversee operations, military engineers were already hard at work developing the vital new Alaska Highway link, and upgrading all airports along the Northwest Staging Route to Whitehorse and Alaska.

Here again, Sheldon had racked up another first, with a local newspaper photographer showing Sheldon accepting a receipt from Kamloops Postmaster W.A. Wylie for the registered mail on board YSAT's Barkley Grow, the *Yukon Queen*.

Publicity such as this suited Kamloops quite well, as it was being promoted as a perfect pilot training centre and was already logged as an emergency landing field for Trans-Canada Airlines.

As important a role as TCAL played in the development of Canada as a nation, YSAT's contributions to the northern and northwestern development of this nation were of no less significance.

## 2. Hopes and Headlines

Sheldon would never have made it to the cockpit of any aircraft had his mother and father anything to say about it. They tried to keep him out of it.

Sheldon, born in Kingston, Ontario, on January 26, 1911, was the third of four children in Rev. H. B. and Minnie Luck's family. His sister, Mae, firstborn, married Andrew Gleddie, a Prairie man, and when the first edition of this book was printed in 1986, were living in White Rock, BC.

Ira, the second child, died in 1979 and the youngest, Donald, retired in Edmonton.

So, why did his parents not want him to become a pilot?

An incident took place in the summer of 1917 which soured Rev. Luck's enthusiasm for anything to do with aviation,

Rev. Luck's Free Methodist ministry had kept the family on the move in the central part of the Canadian province of Ontario - from Kingston in 1911 ... to Bracebridge in 1914 ... and in 1917, on to Holt, near Newmarket, about mid-way between Toronto and Barrie.

The incident which completely soured Rev. Luck on aviation took place after he had closed the parsonage at Holt. He had left Holt to pick up his family, vacationing at Grandmother and Grandfather Luck's home in Hillsdale, some 15 miles (24 km) north of Barrie.

Rev. Luck's horse-drawn buggy was making good time, until a large touring car loaded with young air corps pilots from the military base and airport at nearby Camp Borden came careening down the narrow dirt road.

The car hit the back of the buggy, flipping it and Rev. Luck upside down into the ditch.

The horse took off for parts unknown while Rev. Luck regained his senses. Someone found the horse the following day.

Such an accident could only result in one reaction from hard-working Rev. Luck, who was born in the less mechanized year of 1873. From here on in, aviation had become a no-no, especially where young pilots were concerned.

By 1917, Canadian aviation was only nine years old, having only taken wing in 1909.

But judging from this road accident, as far as Rev. Luck was concerned, aviators were obviously irresponsible fellows… definitely not the type of career for a preacher's son to follow.

He figured that if Sheldon or any other child of theirs was destined to get to heaven, it would be in a dignified manner, and not by flying an airplane.

This attitude put quite a strain on Sheldon over the next few years, as tending to the flocks kept the Luck family on the move again, through to Midland, Ontario, and out into the western province of Alberta, to Ponoka, Edmonton and, for a while, Calgary by 1927.

Despite his parent's frowning on aviation as a career for Sheldon, he already knew who his heroes were: they were the pilots of the day, pioneers one and all, and many of them veterans of World War I.

And in Alberta, Sheldon could match faces to names of these heroes.

As early as 1925, Sheldon had already begun asking questions about flying, even before the family moved to Alberta.

Could the son of a poor preacher man learn to fly?

It seemed almost impossible to make such a big jump, from being a preacher's son in church to being a pilot in the cockpit.

Pilots were celebrities and admired by young and old.

Whenever he and Ira could get away from home chores, they would walk to the Calgary Aerodrome on Saturday afternoons, fists tightly clenching lunches packed by Mother, and watch their heroes at work, both on their aircraft and while they flew.

Sheldon, Ira and other wide-eyed youngsters went so often to the airfields that it did not take them long to be able to identify their favorite heroes from a distance, spotting them by their clothing and the very way they walked.

The pedestal on which young people had elevated these pilots came naturally. Aviation is considered to have five generations, or levels, of pilots, the first generation being the aviators who flew in World War I, risking life and limb with a good chance of never coming back. When one did return, he most likely had become an excellent pilot, well-trained and disciplined… steeled by the rigors of war to meet any coming adversary head-on.

This was the very stuff dreams were made of!

Second-generation pilots, such as Sheldon, would make their mark in their own way, but this would not take place for a while yet.

In the late '20s and early '30s, the World War I aviators were the A-list of the flying elite, the *crème-de-la-crème*... the true-and-tested eagles of the air.

One of these heroes had been Wop May.

For years he had been known, respected and liked in and around the western Canada and especially Alberta, largely due to his narrow escape in World War I from the famous German air ace, Baron Manfred Von Richtofen... better known as the Red Baron.

Probably every school child in Canada knew the story of how Wop had strayed into the Red Baron's gun sights and how his flying companion, another Canadian, Lieutenant Roy Brown, came in from behind Wop, and shot down the Red Baron.

After the war ended, Wop had teamed up with Vic Homer of Commercial Airways, operating out of Edmonton.

In January, 1929, diphtheria had broken out in Little Red River, Alberta, nearly 400 miles (644 km) north of Edmonton. Wop and Vic took Wop's Avro Avian airplane - G-CAVB - and with it, flew enough diphtheria anti-toxin to treat two hundred cases to a waiting dogsled team at Fort Vermillion, about 50 miles (80 km) from Little Red River.

This mercy flight only enhanced their already solid and well-established reputation.

This reputation played a large role in influencing Sheldon to become a pilot. But he knew it would be no easy task to become one. Young men, barely out of their teenage tears, really believed and felt that too many things stood in the way of taking pilot training. They believed they needed a minimum of a university education, or an engineering course at least, if not having joined the Armed Forces.

So, Sheldon took a stab at military training. Rejected by what has later would become the Royal Canadian Air Force because he did not have an engineering-based educational background. Therefore, he set out to acquire this very background at what has since become the Southern Alberta Institute of Technology and Art.

But it wasn't quite enough.

An air force officer strongly urged him to return to school, go to university and work towards a diploma - good advice which would give easy access to flying. But Sheldon rejected this advice. He wasn't alone in this rejection. Many of his colleagues did not bother to take the same advice either, choosing a more direct route into the air.

With a few kind strokes of good luck he met Art and Lowell Dunsmore, who both worked for Bill Rutledge's flying service. Rutledge's service was essentially a flying school, but **not** a flying club which received government support. Flying schools got zip in the way of support.

Art was one of the few men who straightened out Sheldon's misconceptions of what it took to learn how to fly. Hell no, he said, if you had the money, it didn't matter a whit if you weren't a gentleman, or an officer, you could be taught to fly.

Mere money and a great yearning to learn to fly were the key assets to becoming a pilot.

By applying a lot of ingenuity in getting jobs when they were as scarce as hen's teeth, and by putting his back into every job he could get his hands on, Sheldon saved enough to start ground school.

Dunsmore had left Rutledge to return to farm work, but two other pilots took Sheldon under their wing. They were Tom Burney and Max Wisebroad, who instructed him right through ground school and into flight training.

In between odd jobs, he delved deeply into the basics and principles of aerodynamics,. He hung on to every word and breath of his instructors when they met in the rear section of the hangar, which was reserved for teaching fledgling pilots.

A deep sense of respect surrounded him and his instructors; something he insisted is lost today. The two-way rapport between him and his teachers was steeped in traditional value systems which led to a sense of professionalism.

The time had arrived for his solo flight.

He studied hard and finally understood the principles of aerodynamics.

During this time, he also worked, and earned another $116 in cold, hard cash.

He used $100 of it to pay for dual instruction time in the air. The remaining $16 paid for his solo flight.

Christmas Eve 1930, turned out to be a magic day for Sheldon at the Calgary Aerodrome. It had been scheduled to be his last session in dual instruction. He and Tom Burney climbed into CF-AMZ, the American Eagle biplane on which he took hands-on flight training.

He and Tom had already logged five hours and five minutes of flying time in the Eagle.

Unknown to Sheldon, Tom had judged that their graduation time had arrived.

Tom sat quietly in the back of the fore-and-aft cockpit, watching Sheldon make a couple of circuits – basically laps around the airport, some landings and take offs. Finally, he made a smooth three-point landing in front of the Rutledge hangar, letting the aircraft settle down on the two front wheels and tail skid at the same instant, bringing it to a smooth stop in a relatively short distance.

Tom reached over to tap Sheldon on the shoulder, and with a waving motion of his arm, indicated that Sheldon turn the aircraft around and return to the take-off position across the field.

Worried that he had made some goofs on what he knew was to qualify him to make his first solo flight … and that Tom would want him to repeat certain maneouvers before turning him loose alone… Sheldon waited for further instructions, Gosport tube at the ready.

NOTE: The Gosport tube was a primitive forerunner of today's modern radio, and it operated on the same principle as a doctor's stethoscope.

It was the essence of simplicity.

Not much for looks, but it worked.

It was nothing more than a hollow rubber tube which connected the front and rear cockpits, splitting into two components at each location.

One tube went to the student's helmet, acting as an earphone while the second went into a speaking apparatus which served as a microphone.

Vibrations against metal imbedded in the helmet could be readily understood by both pilot and instructor.

Flying students, including Sheldon, were actively encouraged to make their own Gosport tubes as part of their training. This involved going to town to collect the necessary parts, which included a rubber hose, usually borrowed with or without Mother's permission from her hot water bottle or enema tube, a valve cap protector used on automobile tires, a fine piece of thin gauge paper and other odds and ends, such as solder.

As he taxied to take-off position, Sheldon expected to hear Tom's voice asking him to make another circuit. To his surprise, he saw that Tom was climbing out of the cockpit, and so far not a word had been said since he landed.

"How do you feel?" asked Tom, now standing beside Sheldon.

"Fine, thanks," replied Sheldon, not too certain about what Tom was doing, his mind never registering the obvious.

"Do you think you can do another landing, just like this last one?"

Sheldon was now grinning from ear to ear, adrenalin coursing throughout his body. He answered with two words: "Yes, Sir!"

This was it! His first solo!

Without another word Tom walked around the wing and back to the starboard, or right, wing tip. He carefully removed his scarf and carefully fixed it to an inter-wing strut with a pin which he removed from his pocket. He knotted the scarf and secured it tightly to prevent it from coming loose in flight, but in such a way that it would trail as a stream for all to see, both from the air and from the ground.

Sheldon could hardly wait.

Finally, those long months, years, actually, from the time he first asked about the possibilities of learning to fly were about to pay off. It had been worth hauling manure from the city stockyards, getting up at five o'clock every day to spread it out over private farms around the city, and of hunting for every type of job he could lay his hands on. He had become a *gofer*. *Go-fer*-this, *go-fer*-that, digging ditches, carrying plasterers' hods, clerking in a men's clothing store… anything to raise money to pay for his flying lessons.

Within seconds, he would launch a flying career stretching well into his seventies and see him do things no one in his family would dare envision even in the wildest stretches of their imaginations.

That he had taken up flying came as quite a shock to his father and mother, who wanted Sheldon closer to God all right, but by means of the cloth and not the cockpit.

Glancing out now at another piece of cloth, the scarf, he knew it broadcast to all who saw it that this was his first solo. A World War I tradition, it had already become a part of the aviation liturgy of the day.

Tom waved at him and Sheldon prepared to take off.

Here he was 18 years old and ready to fly alone for the first time in his life! A dream was being fulfilled.

### Suddenly, he became a birdman… flying!!!

"Suddenly I was airborne. I was a birdman, flying, and there was nobody else in the cockpit in front of me. I really was on my own. This was an experience I do not think I can ever repeat in my lifetime. They don't have open-cockpit aircraft for new pilots today. The aircraft they use are all closed in from the environment. Gone is the smell of the engine, the grease, the oil which often got into the open cockpit and the hot smell from the engine exhaust … you could smell it streaming in around the windshield. It was all part of the thrill.

"It was a terrific, fantastic and great feeling. Flying is the one thing that we do in life in which man comes very close to being a bird. We weren't born to fly, but humanity has triumphed, with the help of science, over nature. In flight is the one time when one can physically feel very near to God."

Then, all too soon, another nearly perfect three-point landing … and his solo became history. It seemed that everybody in Calgary had turned out en masse at the airfield to do another traditional thing: pat him on the back and shake his hand in sincere congratulations.

In a way, he honoured the intent, if not the detail, of his parents' strongest wishes that he be very near to God.

For the next 54 consecutive years, from December 24th, 1930, to early in January 1984, when he voluntarily surrendered his private pilot's license - he'd let his commercial end of his license lapse some years before - Sheldon Luck spent as many days as he could just… walking on air.

So much for his solo.

Next thing in line, he needed to pass his private pilot's license test. Circumstances dictated that he wait until the summer of 1931 before being tested. Few flight tests were ever conducted in winter in those early days of commercial aviation. He'd have to wait until the testing inspector had more free time and could come to Calgary to test him.

An accident with the American Eagle on which he had soloed added to the delay. Another student had dumped it into a haystack, and the ever-present cash shortage prevented Rutledge from repairing it immediately.

In time, arrangements were made for Sheldon to rent Wop May's Avro Avian, G-CAVB, for his flight test.

The time had arrived to put his young wings to work and earn a living.

But, he couldn't do that either - not yet, not with a mere private pilot's license. He needed a commercial license. And, to get that, he needed more work. Odd jobs were tough enough to get while he was earning his wings and things looked no rosier now than when he had soloed. In fact his right to fly came complete with a restriction: he couldn't be tested for his commercial license, which would legally permit him to fly for money, until he'd accumulated fifty more hours in the air as a private pilot.

He faced the prospect of fifty more hours of air time with a shrug.

It had to get done.

It would be done, as simple as that.

He persevered, scraped up whatever money he could, usually in $16 chunks, which was enough to rent an aircraft and buy an hour's worth of fuel.

Sheldon wasn't the type to do things half-way. In addition to worrying about building up enough air time to qualify for his commercial ticket, he was also busy building a family at age 20. He married Isabel Hunter on Dec. 11th, 1931, and ten months later, earned enough to feed himself, his wife and their first-born child, Jamie. As his family grew so did the list of aircraft types on which he qualified to fly.

Between his private pilot's test and June 1933, when he received his commercial license (No. 102 in Canada), Sheldon strove to not only maintain his proficiency, but to constantly upgrade his personal flying skills. He practiced take offs and landings in bad weather, flew at night, and aroused the interest not only of families who lived near the Calgary Aerodrome, but of newspaper reporters and editors in the region.

And he put in a good number of hours flying local mercy missions as well, bringing food to stranded cattle in winter, and in one instance, flying a man to meet an eastbound train to take him to his father's funeral back east.

However, those night-time flights, especially the ones undertaken in bad weather, drew more media interest than the mercy missions, even though a few of them made their way into print as well.

One typical story, and its headline, is reprinted from Sheldon's massive clippings files:

*Pilot Flies in Rain Because He Wants to*

*Night flights, combined with take offs and landings under unfavourable weather conditions, were practiced by a pilot to the entertainment of scores of Calgarians at the municipal airport Thursday night. He is Sheldon Luck, 123 Eighteenth Avenue northwest.*

*The young pilot made several successful take offs and landings during the evening. Many autos arrived at the field during the evening as occupants braved the elements to watch the flight practices. Flights were made in the course of training as a commercial pilot.*

Both the reporter's and editor's attention focused more on those who "braved the elements to watch the flight practices" than on the daring young man who was really braving the elements to improve his proficiency level. Unknown to them they were watching history in the making, particularly, one history-making flight which would take place but a few years down the road and terminate under just about the same conditions as the above flight.

### The legend of the Whacky Waco – or Whiskey Six

Sheldon developed a great deal of respect for the unknown after he received his commercial license. Especially when he and his friend, Ron Campbell, thought they knew what the "unknown" was.

Take the case of the "Whacky Waco"… it wasn't the aircraft Sheldon remembered it to be, which had been blessed with the name "Whiskey Six," in honour of its rum-running days between Canada and the United States during prohibition.

We'll call it the "Whacky Waco" for now, because the incident deserves to be related and it could teach young pilots a good lesson in self-knowledge, especially those new ones who may think they know a lot about their engines.

A friend, Tim Kirby, at Royalite Oil (now Gulf) had bought a plane and wanted the two-cockpit craft stored nearer his Calgary home so he could continue his flying lessons. The flight provided just the opportunity for more air time for Sheldon as well. Tim asked Sheldon to drive down to Turner Valley, south and a bit east of Calgary, where the airplane was stored, and fly it back to Calgary for him. Ron Campbell, and a helper, drove with Sheldon in Ron's uncle's McLaughlin Buick.

The trip should have been a milk run.

Built of conventional tubing and construction techniques, "Whiskey Six" had a Curtiss-Wright V-8 engine which left much to be desired. Sheldon and Ron drove to the machine, and had a hard time getting it started. He and Sheldon cleaned the carburetor filters and gas line.

At least they looked clean afterwards.

Four gallons of gas went into the tank. It flowed freely and the engine seemed to turn over like well-oiled clockwork. Sheldon taxied for take-off. The Waco climbed nicely and lightly, and Ron began the drive back to Calgary, to pick up Sheldon at the airfield.

Ron hadn't made it to the highway before he heard the V-8 give a gruesome sputter. He knew right away what it meant: no gas. Sheldon had taken it up to 200 feet (61 m) when the engine coughed, sputtered again, and died. No problem from where Sheldon sat. Turner Valley was a broad ranching area with a lot of wide-open fields. Sheldon picked the nearest one, and Ron drove out to meet him.

All three young men went over that engine once again.

Sure enough, the filter was clogged.

At the time, many felt something heavy lay in the air over Turner Valley, but those "many" who claimed this "something heavy" could never describe exactly what it was. But odd, often unexplainable things did happen there every now and then.

Ron and Sheldon thought that this "something heavy" was contaminating the fuel. Whatever the reason, the fuel was contaminated. Car drivers often complained of finding a residue in the fuel tanks of their cars, and blamed it on this "something heavy".

Lines re-cleaned and filter cleared, Ron and Sheldon were absolutely certain she would fly, that the problem would not recur.

Ron spun the propeller once again, waved Sheldon off and went back to the Buick, wondering if indeed it would stay flying.

It didn't.

It got a little bit higher and further than the first flight before the engine died a second time. Ron, wiser by now, hung around the field just long enough to see Sheldon skim over a barbed wire fence in the distance.

Sheldon had pointed the Waco's noise at a nearby oil derrick.

As far as the drill crew was concerned, Sheldon was hell-bent-for-leather on destruction and had that airplane aimed right at them. They didn't know him from a hole in the ground, and for a few frightening moments they couldn't care less who he was.

What he was about to do to them took their undivided attention!

They abandoned that rig in what must have been Olympian standard record-setting time!

Sheldon could see no reason for their alarm and obvious panic to leave the tower because he fully intended to miss it by a large margin, as he had planned to land close by. He was just enjoying the gliding ride down and was taking in some sightseeing, without once threatening either his safety or the safety of the aircraft on its way down.

The oil rig crew did not know what was on Sheldon's mind. The crew was aware that this reckless pilot had scads of room in which to safely land the plane elsewhere.

No way could they be blamed for thinking they were about to be wiped out.

By the time Sheldon and the Waco slid noiselessly past the derrick, every man from that crew was on the ground, looking on in awe.

As far as Sheldon was concerned, he was one more landing closer to Calgary than before.

He'd get that Waco there yet.

He waited for Ron to show up, and they again tackled the fuel lines and filter, cleaning them as clean as whistles.

For the third time, Ron spun the prop and the Waco took to the air cleanly and easily. Once airborne for a few minutes, Sheldon spotted the community of Okotoks, about 20 miles (32 km) south of Calgary.

As he set his sights for the airfield, the engine quit.

Again.

Sheldon admitted that he should have chosen a field more in parallel with the highway instead of crossing the highway before landing a third time. As he crossed over the highway, with about 20 feet (6 m) to spare above the crown of the road to clear the fence on the far side, he had taken notice of the traffic.

It was light traffic and almost immediately below him.

He looked out and saw bodies sticking out of windows of the cars below, heads upturned looking up at him, while the cars were still in motion.

The drivers of the two cars paid more attention to him crossing the highway than where they were going. Sheldon never saw what happened, concentrating on looking straight ahead at his selected landing spot.

The two cars stopped together, in the same spot, with nicks and dents marking their meeting place.

No one saw the third car.

That driver was probably busy as well looking at Sheldon cross the highway and bring the plane down smoothly over the field. The third car's driver realized too late that he was about to plow into the first two, and made an emergency turn into the ditch. Had the ditch been deeper and wider, it would have flipped, but it merely came to rest on its side.

At the end of its landing roll, Sheldon wisely decided to stay in the cockpit. When it came to a standstill, he stood up and looked about in time to see a donnybrook break out on the road, and could faintly hear the hooting and hollering which accompanied the melee.

Thinking that he was to blame for their attention, he decided to remain in the cockpit until Ron arrived.

If he or Ron had any real smarts at all, they'd have abandoned the Waco then and there.

But no, he wanted to keep his promise to Tim, and if he didn't get the Waco to Calgary, he'd have a harder time building up his hours in a rented aircraft which he could ill afford: Tim had offered Sheldon the use of the Waco for free, and all Sheldon had to do was provide the gas.

However, these boys discovered that they were fast learners at cleaning fuel lines and filters.

Within moments of Ron's arrival, Sheldon had the Waco in the air for a third leg of the flight. This time however, he didn't set out in a bee-line for Calgary right away. He climbed and circled for altitude, hoping that, if the engine quit on him again, he could glide all the way in if he got high enough.

Those early aircraft had an impressive and comfortable glide ratio.

The engine did quit a couple of more times, but eventually Sheldon got it close enough to the airfield to set it down in yet another empty field. He avoided flying over populated areas, fearing the worst.

Seven days later, Ron and Sheldon decided to pull the gas tank apart, cleaned the gunk out of it, and put it back together. This time it worked fine, and Tim kept his promise in return.

It was the greatest training he'd ever had, he claims. In years to come Sheldon would experience many more forced landings, under much more adverse conditions than those encountered with the "Whacky Waco."

### A commercial pilot's licence is no guarantee of a flying job

Even with his commercial license in hand, he still had to find work as a professional pilot. Sheldon had first met Grant in 1932, before Grant had formed Independent Airways, the predecessor of United Air Transport / Yukon Southern Air Transport. He'd seen him again in 1933, and got the same answer about a job: not yet.

Sheldon decided to try what other aviators at the time were doing, and went fishing.

In the winter of 1934-35, he teamed up with a friend, North Sawle. North would later die in a jet crash in Karachi, as First Officer on Canadian Pacific Air Lines' first jet-liner, the Comet.

Both Sheldon and North were working on their air engineer's license to add to their skills level. Being able to make repairs to their engines and aircraft, while hundreds of miles from the nearest maintenance base, added a lot of value to a pilot, not only from the boss's point of view, but from a survival basis as well. Sheldon would obtain his engineer's license in 1937.

North had been between jobs in Edmonton, and he and Sheldon were together when Sheldon got a charter.

Fish prospector Red McIntosh wanted a charter in the Wabasca region to scout likely looking lakes for fish.

The fish hunt didn't pan out; Red was having his problem locating the fish in quantities and Sheldon and North were having their share of difficulties with the American Eagle high-wing monoplane and its Wright J6-5 engine. It had a malfunctioning carburetor, resulting in a steady stream of black smoke whenever they started the engine.

Sheldon and North decided that a return trip to Edmonton offered the only chance of a permanent cure; they kept on trying to make minor adjustments, but to no avail. They made alternate arrangements for Red and tried to get back to base as soon as possible.

Another adjustment before take-off.

Sheldon's turn came to try and fix the problem.

He stood on the ski while North taxied out for a run. Not fast enough to take it into flight, just skimming along over the ice. Nearby fishermen watched with ample curiosity, alerted to each test run was advertised by the black smoke belching from the exhaust.

They looked on in awe staring at a two madmen ... one standing on one of the skis outside the plane while other was up in the cockpit, taxiing it along at quite a clip.

Little did they know that the madman standing on the ski was the pilot of this fast-moving aircraft - Sheldon.

He had instructed North to go at it, full bore, just one more time ... so that he, Sheldon, could make one more teeny-tiny adjustment to the carburetor.

He was safe. Five straight miles (8 km) of smooth ice surface lay ahead of the Eagle.

Sheldon stood on the ski, with his head poked inside the engine; the cowling had been removed earlier.

He waved to North to go for another test run. Sheldon hung onto the engine mounting tube with one hand, his other free to reach into the engine compartment with a screwdriver to make an adjustment while the plane was taxiing.

North got the Eagle wound up and going. Sheldon studied the behaviour of the carburetor, so much so that he caught North's attention, which should have been elsewhere – in front of him, not below him.

North thought it would be a good thing to peer over the side of the cockpit to see what Sheldon was doing.

Neither thought of looking straight ahead.

Nor straight down, well below the ski on which Sheldon stood.

Seconds later, some sensation alerted Sheldon to pull his head back just a touch from the engine compartment and greatly inspired him look straight down.

Down… 10 feet (3 m) down, to the ice surface.

Then he looked straight up.

To see North staring down at him.

Both suddenly realized that the Eagle had taken flight.

Sheldon instantly lost all further interest in the carburetor and hung on for dear life.

He was horrified,

North throttled back and gently eased the Eagle's nose back onto the ice, where it belonged. He didn't want to lose Sheldon.

Kaboom!

The landing nearly knocked Sheldon from the ski.

Finally, the Eagle, North and Sheldon were all at rest.

They looked back and saw a two-hundred yard gap missing from their ski tracks. It had been an easy thing for the Eagle to take off under such optimum conditions. Lots of power, unmarked snow without any vertical height reference for North, and a relatively light aircraft all combined for an unplanned flight and prompted their next decision: live with the billowing smoke and head for Edmonton now.

With Sheldon at the controls, they planned to make it to the Big Bend of the Athabasca River, west of Whitecourt and about 90 miles (145 km) west of Edmonton. They planned to fly to Whitecourt, then on to Edmonton.

Still some distance from the Big Bend, the Jacobs engine quit. Sheldon glided the Eagle to the lee of an island where a smooth ice surface afforded a safe landing spot.

The Yellowhead Highway (Hwy. 16) today is on the north side of the river. It wasn't there then when they could have used it. There was a sawmill about 10 miles (16 km) from the Big Bend, closer to Whitecourt, and they knew of a timber hauling trail which led to the Canadian National Railway mainline at Whitecourt.

Safely down and with the aircraft secured as best they could, North removed the carburetor and bundled it into one of the many fish sacks they had optimistically stowed on board. Both packed bush survival kits and took off on foot.

They went downriver, knowing that retrieving the Eagle would be no problem once they got to Edmonton. Getting there turned out to be more difficult than they first imagined. Dark set in and neither knew their exact position, other than being somewhere between forty or more miles (64 km) from Whitecourt.

The best place for walking turned out to be along the edge of the riverbank, using snowshoes. Every now and then one would remove the snowshoes, clamber to the top of the bank, and take a bearing. They'd soon have to stop for the night; breaks in the ice occur naturally even in the coldest of weather, and with the onset of night, they couldn't see clear water patches in time to stop.

Moments after removing their snowshoes and resuming their journey atop the bank, they sighted a small clearing - a natural moose pasture with a good adjacent timber stand.

Both were tuned into each other's wavelength on sighting the clearing and simultaneously said: "This is a perfect spot for a trapper's line cabin." Within moments, they had found the cabin, which their instincts had told them would be there.

It measured about 6-by-8 feet (1.8-by-2.4 m), but with a low ceiling, so low that Sheldon and North had to stoop inside. As with similar line cabins this one also had a small tin heater. The last user, if not the owner, had been true to the code of the wilderness and left enough kindling for the next occupant to start a fire. Soon the interior became cozy. Hay strewn about the floor made a perfect mattress and within minutes, they had forgotten all about the -50°F temperature outside.

A snappy, cold winter day greeted them next morning, cloudless skies above, just right to continue their walk to safety. They replaced the kindling after making a small breakfast, and resumed their walk, parallel to the river. Not too long after, they heard the sound of an engine, apparently coming from the west. They turned towards the source and came upon a trail, obviously cut for and used by a tractor/sled wood-hauling combination.

Soon a Cat 30 tractor came along, pulling two timber-laden sleds. The pair on board the tractor looked slightly nonplussed at the sight of two well-dressed pilots, complete in their furs, and offered them a lift.

Sheldon and North threw their packsacks onto the sleds, eagerly accepted the ride, and took turns warming up in the control seat of the Cat. Within days the Eagle had been recovered and brought back to Edmonton.

Survival tactics such as this, along with many other successful charters improved his pilot skills, while at the same time doing two other things - putting bread and butter on the family dinner table and satisfying his appetite for adventure and excitement.

In time, he teamed up with the Muncaster family at Advanced Air Services, where Ron had already been working as a mechanic.

Sheldon and Ron were destined to make history without any fuss or bother, when they became the first pilot-mechanic team to cross the Canadian Rockies in a single-engine aircraft, at night, from west to east.

A good aircraft, homesickness, hunger and a washed-out sales trip into north-central British Columbia were among the key ingredients to this history-making flight on September 5$^{th}$, 1935, from Williams Lake, BC to Calgary.

**One for the aviation record books: fly over the mountains at night – from west to east, with matches to read the instrument panel**

Such a flight, in a single engine aircraft, is not even recommended today, despite the great improvements in aircraft, instrumentation, navigational aids, the higher reliability of engines, of communications facilities, and weather reporting facilities.

Nor would they realize that they had, in fact, made a historic flight until some time after the deed had been done, dispensed with, and generally forgotten by those involved and those who even heard of it.

It would be nearly half a century before information on the flight surfaced. Twice in two years.

The Canadian public first read about the flight in a trivia article on Nov. 28, 1981, in the *Today* Magazine's *You Asked Us* column.

The second took place when Sheldon told a national television audience in prime time on CBC-TV's *Front Page Challenge* in February, 1982, during the seven-year span in which Sheldon and I carried out extensive interviews to recall his adventures in the air and on the ground, all the while tape-recording them and later me transcribing them into hundreds of single-spaced typewritten pages – now deposited in Canada's Public Archives in Ottawa, ON, under the Fonds Ted Beaudoin – Sheldon Luck.

The late Gordon Sinclair, panelist on the show, told the show's audience that he had vaguely remembered a headline about the event. He couldn't have heard about it, said Sheldon with a slight shy grin ... because he and Ron hardly told a soul about it for fear it would have been considered an illegal flight and they might have been grounded at the time.

They also kept quiet because both men thought little of the flight as an accomplishment.

Much had led up to that flight.

Certainly Sheldon made headlines landing at night, in the rain, at Calgary. Canadian pilot training in the early 1930s concentrated on good weather flying only.

Bush aircraft weren't designed for sustained night flights. Instructors urged their students to avoid, at all costs, the combination of bad weather and darkness.

"Smart" pilots did not fly at night, or in the rain. Fortunately for the world, rapidly improving and developing technology abruptly ended this fallacious line of thought.

Sheldon had joined the Muncaster family's Advanced Air Services in the summer of 1935. AAS was a small family-owned business led by the Mother Muncaster and her son, Phil.

One of the first business decisions taken involved Ron and Sheldon. They would make a good will public relations trip into the north-central regions of British Columbia, and try to promote business in an area which was predicted to boom quite heavily in the coming years.

Concurrently, a suitable aircraft had come up for sale, a deHavilland Puss Moth, registered as AGW, owned by Consolidated Mining and Smelting Ltd., in Trail, BC. The company became Cominco, a CP subsidiary. Its then general manager, William A. Archibald, is the acknowledged founder of business aviation in Canada, who later earned Canada's coveted McKee Trophy for his use of AGW and other aircraft as business tools since early May 1929.

A couple of exploratory trips to Trail by Sheldon saw AGW change hands, and in no time flat, Ron and Sheldon were wending their way to Prince George, their starting point on the sales trip. They got there only to discover they had been beaten to the punch by Grant McConachie.

There wasn't enough business left in the area to make their stay worthwhile.

While in Prince George, Sheldon met the Pan American Airways Lockheed 10 aircrew who were flying the bodies of two famous men back to their families.

Internationally known humorist Will Rogers and his globe-trotting pilot, Wylie Post, had drowned a few days earlier when their plane crashed on take-off at Point Barrows, Alaska. Years later, Sheldon had occasion to recall this event when Archie McMullen, Canadian Airways Limited, gave him two photographs of Rogers and Post, taken at the dock the night before their fated take-off.

Disappointed at having been beaten by Grant, Sheldon and Ron flew down to the next major communities in line, Quesnel and Williams Lake, where they made their last stop. Plans had called for them to round out their trip by flying to Kamloops, and returning to Calgary by following the Canadian Pacific Railway mainline through the mountains in nice, easy stages.

They made just enough money barnstorming to purchase gas when they asked themselves what to do next?

Go home.

Right now.

Both were tired of barnstorming; Sheldon was homesick and Ron was starving for a good home-cooked meal. Since no other business prospects loomed in sight, why not go home, right away?

An Imperial Oil road map served well enough to plot a direct line of flight over the mountains, which would see them pass, in succession, the Columbia, Cariboo, Selkirk and Rocky Mountain ranges.

Sheldon planned to cross them all at an average altitude of 15,000 feet (4,572 m) above sea level.

Neither knew anything about weather conditions en route, or around Calgary.

Perfect weather conditions prevailed at Williams Lake, and both assumed it should continue that way over the mountains.

Their intention had never been to make a night-time crossing of the Rockies.

Sheldon had reckoned that, given the late sunsets and considerable amount of light after dusk in these high latitudes, he could just set down in Calgary shortly before or after total darkness. Waiting around to try and make a long distance call would have meant another hour or two of delay, telephone services being what they were then.

Radio weather forecasts for commercial pilots were non-existent at that time, and there were no weather stations along their intended route.

AGW had been equipped for night flying, but the rating held good only if it had an on-board power supply for its navigation lights.

He and Ron had neglected to mount the spare battery in the aircraft before taking off from Calgary, so it didn't possess the necessary juice to power the navigation lights, or the instrument lights in the cockpit.

In their anxiety to get home, they both overlooked another critical item dealing with sunset: Calgary is in another time zone, one hour later than Williams Lake. He'd forgotten to calculate the extra hour or so of darkness into his estimated flying time.

One more unknown threatened to intrude into their well laid-out plans – a violent thunderstorm which was pummeling Calgary with rain and high winds. If it moved on eastward, it just might clear enough for him to make a safe landing.

One without headlines this time as nobody knew they were planning to come home that night. Given all givens, and whatever unknowns lay ahead, they took off on a perfect pre-autumn day.

The little Puss Moth had ample fuel to handle the 360-mile straight line distance between Williams Lake and Calgary. AGW droned on over the first mountain range, the Cariboos. Shortly before crossing the Thompson River Valley, Sheldon noticed a massive build-up of cloud cover ahead. It would rapidly diminish the remaining amount of visible light along his intended flight path. However, he knew he'd be safe by maintaining his heading and staying at 15,000 feet (4,572 m), room enough to clear the tallest mountains, which lurked ahead for unsuspecting and less experienced pilots.

*Photographic reproduction of a 3'x2' water-colour painting of AGW in flight. I had commissioned and paid Sicamous, BC artist Charlaine Cooke $300 to paint it for me in 1986, to commemorate this historic flight. I also used this painting as the background for the cover of the original book, Walking on Air.*

It got darker all right, and, as luck would have it, Ron had a package of matches.

They came in handy as every now and then he leaned over from his rear seat and struck a match. This gave Sheldon just enough light to read the instrument panel.

Not long after, both were longing to see any kind of light reflected from the cloud layers which were above and below them. They would at least indicate the lights of Banff, Alberta, especially the long string of lights which would identify the Banff Springs Hotel.

Sheldon had lost all visual contact with the ground from the Thompson River Valley.

Seconds later they spotted a familiar and heartwarming sight through a break in the clouds - the Ghost River Dam. They knew they were nearly home. He brought the plane down through the cloud layers in time to see the lights of Cochrane, about 20 miles (32 km) west of Calgary.

Further on, he made out the dim lights of Calgary.

The dimness of those lights gave him the clue as to what had blocked his vision. He had been flying through the trailing edge of the massive storm which had poured over Calgary earlier, while they were taking off from Williams Lake. Had the storm not been there, the city lights of Calgary would have been sparkling like a field of diamonds. The dimness told him something had walked over Calgary, and was still lingering there.

He circled and did what he had practised for earlier, practices which made him headlines: night landings. This time, however, he did not want a headline of any kind: just get into the city safely, and with little fuss and bother.

This landing had a greater element of risk. Since nobody knew they were coming home, the airfield lay in total darkness. He knew Bruce Wadell, a civic caretaker who lived in the upstairs part of the hanger. He pinned his hopes that Bruce would be attracted by AGW's engine noise and wake him, so that he could get up, open the hangar door and throw the light switch inside the hangar.

It would make a perfect beacon.

He guessed right.

Bruce did wake up, flicked on the hangar light then opened the hangar door.

Sheldon landed and taxied up to the hangar.

He had narrowly avoided disaster, but he wouldn't know about it until daybreak.

The weather had been generous to farmers, and the Calgary airfield had yielded a second crop that season. He had no idea that night that he made his landing between parallel rows of haycocks. They weren't there when he and Ron left for Prince George!

The entry in his log book:

| Date | Type | Pax/Ohs. | Height | Air Base | Course |
|------|------|----------|--------|----------|--------|
| 5.9.35 | CF-AGW | SL & RC | 15,000 | 4:05 | Wm. Lake - Cal. |

Officials soon learned of his unauthorized nighttime crossing of the Rockies and toyed with the idea of pulling his license as a penalty for undertaking such a hazardous flight. Ron recalls someone asking if he and Sheldon ever gave any thought to the possibility they might have broken their necks during that flight, and answering a simple: "No."

One government official told Sheldon a few months later that it had been a pity that the flight could not have been sanctioned by the Department of National Defense Civil Aviation Branch, as it might have been a fully recognized aviation first in Canada.

It was a Canadian aviation first, but this was not officially recognized until 1981.

Sheldon's style was always to keep a low profile, especially about his accomplishments, which accounts for the silence about this feat all these many years.

He never pushed the limits of his family name: Luck.

As he said a number of times ... to him, it wasn't a big hairy deal, and neither he nor Ron ever considered it a significant flight in any way.

And, he admitted to having been a little bit worried at the time that he had squeaked in after dark, and that officials might suspend him as punishment.

### Put it down. Now. Here… just to be on the lee side of things

Sometimes nature can whip up quite an emergency without any mechanical thing going wrong, and force an eager and keen pilot to do the right thing: put the plane down.

Right now.

Right here.

This happened to Sheldon one day shortly after he joined UAT. He took on another fish prospecting charter which inadvertently generated more headlines for his scrapbook.

George McInnis, of McInnis Products, and his manager George Schlaedar, had chartered Sheldon to take them to Fond du Lac, at the east end of Lake Athabasca in the northern regions of the Canadian Prairie province of Saskatchewan.

Sheldon filed a flight plan for the Fairchild FC2W2 that called for an overnight stop at Fort McMurray, then to head out the next day, north and east over Cree Lake, out over Lake Athabasca and on into the narrows and land at Fond du Lac.

They made it to Fort McMurray, but the rest of the flight plan fell apart after take-off.

Sheldon and the two Georges had taken off on a cold December Sunday, under a high overcast. Sheldon took the Fairchild as high as he could, but the ceiling kept crowding him, closer to the ground with every passing mile.

It started snowing, lightly at first, then harder, driving Sheldon closer to the tree tops, socking him in on all sides. Just a little more of this, he figured, and forget Fond du Lac; he didn't want to crash through the icy lakes below and go to the real *fond du lac* – French words for "bottom of the lake."

He settled for the first suitable ice-covered lake surface and put the Fairchild down, for the night, or until the snow cleared. Not in the least concerned about being stranded, Sheldon stood in good company - both Georges were excellent bushmen.

Sheldon taxied the Fairchild to a likely looking snow bank, barely touching the wing tip against the top of the bank. His intention was plain: use the area below the wing as a snow-free area in which to set up a tent. The men helped him spread a canvas engine cover atop the wing, letting it hang loose below. It made a good makeshift tent, quite a far cry from its conventional use.

In short order, the trio had built a comfortable niche for themselves between the fuselage, with a snowdrift on one side and the bank on the other. Sheldon spread his caribou skin out as a ground sheet and the three men crawled into their sleeping bags for the night ... a little on the cool side, but comfortable.

They stayed there all the next day, the next night and a good part of the following day, when the weather cleared enough for Sheldon to resume his flight.

Since nobody in Edmonton expected them back for a few days, no one knew that they were being held back by nothing more complicated than the weather.

Sheldon did not expect any publicity from the trip, which he got anyway a few days after they returned.

He thought that McInnis, who always relished good publicity, released their story to the newspapers when they returned. The only value this trip had to Sheldon was of a purely statistical nature: it turned out to be the longest time in his flying career that he'd been holed up by weather.

**Passenger-laden float plane chugs merrily along without its pilot... who was *not* swimming in the water**

Then there were emergencies caused by simple human error. Like in not cleaning a grease glob from a wing strut, something which almost cost him his life and terrified his passengers, who at no time were ever in any danger to begin with. It just seemed that way.

This event took place at Fort St. James, B.C., about 80 miles (129 km) west of Prince George, soon after Grant had instructed Sheldon to look after UAT interests in north-central British Columbia. A government charter had been booked for an early September morning flight. A local Indian affairs agent from nearby Vanderhoof accompanied an interpreter and two federal government doctors. The trip was a regular health-and-welfare visit to remote Indian tribes, and could only be done rapidly by air charter.

First stop was Fort Ware, almost 240 air miles (386 km) due north of Fort St. James, on the Finlay River.

Pete Seeman, his mechanic, helped load the Fokker and stood at the dock to watch Sheldon taxi it out onto the calm waters of Stuart Lake. Ahead of them stretched nearly 35 miles (56 km) of lake, ample room for a smooth take-off.

Few were awake at this early hour: Isabel, usually an early riser, was inside their cabin making her first pot of coffee for the day, and a neighbour, Blackie, was busy hammering on his cabin roof down the shore a way. When it looked like Sheldon was going to put her on the step - a position any float plane assumes just prior to take-off - Pete returned to the UAT cabin to catch up on his sleep.

Since the Fokker cockpit had no heat, Sheldon dressed warmly for the anticipated cold: leather jacket, sweater, flying suit and knee-high flying boots, with mile-long laces.

The four passengers were secure in their cabin, aft and below the cockpit. This cabin could only be entered by one door, on the left or port side of the fuselage. The tops of the port floats served as a walkway for passengers and pilot. Wing struts made it awkward to travel fore and aft with any ease when the plane was at dock.

Once the passengers and cargo were positioned for correct weight distribution as the pilot wanted, he would make certain the door was secured, then ease his way forward past the large cabin windows, climb the few steps up to the cockpit and close the canopy as he settled in.

A small slot in the bulkhead separating the cabin and the cockpit permitted the pilot and passengers to see each other and talk when needed.

Sheldon taxied out some distance from shore and retracted the float rudders before he poured on the power.

No need to wake anyone else.

However, the Fokker wouldn't rise to the occasion. (*Pun intended.*)

He nearly cursed the badly-underpowered aircraft and the calm autumn morning. A headwind might have helped provide more lift when he applied power, but the lake surface was mirror-smooth.

He notched the power back to engine idle, and, squirming around in his seat, opened the slot to the passenger cabin. A fast visual check revealed that they and the cargo were all in the correct places for centre-of-gravity positioning. However, it wouldn't hurt to get down and just take a closer, more intimate and personal look, and see if he could reshuffle the load distribution a little better.

The Fokker had travelled quite some distance from shore, but that was all right. Ahead lay plenty of clear water to continue the take-off. He put the engine in idle. His plan was to shunt more weight forward.

With his back to the wing struts, Sheldon began to descend the ladder, unable to spot the grease glob which lingered just a few inches lower, where his hand was heading.

He reached out, grabbed the strut, lost his balance as his hand slid on the grease, and plunked into the water.

The Fokker engine continued its casual idle.

It seemed to him that the moment he entered the water, it triggered the first breeze of the morning.

A light breeze, nonetheless, but enough of one to put some distance between him and the Fokker, which was behaving more like a sail boat, trapping the wind, than an airplane.

He caught a better glimpse of his passengers… confirming that he had seen a look of sheer horror on their faces.

What was their pilot doing in the water, getting farther away by the second?

Was the plane in motion?

Nothing would stop that Fokker now, unless one of his passengers could get out and stop the engine, or bring the plane around to pick him from the ice-cold water.

Sheldon looked around, estimated he was nearly two miles (3.2 km) from shore. His gaze fell on the very spot which in twenty years would become the family ranch.

Right now however, he had to shed clothing.

He tried to remove his leather jacket, but couldn't.

His hands were numbing.

He reached underwater, trying to bring up a knee to remove the cumbersome boot.

Couldn't do that either.

Only one thing left to do if he didn't want to drown was to tread water.

In the meantime, back in the Fokker, his passengers were over their initial shock of seeing their pilot fall overboard.

This motivated them rapidly into a flurry of helter-skelter activity. In the excitement, one of the passengers grabbed the interior door latch, hoping to get out, but broke the latch instead.

Now they were locked inside a slowly moving, airplane. Without the benefit of a pilot in control!

Another passenger broke one of the large cabin windows and Sheldon watched, wanting to laugh, but unable to do so.

His fellow passengers didn't want this passenger to fall into the water with Sheldon. They had wrapped his waist with rope - standard equipment for bush aircraft. He made it safely, rope trailing behind, out the window and went straight for the cabin door, opening it from the outside.

With each passing moment, Sheldon felt colder and colder and felt himself getting weaker and weaker. He watched, helplessly, as the man on the floats had made his way to the cockpit.

Now what?

Obviously, he'd had some experience with boats, and under the right circumstances, an aircraft with an idling engine and float rudders lowered, could be handled like a power boat. But Sheldon had raised the float rudders and the aircraft went to where the wind blew it.

And Sheldon simply did not have the energy to yell to the man in the cockpit how to lower the rudders.

Nearing exhaustion, Sheldon looked to the Fokker and saw it heading for shore under its own power. He saw the reaction before he heard the engine revolutions increase.

Its nose reared to the air and the tail dropped in response to the power thrust.

The nose went up and the tail went down.

Whoosh!

A second time, nose down and tail up.

More power.

He could clearly hear the clamoring of the passengers inside the cabin over the noise of the engine, and could make out the demands from the passengers in the cabin that their new pilot cease and desist immediately, lest they all fall out and drown.

The Fokker came to rest on a beach, engine still ticking over.

He saw the passengers descend from the cabin and cockpit, mill about for a few seconds, then pick up the plane, turn it around and point its nose at Sheldon.

This time they wouldn't fail in their rescue attempt!

Sheldon, frustrated, thought: they were just moments away from first-class help - if they had just gone through the brush which hid the B.C. Police constable's cabin. Sheldon knew exactly where the plane was but the passengers did not know how close they were to land-based help.

Then, it seemed as if in no time, they were all back on board.

One in the cockpit, the others in the cabin.

Off to the rescue! Again.

The man in the cockpit was a little more certain of himself this time, and knew that he could risk putting on more power without the danger of having the plane take off.

As the plane headed downwind, he poured on the power.

Up nose.

Down nose.

Up nose.

Down nose.

Sheldon knew exactly what the distraught man was trying to do.

Every time the Fokker's nose came down, the plane weather cocked into the wind. He'd try to overcome this effect by putting on more power, hoping to compensate and tried to steer a straight line to Sheldon by using the tail rudder, which tended to respond when the propeller, under power, threw a slip stream over the fuselage.

As the Fokker closed in on Sheldon, a new fear overwhelmed the driver.

The Fokker passed him by, and Sheldon stared in disbelief!

"He went right by me, the dumb —."

He later learned that the man in the cockpit was worried that the spinning propeller might decapitate Sheldon if he got too close, never realizing that the propeller tips were quite a safe distance above the water level.

He swung around for another try.

This time the floats eased beside him and he saw two men leaning over the float.

They were secured around their waists with a rope which went into the cabin and which was being held fast by two men inside the cabin... a five-man rescue attempt – 1 novice pilot, 2 ropers and 2 grabbers ready to reach out and haul Sheldon up, and out of the water.

Within seconds, they reached out, grabbed him by the underarms, flipped a rope over his head and shoulders, and yanked him onto the floats.

Sheldon then dimly became aware of being jostled into the comfort of the cabin, eyeballing a scene which always brought a smile to his face whenever he recalled it in years to come: another rope led out from the cabin door and snaked its way along the side of the fuselage, up the ladder and disappeared into the cockpit. No way were they going to lose their second pilot!

Somewhere between alertness and passing out, Sheldon collapsed onto the cabin floor. He looked up to the peephole in the fore bulkhead and found an eye looking back at him: their new pilot.

He's certain he detected a note of great concern in the part of the face which was visible to him.

Under an explosion of noise, everybody began speaking to each other, all at once, and Sheldon broke out in gales of spontaneous laughter, howling until tears cascaded down his face.

The emotional release helped ease the shock on Sheldon's system, and he was able to, at last, issue verbal instructions on how to lower the float rudders. In what seemed like no time flat, the Fokker was safely moored to the dock.

Sheldon was entering late stages of hypothermia - severe loss of body heat - and wouldn't have lasted much longer in those frigid waters. Normal survival time in cold northern waters is usually about fifteen minutes. Much credit goes to his pilot's leather helmet, which capped his body heat. Most heat in a person treading water is lost through an unprotected head.

Returning to the UAT cabin-office, they woke Pete and trundled Sheldon into a sleeping bag, piled another on top of that one, and poured a rather large quantity of 35-overproof rum down his willing and dry throat.

Purely for medicinal purposes!

It was a frustrating thing back then having an engine failure on the highway because there was just no easy way to "call" for help in such a dilemma. There were no cell phones in those days, and farm phones were few and far between.

However, with today's modern highway and communications systems with cellular telephones, GPS systems, various automobile associations, and regular police patrols, it's often just a matter of time before help is on the way.

But an engine failure in the air, particularly during the early days of commercial aviation, hundreds of miles from nowhere, was a harrowing, mind-bending thing for the pilot.

It was always best to pray heartily, and hope some almighty force would keep that propeller turning when the pilot knew that it couldn't turn any longer.

Sheldon had just this happen to him, on two aircraft, one after another, on the same mail run, on the same day.

### FOO-FOO's engine does well on seven of its nine cylinders...

He'd been assigned a Fairchild 71 on the Whitehorse-Fort St. John leg of the air mail run. Returning on the southbound flight from Whitehorse, he planned a stop at Watson Lake. The base had since been moved from Lower Post, an incident detailed elsewhere in these pages.

The Fairchild had extra fuel, a light load of air mail and cargo, and if he didn't have to buck winds in the expected overcast en route, he'd make it to Watson Lake in good time.

Shortly after taking off from Whitehorse, visibility dropped by a sizeable margin; by the time he was half-way to Watson Lake, the ceiling continued to drop and incoming snow reduced forward visibility to a few miles in front of the Fairchild's nose. The flight path, roughly 120 miles (193 km) in a straight line, passed about 40 miles (64 km) north of Teslin, a few miles north of the Yukon / BC border. Had visibility been reduced more, he could always cut around to the right and make Teslin without too much worry.

Things hadn't gone completely sour, yet.

Every now and then, he'd go left, to the north.

Then right, to the south a bit, always hugging valleys as the snowfall increased in intensity. He aimed to fly over the north end of Wolf Lake, as he had in mind a relatively low pass which would put him on an easy course to the upper Liard River, which he could then follow downstream into Watson Lake.

He could not afford to relax now, as forward visibility was dropping to less than two miles (3.2 km), often dipping to less than a mile (.61 km), crowding his operating limits. It could drop to zero without warning, and he'd be in serious danger of flying into a solid wall of rock if he wasn't on the ball.

Wolf Lake and the pass behind him, he spotted the Liard River at the same time as the engine started to miss and do strange things.

He had no inkling as to the cause of the problem, but he did find some relief by experimenting with reduced power settings. They seemed to do the trick, for a bit. Just fast enough to stay above the Fairchild's stalling speed, that critical point at which an aircraft assumes all the flying characteristics of a falling rock.

Nor was there any place to let down below; the Liard River in these northern regions is a wild one. He kept on flying, 150 feet (46 m) above the river's mottled and jumbled ice surface.

Visibility now down to a mile-and-a-half, Sheldon knew he had one more

*Photo from Sheldon's personal collection (one of many now housed permanently in the Public Archives of Canada) shows FOO-FOO, with Grant McConachie at the controls atop the plane and Sheldon, giving the plane a push from behind the struts, at Peerless Lake, Alberta, winter 1936.*

hurdle the aircraft had to clear. It lay smack dead ahead: a huge hump across the east bank of the river, then downhill four miles (6.4 km) into Watson Lake.

Would the Fairchild make the grade?

Not all UAT aircraft were radio-equipped, and without his radio in the Fairchild, there was no way he could get word out about his developing emergency.

Those waiting at Watson Lake knew he was already late, but they didn't know why. They could only speculate; either he had set down at Wolf Lake or had taken a detour down to Teslin to wait for better weather. Anything else was basically unthinkable at the time.

He managed to coax more altitude from the Fairchild, almost stroking it to greater heights to at last barely clear the tree tops of that clump of ground... so close to safety.

The Wasp C engine just about didn't make it. Within minutes, everyone, including Sheldon, was tickled pink to see the Fairchild make a smooth landing.

While mechanics went to the engine, Sheldon called Fort St. John to make arrangements for another plane to be flown up the next day so he could continue his flight. The mechanics discovered the flaw in the Wasp C engine - a broken valve which had cracked a cylinder. A radio call to Fort St. John produced the spare part needed to repair the engine.

Sheldon's friend Alex Dame arrived the following morning with a Fokker, the affectionately dubbed FOO-FOO. Alex, an excellent two-hit man was as good an engineer as he was a pilot, and stayed at Watson Lake to repair and fly the Fairchild. Sheldon resumed his air mail flight in the true tradition of the postman, even if airborne, and a wee bit late.

He lifted off from Watson Lake at two o'clock the next afternoon, FOO-FOO's tanks topped off, heading for Fort St. John. Since there was no mail for the interim base, Fort Nelson, some 270 miles (247 km) down the leg, he planned to overfly Fort Nelson and continue south about another 195 miles

(314 km) into Fort St. John.

FOO-FOO, built in the 1920s, could clip along at 80-85 miles an hour (129 km – 138 km/hr), and he estimated a little over six hours for the 465-mile (748 km) hop, planning to land in Fort St. John around eight o'clock, a bit after dark.

The beautiful, cold clear afternoon sky hinted at an easy flight, and both Fort Nelson and Fort St. John reported similar good weather around them.

Sheldon coaxed a few more miles an hour from the 300 horsepower J5 Wright engine, despite the fact that the Fokker was underpowered.

This was the same make of engine which Lindbergh used to power his *Spirit of St. Louis* across the Atlantic Ocean.

Now that he had FOO-FOO flying a little faster, Sheldon calculated he'd save nearly an hour's flying time.

Things continued fairly smoothly until well past Fort Nelson.

At about 8,000 feet (2,438 m), the J5 Wright tried to make minced meat out of itself when a cylinder packed it in. He'd reached a point between the Sikanni Chief River and Charlie Lake, the company's float plane base a few miles outside of Fort St. John.

Whatever the difficulty was now, he faced similar height-of-land problems that he had to deal with the day before. There was one more height of land which he didn't think FOO-FOO could climb over with its engine throbbing away on a missing piston.

Sheldon worked hard to keep the plane at 2,000 feet (609 m) above the river valley, and began looking really hard for a place to land. There just didn't seem to be any safe place in which to set down, not with the ice jams on the river and its numerous bends.

He had no choice but to make a 180-degree turn and head back to Fort Nelson, by following the Sikanni Chief River to where it joined the Nelson River, and over the Nelson River into Fort Nelson.

At exactly the same moment he made the decision to turn, a second cylinder in the engine gave up the ghost. Amazingly the Wright continued to function on seven of its nine cylinders.

Definitely a tribute to a Superior Power, the engine's manufacturers or engineers, or to someone, somewhere.

And in that order too, most likely.

Looking down between his feet, straddling the rear of the engine, he could see red coming from the engine compartment. The Fokker had no firewall separating the pilot from the engine.

In what seemed to him to be an eternity later, Sheldon sighted the junction of the Sikanni Chief and Nelson River banks barely 50 feet (15 m) below his seat.

FOO-FOO still chugged along.

Every now and then the J5 Wright would lose a few revs, and FOO-FOO responded accordingly by dropping a few feet.

Mysteriously, the Wright would regain the lost revs, lifting the Fokker and elevating Sheldon's spirits by that much more.

This maddening cycle continued as he slowly made a left turn over the Nelson River.

Each time the engine lost some revs, his heart rate increased; it dropped whenever the revs picked up.

The longer he spent so close to the Nelson, the more he appreciated the vast differences between it and the Sikanni Chief River. If needed, he could easily make an emergency landing immediately, in the moonlight.

Yet, FOO-FOO was still airborne, though why he never found out, and this was no time to ask silly questions of the Powers That Be.

If he could just get FOO-FOO as close in to Fort Nelson as possible, and delay a forced landing to the last possible moment, he could even walk into town!

All the bases knew something else had gone wrong; they consoled themselves in recalling yesterday's incident and in their knowledge that Sheldon would never be a bold pilot, that he'd probably live to be an old pilot, one never known to push his luck, always living up to his family name.

Chris Christensen, Fort Nelson base manager and radio operator, had been in touch with Grant and the company's chief pilot, Ted Field - before Ted was promoted to general manager - to let them both know that Sheldon was overdue again.

Grant and Ted suggested that Chris round up a good supply of gas lamps from the building which houses the base's 32-volt electrical plant, common to remote trading posts.

Chris did just that, preparing to light them and mark out the ice strip for Sheldon.

While Chris was lighting the lamps, a couple of them fell sideways, spilled their volatile fuel and flame from hell broke loose in the radio shack.

At that same instant in time, somebody ran into the shack saying he'd heard the sounds of an aircraft engine nearby.

Chris had burned his hands badly in trying to put out the fire, feeling guilty at not being there to light Sheldon's way in, but knowing he couldn't let the radio shack burn to the ground. He managed to contain the fire before too much damage was done inside the shack.

Sheldon didn't need the lanterns. He had spotted the lights of Fort Nelson from a distance. Maintaining a height of 25 feet (8 m) above the river ice, he now nursed one worry: would that engine hold out, just a few minutes longer?

The skis kissed the ice.

He pulled back on the throttle.

Just as he started doing this, the engine died.

He looked up and saw a row of swinging lanterns coming down the bank. In moments men were swarming over him and FOO-FOO, critically eyeballing the battered J5 Wright engine.

Oil covered the fuselage surface and a large pool lay limpid on the ice below. Sheldon grabbed a prop blade with one hand and he and a friend physically lifted it vertically about a quarter of an inch.

The big end bearing was shot. Then they checked the oil tank to see how much was left: dry as a bone. Within seconds flight would have come to an abrupt end if the engine had seized.

When the replacement engine arrived, engineers carefully removed the bolts from the old one and gingerly laid it on the ice. The old engine sank when the ice finally melted.

In all probability, is still there today.

Grant later commented that he and Sheldon should retrieve the engine and send it to the Smithsonian Institute with the story of how it kept Sheldon and FOO-FOO in flight despite a diminishing oil supply.

At one stage, Grant needled Sheldon.

He loved doing this to get a rise out of the man.

"Why the hell didn't you bring FOO-FOO right on into Fort St. John, instead of returning to Fort Nelson?"

Sheldon missed the twinkle in Grant's eye, and was about to blow his stack at him for this unnecessary needling. He only prevented himself from plowing him one when he realized that Grant knew full well the Fokker would never have made that hump of land on seven cylinders and a dwindling oil supply.

### Landing fully-loaded airliner on sandbar in 1947 likely made aviation history (Does a remote sandbar a runway make?)

Sheldon had to execute an emergency decision in the spring of 1940 which was probably a first in Canadian aviation history where an airliner is concerned, and is likely a world first as well.

The incident drew so much private, government and public attention that it stood a retelling on an Edmonton radio station, CKUA, seven years later, in 1947. Listeners were amazed as they heard the narrator relate the story which follows.

Sheldon taxied the gleaming YSAT Barkley Grow out to the runway. Receiving tower clearance for take-off, he lifted cleanly from Whitehorse one sunny afternoon.

Balmy spring weather hinted at a smooth flight at 10,000 feet (3,048 m).

Vancouver, the end of the run, lay almost 920 miles (1,481 km) due south. But Sheldon and this plane were scheduled to make a 1,170-mile (1,609 km) flight, stopping at Fort St. John and Prince George before going home.

Normally the aircraft would have been on skis and due to call in at Fort Nelson, about 440 air miles (708 km) southeast of Whitehorse. Then it would have gone on to Fort St. John, another 195 miles (314 km) south and east of Fort Nelson, before flying to Prince George, 180 miles (290 km) south and west of Fort St. John.

Sheldon had flight-planned a 600-mile (966 km) direct flight from Whitehorse to Fort St. John, which would take him about 110 miles (177 km) abeam of Fort Nelson.

Warming temperatures were thawing ice on the lakes and rivers below; YSAT had put its airliners on wheels, and was not landing either at Watson Lake or at Fort Nelson where their ice runways were rotting and breaking up. Conventional runways had not yet been built at those locations.

His load included passengers, air mail, cargo, a gold shipment and his mechanic, Stan Emery, who sat next to him in his gleaming whites in the co-pilot's seat.

On reaching the towering eastern slopes of the Cassiar Range, the first group of mountains southeast of Whitehorse, Sheldon noted Watson Lake far to his left. Straight ahead, he expected to sight the Liard River Valley.

A flickering instrument needle drew his attention from outside. Seconds later his number two Wasp engine began losing oil pressure. Engines are usually numbered from left to right, using the numbers one, two, etc.; number two on a twin-engine plane is on the right wing.

The emergency had begun.

The propeller went into automatic coarse pitch, then wind-milled. The slowly rotating prop acted like a solid brick wall, reducing the plane's speed considerably and imposing imbalanced forces on the ship. Immediately, he radioed the loss of oil pressure to Fort St. John, while Stan opened the cockpit window on his right to make a visual check. He reported a lot of oil on the trailing edge of the wing and tail surfaces.

The oil pressure needle hit the zero mark, indicating serious trouble.

The engine could seize any second, or worse yet, start an engine fire. He had flown too far now on his number one engine to be able to make a safe return to Whitehorse. He was still about 100 air miles (161 km) from Fort Nelson, but he couldn't land there even if he wanted to. Nor did he think the plane could make it that far on one engine.

Circumstances had pushed the Barkley Grow irrevocably past the point of no return, yet hundreds of miles from safety. Densely wooded forests and mountain flanks lurked below.

Everything normally beautiful about the mountains when seen from the air instantly lost all of its beauty under these conditions.

The crippled BG could not maintain 10,000 feet (3,048 m) altitude on one engine. Nor could he risk going much lower. This Barkley Grow wasn't going to make it to Fort St. John; that much was certain, at least not in its current condition.

However, he wasn't in a panic. His passengers knew something was wrong, but they seemed to hold their own emotions in check, as Sheldon assured them he had a solution in mind.

They can be forgiven their doubt at the time.

He knew the capabilities of this aircraft, as well as the terrain below, like the back of his hand. A long gravel sandbar on the Liard River would serve nicely as an emergency landing strip, if he could just reach it.

That pioneering work of the mid-to-late 1930s was about to pay an unusual and unexpected dividend: the possible saving of passengers' lives, the crew and a valuable airliner, all in one shot. Sheldon had Prospector's Bar in mind, one of the many on which fuel caches had been established on the Liard River. He and many other UAT / YSAT pilots had used it, and others, a number of times before.

Not in an airliner, however.

There was just the slimmest chance he could set the plane down onto that sandbar. The BG normally required about 4,000 feet (1,213 m) of clear, paved or hard gravel runway, for a safe landing.

Aware of these safety limits, he also knew that the gravel and sand combination at the sandbars had a compaction factor which should slow the aircraft in sufficient time to prevent it from going into the Liard River. And if he was wrong, well it would be at a slow enough speed that none of the passengers would be seriously hurt. They were his foremost concern at this time.

If he could save the $75,000 aircraft in the process well all the better.

All he had to do now was find Prospector's Bar before number one packed it in from being pushed so hard. A few moments before Prospector's Bar crossed his mind, he cut the fuel supply to number two. He didn't want to face a mid-air fire in addition to his other problems.

Sheldon routinely radioed Fort St. John as the emergency took him through successive decision stages, including the one to try for Prospector's Bar. Events unfolded with dizzying speed. If one can imagine listeners glued to their sets in 1947, seven years after the incident, one can only speculate as to how YSAT base personnel were handling the tensions as the gripping drama unfolded over the airwaves.

Base personnel at Fort St. John, were no doubt passing information down the line, right into Vancouver and Edmonton headquarters.

Sheldon's voice rose in pitch with every new radio report.

Things weren't getting any better - he couldn't find Prospector's Bar.

The plane steadily lost altitude as he guided it over to the Liard River Valley, no longer worrying about losing all power over a mountainside.

Any good-looking sandbar would do, if his number one engine would just hold out.

Plenty of fuel left for it.

Reducing speed, he ordered Stan back to the passenger cabin with instructions to open the cabin door and lighten the load: he could keep the BG airborne for a little longer with less weight on board.

Stan opened the cabin door, then lying on the floor, he propped it open with his feet, overcoming the airstream pressure outside. The door hinged toward the front of the aircraft, making it possible to open it wider in flight. With his hands, he now could shove cargo and everything else he could get his hands on.

Passengers handed him their own personal luggage, which Stan thankfully and promptly ejected.

Turning to see how things were going on in the back, Sheldon saw Stan look wistfully at a large red tool box. His very own, but it weighed thirty or forty pounds. A few moments later, he looked again: the box was gone. Stan later submitted an expense claim to replace the box and his precious tools, but YSAT finances weren't anything to write home about, let alone cover the cost of a mechanic's tool box and tools. Much later, he got a new one, complete with new tools.

Feeling that time had run out, and having given up on Prospector's Bar, Sheldon spotted another sandbar. He recognized it from having flown over it many times before. Although he'd never landed on it, a gut feeling told him it could do the trick.

Maintaining a running radio commentary, he gently brought the airplane down, lower and lower, to a point where if he did not land it purposely, he'd never recover the lost altitude on the remaining engine.

He recalls thinking that the bar looked s-o-o different from this close than it had from previous sightings, but still it was the only solution to the dilemma. The spring run-off hadn't started in full force yet, and the available space on the bar looked just about right. Somewhat of a tight squeeze but better than trying to walk a passenger-laden airliner into the tree-tops.

Listeners at Fort St. John and down the line froze at their sets, unable to help or do anything.

Their emotions ran the gamut from the worst scenario they could visualize to the wildest of fears, yet all were somehow confident that, according to the commentator on radio, the best pilot in the company could pull this one off.

Time was up.

He pointed the Barkley Grow's nose straight toward the sandbar... relaying every action that he took on the radio ... his voice strained ... but clear and crisp.

Almost too crisp, some thought, as they tried to see in their minds' eyes what Sheldon was looking at with his own eyes.

For the first and only time in his flying career, Sheldon forgot his manners on the air.

The Department of Transport frowned then, and still frowns today, on profanity and unnecessary speech over commercial airwaves ... sending reminders to careless voices. Sheldon never did receive a printed notice for his next statement, though doubtless overheard by many DOT inspectors:

"Here we go in for a landing, and by the holy Jesus it better be a good one, and I don't give a good God-damn who's listening!"

Easing the craft low over the trees, he kept the river and bar to his left. He also took advantage of the one little help from above he'd had during the past half-hour: a tail wind. He made a pass and turned around to come in against that wind, which would give more lift and help in slowing the plane once it was down.

He judged it so finely that the landing gear slipped by inches above the water surface as the plane crossed the shoreline of the bar.

In Sheldon's words:

"It scooted along the gravel, with the water to my left, below the wingtip. I suddenly spotted a snag which I missed from the air. You find a lot of these big dead Cottonwood trees all along the river, and this one had hooked onto the bar in the previous year's high water. The right wheel missed it by a hair's breadth. It would certainly have snapped the landing gear. As it was, we rolled to a stop a few feet from the water's edge at the far end of the bar."

Breathing collective sighs of relief, everybody deplaned and milled around the sandbar, looking around with mixed emotions, but all alive and safe. There's nothing like a brief excursion to the edge of infinity to convert a remote sandbar into a haven.

Sheldon and Stan paced the length of the sandbar. They calculated that, from where the tail wheel made its first impression to where the front wheels now sat, short of the water by a few feet, the plane had traversed 1,000 feet (305 m).

They also left a set of arrow-straight furrows which were clearly visible in the sandy surface of the bar.

This furrowing activity is exactly what Sheldon predicted would happen on landing the heavy machine, helping it roll safely to a stop in less than a quarter of the distance normally required on a hard surface such as those at larger airports.

Stan wasted no time in identifying the problem with the faulty engine. An oil line from the engine to the propeller was joined to a small length of yellow hose by a clamp. This clamp had broken off. With the oil pressure at eighty pounds per square inch, it didn't take long for the oil pump to empty the system, right out onto the wing and tail surfaces. Later inspection revealed that the number one engine, the good one, took a much greater beating than number two. It worked so hard to keep the Barkley Grow in the air that all its seals and gaskets developed serious leaks.

One hour and forty minutes after they left Whitehorse, Sheldon, Stan and his passengers were comfortably set up for a night on the sandbar. Fortunately, both crew and passengers all had extensive bush experience. A lady passenger prepared supper from the ample emergency rations on board. What could have been an uncomfortable ending to a hair-raising flight turned into an adventure.

Afternoon gave way to early evening, temperatures stayed pleasant, everyone was alive and well, and so was the Barkley Grow.

All in all, a good day's work.

However, they were still hundreds of miles from their first stop, Fort St. John, and they had to get out of there. While the passengers prepared for their overnight stay, Sheldon and Stan reeled in the long radio antenna. It normally trailed behind the aircraft in flight, but it was now strung out behind the ship on the sandbar.

Radio reports resumed, Sheldon and the base worked out his position, and made plans for help to be flown in the next morning - to evacuate his passengers and the air mail; the gold shipment would stay on Sheldon's plane. Stan radioed his report on what he needed to fix the engine.

No way would Sheldon leave the Barkley Grow. He landed it and had every intention of flying it off the bar the next day.

Alex Dame flew in with a Fairchild 71 shortly before noon the following day, with the necessary repair parts for Stan and a new oil supply for the right engine. The men went to work, cleaning the strip, removing the large snag and turning the Barkley Grow around so it faced its incoming tracks. Sheldon planned to take it off in its own tracks. He and Stan had calculated exactly how much weight the plane could tolerate taking off under these unusual conditions, and both agreed there was ample fuel to continue the flight into Fort St. John.

The Fairchild had a payload capacity almost that of the Barkley Grow's, so taking all the passengers and some of the air mail represented no problem for Alex.

Soon Alex was airborne and circling overhead, waiting to see how Sheldon would make out on his take-off.

Alex later told Sheldon that he could see the river surface shimmer behind the Barkley Grow's propellers as they clawed their way into the sky, leaving a page of history behind on a sandbar.

Sheldon's and Stan's handling of this emergency radiate volumes about the level of competency which most airline personnel gave to convert a primitive air service into a forerunner of a first-class global airline system, which Canada and the world take so much for granted today.

Sheldon faced this, his first airline crunch, as a twenty-nine year old man. He relied on his experience as a bush pilot, adapted it to conform to airline emergency procedures and struck a new legacy for all future pilots. Yukon Southern had never lost a passenger yet, nor would it.

He had been flying for the better part of a decade and reacted in a cool-headed professional manner to avoid what would otherwise have certainly been an aviation disaster.

He telegraphed forward into time the professionalism with which he and many other seasoned professional pilots would practice in handling future serious emergencies.

## 3. Search and Rescue and other Mercy Missions

Canada boasts a geographic mix which makes it a dream for geologists, geographers, explorers, adventurists, resource developers, and generally those who want to get away from the hustle and bustle of civilization to roam and enjoy a spectacular wilderness.

For some that means the barren tundra of the high northern regions, up into the Low and High Arctic. Others prefer the gentle slopes of eastern Canada, while for some the mountain regions represent the best nature has to offer.

By and large, remote areas offer a lure hard to resist, whether it be for a vacation, aesthetic value, to enjoy the environment, or live there as a way of life.

There's one drawback: some of these regions are so remote that in case of an accident, the wilderness can turn into a nightmare which can lead to death. Fortunately in such distress situations, modern communications systems and reliable aircraft can quickly come to the rescue to bring a victim medical aid … often within hours.

This wasn't the case in the early decades of the 20$^{th}$ Century, when the bush pilots arrived on the scene.

Miracles in the wilderness are few and far between.

Aircraft have offered and continue to offer various types of emergency airlift services to and from the wilderness. One of these is a known as a medevac, a compound abbreviation for the words "medical air evacuation". It's often been called a "Mercy Mission" as well.

The other is referred to, especially within military circles, as a SAR – the acronym for a Search and Rescue mission, in the case of a downed pilot, and passengers, or anyone who is reported lost far from road traffic.

Mercy flights and medevacs had become almost a matter of routine for Canada's air service pioneers. On each and every charter flight... on regular flights when they became scheduled, pilots were always on the lookout to spot the unusual... and be there to help. In many respects it was and is identical to the laws of the high seas... that when a ship's captain receives word of another ship in distress, the nearest captain to the ship in distress alters course to immediately try and help.

Almost to a flight, each mercy mission flown resulted in a fair amount of publicity for the pilot and aviation company involved; sometimes the news articles were of local interest, at other times they made regional or even national headlines. With each such set of headlines would come a new business awareness of the presence in the bush of such-and-such aviation company. It was worth a whole lot more than just "free" advertising, because most of these mercy flights seemed to come loaded with hazards and danger both for the pilots and the victims they were trying to bring to safety.

Quite often an emergency signal can be spotted from the air. On one flight, Sheldon and mechanic Danny Trousdell were northbound in the Fort Nelson region, flying high enough so Sheldon could keep the Liard River in sight through the snow swirling about them.

Danny told Sheldon he'd seen something unusual on a lake surface to his right. Both he and Sheldon recognized the lake, even from this distance and in the limited visibility: they and other UAT pilots had often flown supplies to trapper Carl Norquist and his family at that lake.

As he flew nearer, something out of the ordinary began to show up. A closer look, while keeping a constant guard against whiteout and loosing sight of the Liard River, confirmed Danny's suspicion something was wrong.

Both spotted the letters "HELP" on the ice. Sheldon quickly landed the aircraft. It would mean that he and Danny would have to off-load the plane for a take-off as the small lake was surrounded by high trees. But the next flight, in or out, could readily pick up the material left behind.

Carl's wife had trekked out to the ice surface, tramped out the letters, and filled the spaces with boughs so they could be seen by passing air crews.

Carl had severely wounded himself with an axe while he was out on his line about four days from home. By the time he returned to his homestead, blood poisoning had set in.

It didn't take Sheldon and Danny long to lighten the cargo just enough to match Carl's weight, and soon enough, they had brought Carl to the hospital in Whitehorse. They arrived after dark and in time to prevent the blood poisoning from doing more damage to his body.

Another pilot later flew Carl back home.

Flights such as these made good copy for reporters and editors. Mistakes were unavoidable as sometimes the situation details got lost in the telling and re-telling to distant editors who never had a chance to talk to the pilot or victim involved.

Although the intent was certainly the best, the message would be hopelessly garbled as to what actually happened. Take the case of the *Wild West* magazine article in February 1939.

First, the newspaper report:

> *Two thick columns of smoke, the old Indian signal of distress, were understood and promptly answered last winter by a pilot of the United States Air Transport.*
>
> *One would hardly expect Indian signals to be known by flyers, but these men familiarize themselves with every sign that might mean something. Sky, sea and ground are all alike to them, and no matter where they may be, they are always on the lookout for something.*
>
> *When Sheldon saw smoke signals rising in the solitude of the snow-clad wilderness, he knew that something was the matter and came down to investigate. He saw a cottage near a small lake in a deep mountain-rimmed valley, about 100 miles (161 km) west of Watson Lake, on the British Columbia-Yukon border.*
>
> *Weather conditions had been very bad for some weeks throughout this isolated section, and it was feared that some of the lonely dwellers of this sparsely inhabited country might be in need of help of some sort. As a result, orders had been given that planes should make frequent trips, and look for any sign of trouble.*
>
> *Pilot Sheldon Luck was flying the mail to Whitehorse, and as soon as he saw the smoke rising, he knew what it meant. He spotted the collage. Billy Smith, who occupied it with his family, was watching eagerly for help to come from anywhere for he neared the end of the only food they had on hand, moose meat, and were feeling the pangs of hunger.*
>
> *When Pilot Luck resumed his trip, he left Billy Smith with a supply of fifty pounds of emergency rations, which all pilots flying into the Canadian northland carry. On his return from the Yukon, he did not forget to bring additional supplies for the trapper and his family.*

Now, what really happened:

Billy Smith and his family really did live there, in a crude log cabin.

He wasn't just running short on food and feeling hunger pangs: he only had one day's supply of moose meat on hand. Since even a small supply of moose meat can be stretched out over many days, Billy was really down and out, and desperate.

The fifty pounds of supplies Sheldon left behind consisted of a few pounds of standard emergency supplies consisting of dehydrated food packages common in those days.

The article led readers to believe that Sheldon reacted with alarm to what was a normal sight in the winter: chimney smoke.

Billy had in fact built a real signal fire, something completely different from ordinary chimney smoke, which a pilot would ignore. Billy heaped green wood onto the fire, which created a huge amount of dense black smoke. This is what drew Sheldon's attention.

There was no lake, except in the writer's imagination; that region is still muskeg country today and on the day Sheldon flew over, the area was thinly blanketed with enough snow to offer a safe landing on skis.

Obviously desperate for a good "rescue" type of the story, the writer never stopped to realize that *all* air crews flying in the north kept their eyes open for *anything* that appeared to be out of the ordinary – which usually meant that someone was in trouble.

On the issue of orders having been given that all planes should make frequent trips back and look for any signs of trouble: *poppycock*, said Sheldon. The writer or editor just didn't know the situation. Never did pilots simply take to the air to look for any sign of trouble. They don't even go up on speculation unless they know someone is in trouble.

Such was the mystique and lure of the north to far-away editors who probably didn't have the budget money to make a long distance call to the pilot involved to check out the story first-hand.

Readers loved it, whether such stories from the bush "checked out" or not.

Many of the "mercy" missions turned out to be routine flights looking for specific hunting parties, to deliver messages of importance, for humane or business reasons.

At all times, they presented the pilots with a certain element of risk and adventure, because they were flying into less frequented regions, and had to bank on their experience and general knowledge of the convoluted terrain below.

One such incident stands out in Sheldon's portfolio because of an odds-bodkins expedition which had preceded it a few years before, and because this same expedition provided him with needed fuel, hundreds of miles from Fort St. John.

### Daring '34, Bedaux Expedition hit snags while trying to drive across roadless mountains

The charter called for Sheldon to fly BC Game Department Inspector Van Dyck from Fort St. James to track down a VIP party which had been on an extended hunting trip many miles north of Hudson's Hope, itself about 40 miles (64 km) west of Fort St. John. He and the inspector had taken off from Fort St. James for the 140-mile (225 km) flight to Hudson's Hope, from where they would begin looking for the party in question. Sheldon did not remember the reason why Van Dyck was asked to locate this VIP party, suffice that it provided another revenue-generating flying contract.

But first, back in time to June, 1934, to the ill-fated Charles Bedaux Expedition.

Google *"Bedeaux Expedition"* today and you will uncover an enormous amount of information about this zany, but ever-so-adventurous explorer from France.

Nothing like him had hit British Columbia in the early 1930s, nor has anything like it ever since tackled its bogs, muskeg and mountains so ill-prepared but amazingly equipped – with all the wrong stuff, like half-track vehicles to go where no roads existed.

It came into the wilderness from out of Edmonton surrounded with booze, fanfare, horses, ladies, a Hollywood cameraman, his assistant, five Citroen half-track vehicles, and a number of advance trail-marking and fuel cache parties … mesmerizing cities and small towns along the way.

The notoriously publicity-starved Charles E. Bedaux, millionaire and one of the 1930s high-rollers was setting out to conquer the Canadian Rockies - on wheels.

He had already tackled and conquered the African jungles and the Sahara Desert with his half-tracks, led by visions of exploring where no man had gone before, with the latest technology of the time at his disposal.

Therefore, what could mere mountains do to stop his latest venture… to pioneer a road over the spine of the Rockies?

Bedaux and his party left Edmonton on July 6th, 1934, at the head of a festive parade down Jasper Avenue and a grand farewell by the Lieutenant-Governor of Alberta.

Eleven days later the party bogged down a few miles north of Fort St. John, unable to make any more progress with their vehicles, but able to continue on horseback for another 400 miles (644 km) to Fort Ware.

The entourage: Himself as the financier and expedition leader, his wife, her lady friend and their maid. He had the entire group fitted out with every detail of camping gear imaginable, and then some. According to an account from

Gordon E. Bowes' *Peace River Chronicles,* who borrowed a few pages from a provincial government surveyor and geographer who accompanied the expedition, it required:

...more than one hundred and thirty horses to carry supplies and equipment, including luxuries such as canned Devonshire Cream, pate de foie gras, silver cutlery, and cases of champagne, (and) the expedition is still vividly remembered at Fort St. John. Packers were paid at the rate of $4 a day, twice the going rate ...

...the Peace River gumbo proved too much for the half-tracks. They were abandoned less than a 100 miles (161 km) north of Fort St. John. Movie cameras recorded their mock destruction.

Bedaux is reported to have dished out $250,000 for this trip ... it is unknown whether this money was in Canadian or American dollars, French Francs or some other currency.

A good part of the money went to depositing large fuel caches throughout the anticipated portion of the route, fuel which in 1935 would have provided relief for Sheldon and Inspector Van Dyck.

Sheldon had made it to the high-level Deadman's Lake, about 4,000 feet (1,219 m) above sea level, as desolate a locale as one could imagine. On the way there, he worried about weather suddenly turning bad and marooning him there with Inspector Van Dyck.

The VIP party which the inspector sought was in far better shape to survive a long period of time in the deep northern reaches of the province than were Sheldon and Inspector Van Dyck. The hunting party consisted of several men and about 18 riding and pack horses, necessary firearms and ample camping gear.

Sheldon still could not understand why the need to locate this party, whose members could have wintered comfortably in the region.

All Sheldon had on board the Fokker was the conventional survival pack which contained a rifle, a light .410 shotgun, handy for game birds such as ptarmigan, along with staples, warm clothing, two sleeping bags, a lot of rope, tools and cutlery.

As he feared, the weather did sock him into Deadman's Lake.

He had to land, as a flight back to Hudson's Hope was too risky and the lake was ice-free except near the shoreline.

He taxied to a reasonably good beach near one of the many trappers' cabins which dot the north, and secured the aircraft for the night. The six-by-eight-by-five foot cabin had a small tin stove, a lot of old grass and bark scattered about the floor, perfect for the night. They broke out rations, made themselves comfortable, and during the evening's conversation, Inspector Van Dyck regaled Sheldon with accounts of the Bedaux Expedition.

What made it more exciting and hopeful for Sheldon was the fact that the inspector recalled reading that the Bedaux Expedition had stored some fuel at Deadman's Lake, causing Sheldon to wonder if he could find it now ... and fuel the Fokker with it the next morning. Van Dyck had also seen notations on a map and thought he could find the fuel for Sheldon.

Next morning, after cleaning up, replenishing the wood chips and bark, Sheldon left a note for the owner before leaving. Since he had no cash to leave behind, he invited the trapper to send an invoice to UAT head office in Edmonton for reimbursement of some of his supplies which he and the inspector had used.

Sheldon taxied to the location which the inspector had identified from his memory... sure enough, there was the fuel cache.

The low octane fuel was never intended for use in an aircraft engine. Bedaux's large and cumbersome French-built half-tracks were powered by six cylinder engines which ran on low octane fuel.

The Fokker's J5 engine required high-octane stuff.

However, Sheldon knew his engine and reasoned that the fuel wouldn't harm it.

They opened the seals and emptied the contents into the Fokker tanks. After take-off Sheldon circled the lake and climbed for altitude before resuming his flight to locate the VIP party. Just in case the engine did conk out on him with the low octane fuel, by flying high, he could use the altitude to make a safe return to Deadman's Lake.

The engine took the fuel without any difficulty.

Failing to spot the party that day, they returned to Hudson's Hope that night to overnight, and refueled with high-octane the next morning. He also brought along a spare fuel supply to avoid having to rely on Bedaux fuel that day.

Hours later, they located the party, dropped messages and met the men at a nearby lake.

When Grant found out that Sheldon had poured low octane fuel into the tanks, he seemed outwardly pleased at the decision, tickled that a company aircraft could use the substitute in a pinch.

Fellow mechanics and engineers weren't so forgiving. They claimed he risked wrecking the engine and losing the aircraft, to say nothing of endangering his life and that of Inspector Van Dyck.

Risky, maybe, but it was a decision only a pilot in the wilderness could have made under the circumstances.

As these "message" missions constituted normal charter flights and did not generate publicity as such, they were valuable in their own way in that they served a dual purpose - not only did the message get through but the pilot could chart, at least by eye and memory, new territory never before explored from the air.

## Routine request: be alert for a man (not knowing that the man was former U.S. President Herbert Hoover)

A routine charter could be turned into something slightly less routine, made more interesting and possibly exciting by a request received from afar.

Such as the day Sheldon was asked to keep an eye out for a very important person, a true VIP – a former president of the United States of America.

But Sheldon did not at first know who he was keeping his eyes opened for.

This was not in any way a search for a missing American president.

There never was any doubt he was missing at all in the summer of 1938. What took the flight out of the routine category was the fact that Sheldon would only learn later the identity of the man he was asked to be on the alert for.

It all began during a freighting charter, ferrying men and mining equipment from Takla Lake north 75 miles (121 km) to the Aiken Lake region. While at Takla Lake, Sheldon received an interesting radio message from Fort St. James: would he keep his eyes open on the way home for Ed Forfar's boat. There was a special VIP with him, and those back at Fort St. James simply wanted to know how they were making out.

Sheldon didn't think it too strange that he was asked to look for a VIP without being told who it was. Even though radios were far and few, listening ears were many. Sheldon and his team maintained a portable ground radio at Takla to keep in touch with the client, Consolidated Mining and Smelting.

Lakes and rivers form an intricate and well-travelled network throughout British Columbia – a boon for riverboaters and barge operators in late spring, summer and early fall, and of equal value to pilots who could use it on skis or floats when the seasons were at their peaks.

A good riverboat operator could head north up Stuart Lake from Fort St. James and connect with other lakes a good 130 miles (209 km) or more to the north.

VIP fishing and hunting parties provided good revenue for such men as Ed Forfar, whose wife Molly operated the hotel in Fort St. James when he was away. Ed had a distinctive vessel, easily identified from the air, and this was the one Sheldon was looking for when airborne.

No one was alarmed at Fort St. James, but Ed had been scheduled to return soon, and the wind had been blowing very hard the last few days, making the water excessively rough even for a boat his size. It was just a routine request.

On his last flight of the charter, Sheldon returned to Fort St. James. On the way home, he did as requested, detouring a bit here and there to check out this bay and that one. Soon, he spotted Ed's boat and party near the shores of Peaceful Bay on Stuart Lake.

He saw men milling around the boat, which was drawn up on shore. They spotted him and waved to the unknown (to them) pilot. Sheldon, knowing all was well with the party, simply continued his flight into Fort St. James to make his report that all seemed well.

Out of curiosity, he asked who the VIP happened to be.

It came as a pleasant surprise when he learned it was none other than Herbert Clark Hoover, the 31$^{st}$ president of the United States who had served his term from 1929 to 1933. He and some friends had been on an extensive hunting and fishing holiday, making headlines as they stopped in at various spots.

The request to Sheldon, and the refusal to give Hoover's name on the air was just plain common sense.

## While airplanes served the law well, they also ticked off the aboriginals

The aircraft also served law enforcement agencies well.

Aviation made it possible for police to take to the air to track suspects and bring them back to face charges to be tried for their alleged crimes.

Sheldon participated in the medical evacuation portion of the following incident, and a colleague flew the remaining part. All told, it generated considerable printer's ink not only for him, but his colleagues, the company and the resourcefulness and wit of the police.

First Nations tribes resented, often with justification, the white man's intrusion into their territories. Many aboriginals in the wilderness had not yet seen an automobile in the mid-1930s, but were familiar with the sight of an aircraft.

But, white man, him, they had seen plenty of.

Trappers and part-time traders such as Hugo Stalberg and his brother, had penetrated into Bear Lake country, about 165 air miles (266 km) northwest of Fort St. James.

The tribe didn't take kindly to the large, husky Hugo or his brother, and vicious scraps often broke out between the pair and the natives. At one stage, rumour had it that the natives had ordered Hugo out of their territory.

One of them was believed to have ordered Hugo and his brother out of his region, Hugo is reported as uttering a three-word sentence: *go to hell.*

Understandably so, this created a brawl. Hugo and his brother physically threw the native out of Hugo's cabin, on a creek close to where it emptied into the Finlay River.

Hugo's brother returned that night to his own cabin, some distance away, leaving Hugo to nurse his wounds alone.

When Hugo stepped outside his cabin door next morning, someone took a shot at him, tearing a hole in his right arm.

He went back into the cabin, wasting no time, and managed to apply a tourniquet.

He hastily threw a few things together, and cautiously made his way to his boat nearby, threw his gear into the boat and managed to shove it into the creek, bow pointed down stream.

It made its way into the Finlay River which flowed by Fort Ware, where he hoped to find medical aid and refuge… if he could survive his ugly wound.

Unable to endure any more pain, he passed out as his boat drifted downriver. Over the next 75 miles (121 km) he wafted in and out of consciousness, his arm throbbing and pulsing. It took a couple of days before he reached Fort Ware.

It was all he could do to lay still and remain covered against the bitterly cold nights and mornings.

On reaching Fort Ware, the trader radioed Fort St. John, and soon Sheldon was airborne. When he picked up Hugo, Sheldon noticed that his right arm had swollen to football-size proportions, and that his shoulder was a tattered mess. Doctors at Prince George hospital later told Sheldon that they were amazed that Hugo had made it so far, on his own, without having died on the way.

It didn't take too long before Hugo began recovering in style.

When well enough, B.C. Police Officer Frank Cook, from Fort St. James, wanted Hugo to return north with him to help him track down the man who shot hum. Frank knew Hugo and his brother were unwelcome immigrants to the woods, but a shooting is a shooting and this wasn't the civilised or legal way to settle disputes.

Authorities gave Frank carte blanche to bring the gunman to justice.

This resulted in weeks of probing, including a foray piloted by Ralph Oakes to Hugo's cabin. There, police found empty Winchester rifle cartridge casings at about the point where Hugo suspected the gunman had stood to take his shot.

But Hugo didn't have a Winchester rifle.

This led Frank directly to Carl Hanewald's trading post at Bear Lake, the only source for automatic rifles and ammunition for miles around. Records kept by Hanewald gave Frank the name he was looking for: he had recently purchased a fresh supply of ammunition, and all sales of rifles and ammunition had to be recorded.

He also learned that a suspicious lot of supplies had recently been moved from Hanewald's, northwards, by way of an Indian trail which was hundreds of years old.

Frank knew the trail well, one of many in the area. He also knew there was one special place, a ravine, where he could trap whoever was ferreting out these supplies to his still at-large suspect.

Unless the suspect's supplier intended to tramp miles around dense forest underbrush to get to the suspect, that ravine would have to be crossed sooner or later.

Frank laid the trap.

He had Ralph Oakes fly him into Bear Lake, taking Bill Forrester with him. Following a brief, police-type chat with Hanewald, Frank learned the identity of the suspect's friend who was bringing in those supplies. Thanking Carl, he returned with Bill to the plane, and instructed Ralph to fly out of sight in a direction opposite to the one he wanted to go to.

Safely out of sight from the post, Ralph returned to near where the trail led by the lake and de-planed Frank. With a few days' supplies in his backpack, Frank took the trail, and lay in wait by the ravine, screened from passing pedestrian traffic.

Soon a young girl came along and before she set foot on the fallen trees which bridged the ravine, Frank stepped out of hiding and nearly frightened her out of her wits. Within minutes, she handed a letter to Frank, addressed to his suspect, Charlie Fox, warning him that police were after him, and urging him to stay in hiding for a while. Additional instructions told him to go to a certain place on the lakeshore where he'd be looked after, and he could sell his furs. The shooting had taken place in the spring and Charlie, knowing he was the object of a police search, hadn't been able to sell his winter's fur catch yet, and summer was on strong now.

Charlie had spent four years at what was known as the Indian school in the small town of Lejac … which is now on the Yellowhead Highway between Prince George and Prince Rupert, and which boasted of one of the few literate native communities in the region.

It didn't take much longer to apprehend Charlie and bring him to trial.

Found guilty of the attempted murder of Hugo Stalberg, he received an eight-year jail sentence.

## BC newspaper credits Sheldon with "most dramatic mercy flight in history of the north"

In the spring of 1940, the Vancouver Sun credited Sheldon with participating in one of the "most dramatic mercy flights in the history of the North."

Yukon Southern had three Barkley Grow aircraft in its fleet: one was on floats and the other two, BLV and BMG, were on wheels, operating regularly between Vancouver, Fort St. John and Edmonton.

During late spring, summer and early fall all flights north from Fort St. John were carried out on the float-equipped BMW.

On one routine flight with a landing gear equipped Barkley Grow, Sheldon answered a radio plea for help while still over Moberly Lake, a few miles south of Hudson's Hope.

Young Jimmy Vance had put the blade of an axe through his foot at Watson Lake, almost severing his heel, and needed extensive medical care which could only be had at Fort St. John.

Sheldon continued to Fort St. John, and after deplaning his east-bound passengers, cargo and mail, resumed the flight at the controls of BMW. As he flew over Watson Lake, alongside the Liard River, he looked for possible landing areas. The lake itself was in the process of breaking up, making it impossible to use, and the river seemed choked with ice floes. Finally sighting a likely looking spot which seemed free of floes, he radioed that he'd continue his flight to Whitehorse and would pick up Jimmy the following morning.

A dramatic move took place during the night as three men helped relocate Jimmy from the Watson Lake base, over an old Indian trail from the northwest side of the lake, down to the Liard River where Sheldon had directed them from the air during the afternoon. An Alaska Highway bridge marks the site today.

The burly construction workers who offered to move Jimmy had fallen through the rotting ice on Watson Lake four times, nearly drowning themselves and their charge and making it hellish for Jimmy, who lay helpless on a stretcher.

As the Vancouver Sun put it: "...they laboured on through soft, treacherous muskeg, enduring untold hardship."

Sheldon had planned to take advantage of the natural current at that location, knowing that the ice tended to follow the outer fringes of the river, resulting in a relatively ice-free inside turn at the location he had spotted.

He timed his arrival for eight o'clock, unaware of the drama which had nearly drowned the entire party overnight.

As he flew to the site, he wished he'd had been in the smaller Fairchild or Norseman instead of BMW... totally the wrong aircraft for this kind of mission. She was a bit too large for the ice break-up conditions this far north, but Sheldon knew both the plane and the river, and counted on this to see him through a tricky landing and a trickier take-off.

Pilots have to take a certain amount of risk under emergency conditions, counting on the fact that rules and regulations have always built-in safety factors for just such occasions, and that aircraft can sometimes do the impossible.

The critical factor in this landing and take-off involved river ice conditions during break-up. Lake ice breaks first and works its way into river systems, plugging them solid later in the day, rendering them useless for float operations. Ice tends to refreeze at lake outlets during cold spring nights, making it possible for strong river currents to dislodge ice build-ups from the previous day.

These currents free large portions of a river from all ice until late afternoon and early evening.

When Sheldon arrived at eight o'clock, he noticed that all seemed in readiness. His predicted clear path on the river was in fact clear, giving him adequate clear water for a short landing run against a swift current. Dense willows on shore gave him some difficulty in tacking BMW into position.

He closed in to the site, keeping the propellers turning to check the force of the current as the men loaded Jimmy on board. Once he knew Jimmy was secured, he reversed his landing procedure. He kept the nose of the plane pointed against the current, tacked out into the centre of the river, and let the current take him downstream, tail first. There had been no room to turn the aircraft around.

Sensing the stern of the floats gently hit the ice down stream, he set his flaps for maximum take-off position, adjusted engine settings for maximum power and took off without any difficulty.

In what seemed like just a few minutes, but was actually longer, Jimmy was on the mend in Fort St. John hospital.

### To rescue others is fine, but to rescue yourself? That's a horse of a different colour

It's all right to rescue someone, but when you have to be rescued yourself, it can be a bit embarrassing.

Sheldon, who helped so many during his flying years, never banked on being the object of a mercy mission himself. The thought might have occurred to him during some hair-raising experiences, described in the next chapter, but for him to be the victim?

Unthinkable.

Until it happened.

Sheldon and his fellow pilots were all over the western and northwestern map of Canada in the mid-to-late 1930s doing what they did best – pioneering an air service and turning it into an airline while serving the needs of the wilderness regions.

One contract had Sheldon flying the Norseman, AZE, while ferrying supplies to a Japanese-financed mining camp on the west coast of Vancouver Island. After unloading at his first stop at Sydney Inlet Mines, Sheldon and his passenger, Stan McLay, headed to the mouth of the inlet, out over the Pacific Ocean, for the flight to Zeballos, about 45 miles (72 km) north.

The heavy seas, rising under a stiffening wind, presented no real take-off problem and AZE made it easily to 4,000 feet (1,219 m) where Sheldon set it on course.

At this time Sheldon wished that he'd been flying the company's second

Norseman, BFR, because it had a better engine - an H-Wasp.

Why?

Because without warning, parts of the Wright Whirlwind engine that pulled AZE through the air blew up.

Then, of course, it simply packed it in and quit.

A cylinder head had left the block and was later found lodged against the engine cowling.

With a dead engine, good altitude and a strong wind blowing in from the west, Sheldon began a forced glide, searching for an ideal location, preferably an inlet, a small one. He quickly found one which backed off from the ocean about a mile, offering what looked like good shelter. He briefed Stan on what he was doing, and lined himself up for the inlet entrance, targeting to arrive as close to the shore line as possible so he could nudge AZE up onto the beach.

Working hard to avoid an illusion common to such landings, in which the waves appear to be as high in an inlet as they are on the open waters, Sheldon eased the Norseman to about four or five feet above the waves.

She hit the water hard.

First the stern of the float went under water.

Then AZE pitched forward to a point where the front of the float submerged.

Waves cascaded over the top of the high wing, covering the windshield and shaking the fuselage and Sheldon and Stan along with it.

Had any structural damage occurred, at least they wouldn't have drowned as Sheldon had AZE close enough to the beach so they could swim if they had to.

However, the water buffeting stopped and the aircraft regained her composure.

Wind had drifted the plane tail first onto the beach, not exactly the way Sheldon wanted it, but it would do. UAT aircraft operating over coastal regions always flew with many long lengths of rope on board for such eventualities, along with some paddles.

Sheldon broke out a paddle and lengths of rope, and he and Stan took up positions on the port and starboard floats to try and re-position her. They had to give up as the stronger winds pushed her back tail-first onto the beach. Sheldon decided to just secure it there, to large rock formations near the water's edge.

He began to work the radio to tell Vancouver of his predicament and position.

With voice contact established, he learned Vancouver would raise a nearby Canadian fish packing vessel, who in turn advised that a closer American fishing vessel would come down the coast to help them out, but not until eight o'clock that evening.

Sheldon next went to his tide book, another standard survival gear item for coastal pilots, and studied the ebb and rise tables.

It would be a nip-and-tuck situation at eight o'clock. He wasn't worried about the beach being submerged at high tide, but there was inadequate room for the Norseman, which would be destined to head for rock and debris on the high side of the beach, pushed there by a high tide.

As the pair waited, they took turns taking up the slack on the line, or letting it out, to prevent AZE from wandering sideways in the surging ocean. As the tide rose Sheldon and Stan wondered if they'd make out all right. There seemed to be no room to shelter the aircraft tail under the rocky overhang above.

The American fishing vessel rounded the bend in the nick of time.

The captain soon understood the nature of Sheldon's concern, and ordered two men to a power boat and sent two others along to handle lines.

They told Sheldon and Stan to board the vessel while they towed the Norseman out to deeper waters so that they could secure the plane for a proper tow.

On board the vessel the captain explained that he didn't want to be late arriving in his home port, slowed by a tow, and asked if Sheldon wouldn't mind his being transferred to a Canadian fishing vessel which was but an hour behind the American?

Not at all, thank you.

The two skippers briefly conversed on the radio, and soon Sheldon and Stan were on board their third carrier that day. By morning, two refreshed men peered outside to a bright day at Ahsusat, where they waited another couple of days for a new engine to be flown in, installed and checked out.

He had often wondered idly in the past, when he was the doing the rescue, what it would fell like to be rescued.

Now he knew.

## 4. All for Laughs

While the events and incidents in the previous chapters generated exhilarating reactions, there wasn't too much humour in them.

When times were tough financially, a good joke often eased the pain somewhat. At least that's what an honest economist would say, regardless of whatever other theories are favoured.

During the morphing stages for UAT / YSAT and when it finally merged with nine others to become CPAL, things were so tough that salaries had become the standing joke of the week.

Things did get a bit better when the giant Canadian Pacific Corporation took over, but until then salaries were minimal and left much to be desired.

Grant McConachie knew the gambles he and his crews had taken were nothing less than calculated risks. He knew they'd pay off handsomely some day, but when, he didn't know. Grant promised many better things were coming, and asked all employees to tough it out with him, week after week, and share in his beliefs and visions.

Jokes made it possible to accept the reality of promises which Grant just couldn't keep... not because he didn't want to, but because the money just wasn't there in sufficient quantities.

For a while it seemed as if life was a wait-until-the-next-contract-comes-along situation.

Gruelling workloads demanded much of the men and women who worked for UAT / YSAT. Being posted to a remote base meant long lonely periods of waiting. Communications were reduced to letter and report writing, as well as occasional telegrams – if one was lucky enough to be posted near a rail line, or what were known as Continuous Wave (CW) radio and telephones, where such services existed.

### Practical jokes were a necessary way of life

Practical jokes were the release valves which made bearable the daily grind that came with risk-taking; they made bearable the agonies of working impossibly-long hours for ludicrously-low wages, and being away from home for weeks, sometimes months, on end in wild, desolate but beautiful regions of the country.

Grant knew his whole outfit came on strong with long-standing practical jokes, and were even better at creating new ones to meet changing conditions.

His crews developed a wealth of experience on which they could draw. They had a number of practical jokes which they pulled on themselves, members of their families, friends and customers, under special circumstances of course.

Newcomers to the company were prime targets.

Pilots' wives and lady friends often found themselves at the total mercy of UAT / YSAT's practical jokers.

The favourite trick often pulled on newlyweds within the company involved shortened bed slats at remote bases. The pranksters would shorten the bed slats, which were thick boards, or planks, lying across the width of the bed frame and supporting the mattresses above. To be effective, they only had to be trimmed to be less than a sixteenth of an inch longer on each side than the width of the frame.

Simply lying down quietly on the bed wouldn't produce the desired effect. Any gymnastics on that mattress however would see the mattress collapse with a resounding thud onto the floor, spilling contents and generating gales of laughter below. Most of the remote bases had bachelor, or crew quarters on the main floor and reserved upstairs rooms for married couples, or customers.

Many marriages had to be consummated elsewhere if newlyweds were in transit.

Indelicate though a joke like that may seem by today's sophisticated standards, they were always executed in good spirits, were well-intentioned, and certainly meant no harm.

### Electrical jokes were truly electrifying

Some jokes however, were downright shocking.

Such as the electrical kind.

UAT / YSAT crews really excelled at this one.

Winnipeg couches were stock items just about everywhere. And they came with bare metal spring frames, and often, with hair metal springs, exposed along the front of the couch.

Some time before a party, a reception or simply during a good-natured get together, the jokers "hot-wired" the couch to an aircraft magneto hidden elsewhere in the cabin.

Rubber tubing under the legs ensured that the juice would flow through the frame when one turned the magneto crank. A carefully hidden wire ran to the magneto, usually hidden in the kitchen or an adjacent room.

Women were few and far between at those bases, and when they arrived, they'd readily accept an invitation to a party. Any reason would do to hold a party in those days, at those remote locations. Since jeans or trousers weren't in style they invariably showed up wearing skirts. Their legs were usually bare, as nylons and silk stockings were in short supply.

The men rarely had a problem getting the lady guests to sit where they wanted them, on the Winnipeg couch. The calves of their bare legs would frequently rub against some part of the metallic frame; it couldn't be helped. One of the guys would keep his eyes posted, and at the right moment, by a pre-arranged but subtle signal, another would excuse himself and leave the room on some pretext.

Kitchen-hidden magnetos were usually under a tea towel in case one of the lady guests happened to be in the kitchen for any reason. At the right time, the one who left the living room headed for the crank, which just lay there begging to be turned.

A momentary squeal accompanied by a jerk or jump usually resulted. When done properly and over a sustained period of time, the effect could be repeated. It never harmed any woman as the shock was quite a small one, but distinctly there nevertheless. In the meantime, all the men in the room acted nonchalant, never once noticing the momentary look of puzzlement and discomfort which would accompany a jolt of juice.

Luckily for the pranksters, all victims were good-natured when told how they'd been set up.

Radios were few and far between in the bush. Movies were unheard of outside of larger communities and extensive libraries were the exclusive domain of the well-to-do.

Men and women in remote regions just had to have something else to do beside work and wait. They needed emotional outlets … otherwise they'd simply blow up at the worst possible time, and under the worst possible conditions.

As childish as these jokes seem now, they served an important bonding role in wilderness regions, and continue to do so today.

### Some jokes took a long time to set up

Some of these jokes were quite complicated and took a long time to prepare... such as when Sheldon thought he'd been called for and forgot to answer at Charlie Lake, the float plane base near Fort St. John.

Red Powell and his wife, affectionately known to UAT / YSAT crews as "Ma", operated a rooming and boarding house, which served the company until the airport was built.

Red established Charlie Lake in 1919 in a homestead search, about seven miles (11 km) north of Fort St. John, because he wanted to get away from being a carpenter in Alberta and become a farmer in BC.

He described the area as "...an 11-mile (18 km) stretch of muddy liquid entirely surrounded by unbroken land..." *(Peace River Chronicles,* by Vera Kelsey, author of *British Columbia Rides a Star.)*

He brought with him to Charlie Lake his wife, Evelyn, and their children.

When Grant first flew into the area, he landed there and asked Red and his wife if, for a fee, his company could use the lake and whatever other facilities they had on hand. She wasn't known as "Ma" yet —that would come when Grant's crews moved in.

Seems Red didn't like farming any more than carpentering, so the Powells quickly adapted their life styles to serve the needs of a growing airline instead.

Their good will and reputation had spread favourably far and wide in the wilderness. Trappers, prospectors and traders all soon learned to make Charlie Lake their own drop-in centre while they waited for UAT / YSAT planes to take them out to civilization or back into the wilderness.

Ma put them up, fed them and their dogs, transforming the Powell homestead into a regular wayside inn for air travellers. Soon, she was preparing meals and beds for twenty or more at a crack. She could handle the increased load but their original cabin surely couldn't.

A new dormitory addition, complete with double bunks, took shape. UAT / YSAT expanded services, and needed a radio operator, so naturally Red added a radio room. Now the household was complete with radio equipment, static and demands that the children "be quiet, please, Ma, I'm on the radio!"

Time for yet another addition, this one away from the original house.

A bunkhouse to be precise.

It served both the company and its passengers quite well.

Sheldon made frequent use of the bunkhouse. Each crew member usually gravitated to a favourite bunk, seldom used by anyone else even in his absence, unless the Powells had an overflow crowd. Red and Ma built cupboards for stashing personal items which remained in the bunkhouse while the crew member left for a few days, up or down the line, or to go home.

On one occasion, weather forced Sheldon to remain a few nights more than usual.

He got into the habit of burying his nose into a book as he lay on his bunk.

His keen, sharp-eyed bunkmates were never ones to let a first-class opportunity go by and took due note of this creature's nocturnal habits, repeated faithfully night after night.

One of these routines carried all the trademarks of a prime sucker-ready-for-a-practical-joke. Sheldon usually waited until everyone else seemed to be fast asleep, then carefully got up and took his nightly trek to the outhouse.

Most men rarely made it to the outhouse on warm summer nights. Relief would often come but a few steps away from the bunkhouse, in the great unspoiled outdoors.

Breath-taking stuff, this nightly whizz under the stars.

The night before his departure, Sheldon, true to his habits, took a casual look about the room… everyone was asleep… or seemed to be.

Rising, he carefully walked to the door, not wanting to wake anybody, to take his nightly constitutional. He turned the handle to open the door. A shotgun went off!

That door had led to the woodshed, which also at times served as a mudroom, and it was between the house and the outside, the only way into, or out of, the house. Unknown to Sheldon, his buddies had rigged a shotgun inside this woodshed, in such a way that when the door handle was turned, it fired a shot … but harmlessly into the woodpile.

Not knowing this, Sheldon immediately became convinced somebody was gonna blow his brains or guts sooner or later. He ran hurriedly from the woodshed and did not get far before he realized that he had been so frightened by the shotgun blast that he did not even have to go to the outhouse to complete his business.

As stated earlier, passengers were usually bunked upstairs in the Powell home. And if the paying passengers were regulars, well-known by the crews, and well-liked by them, they sometimes became the victims of practical jokes as well. Why save the good ones for employees only?

Sol Schubin, from Winnipeg, had been one of these seasoned air travellers. He often carried large quantities of cash to compete, successfully in most cases, against large fur buying corporations by being Johnny-on-the-spot with cash.

Many fur trappers were notorious for their jawbone-size debts, frequently underwritten by the larger fur-buying companies to the tune of thousands of dollars. These debts would be paid off when the furs were bought in the larger cities.

However, when Sol came around, he'd be carrying a poke of up to $50,000 in cash and could buy the furs on the spot in Fort St. John. The trapper would then fly into the city, usually Edmonton, pay off his debt, restock his supply list and return promptly to his line, debt-free until the next time.

In the meantime, Sol wound up with the furs.

He nearly went berserk when he couldn't find his poke one morning!

### Two jokes for two prime suckers

Two practical jokes were in the making at once. This time, Ma was behind one, while the crews were responsible for Sol's missing poke.

She was out to get Sheldon.

He'd asked her to do his laundry while he was out on a charter.

She obliged by taking his pyjamas and smearing their insides with jam, folding them neatly and tucking them into the cupboard beside his bunk.

In the meantime, Sol searched frantically for his lost money, warning one and all that he'd report the theft to the police if this money didn't show up at a specified time. He honestly suspected he'd been robbed blind, never once thinking that a practical joke was being played on him.

Noticing his obvious discomfort and the steel-eyed glares from Red, the boys coughed up the cash, sheepish looks on their faces. Sol later relayed his suspicions to Grant, and asked him to curb the severity of the jokes, saying they'd gone too far with hiding his $50,000.

By the end of the day, all had a good laugh over the re-surfaced missing poke.

But the best laugh took place later that night, long after Sheldon returned from his charter. The strangest look crossed his face as he pulled his pyjamas tightly around his waistline.

Some rather special passengers never once had a practical joke played on them, nor were they ever touched.

Such as prostitutes.

They really were left alone. Ma saw to that.

Ladies of pleasure, who were headed to Whitehorse, Alaska and points beyond relied totally on the airplane to take them north. All of Grant's aircrews treated them with utmost courtesy and discretion.

They took to the air to promote their wares in the north rather than waste their valuable time on a long ocean voyage up the Pacific coastline.

Whenever they overnighted at the Powells, one could always count on fun.

Good, clean fun, insisted Ma.

### The bombing in Fort St. John

Other interesting things of note happened at Charlie Lake, such as the near-sinking of an airliner which led to the practical joke fondly remembered by long-service employees of CPAL and known as the "Bombing at Fort St. John."

Once again, the company's "Barkley Grow" aircraft were involved, along with Ted Field in the first one and Sheldon in the one that followed about fifteen minutes later.

Heading north from Prince George over Moberly Lake, Sheldon noted that the ice below showed signs of rapid thawing. At the same time he heard Ted Field radioing his approach to the Charlie Lake ice runway. Since the ice was showing signs of breaking up at Moberly Lake just below, only 30 miles (48 km) south of Charlie Lake, Sheldon wondered about the quality of the ice strip on which Ted would land.

Jimmy, the radio operator, assured Sheldon that the strip was in good shape. Taking him at his word, Sheldon brought the flight in for one of the most interesting landings in his career.

### No time to stand on ceremonial evacuation ritual

All went according to the book until the aircraft slowed to a stop. He started to reverse the direction of the plane to bring it to the deplaning area, and hadn't completed a quarter of the turn when the wheels broke through the ice surface.

Its wings, spread out on the ice, prevented it from sinking into deep waters, which threatened to drown everyone on board.

This made no sense at all!

Ted had just landed there minutes ago, in almost the same spot, in a sister ship.

A later investigation revealed that nearby underground springs had weakened the ice to a point where, had Sheldon landed first then Ted's aircraft would have gone through the ice instead. The first plane landing and then coming to a rest before turning at that same spot had weakened the ice sufficiently to jeopardize the safety of the next one to land.

There was no way or time to deplane the passengers in the conventional emergency manner: women and children first.

Sheldon's plane had to be lightened immediately to reduce its chance of going through the ice, and the fastest way to shed the plane of its excess weight was to get the men off first.

With no time to explain why, Sheldon ordered the men to leave the plane first, asking the women to remain on board.

He and crew member Vic Webb carefully escorted each man out of the rear door, over the wing and out onto firmer ice, where ground crews took over.

Their combined weight lightened the plane by almost a thousand pounds in less than ninety seconds.

Had the ladies gone first, the weight of the men who would have remained on board might have been enough to send the plane down through the already broken ice.

Mrs. Jimmy Bell, wife of the Edmonton airport manager, was among the last to leave the craft.

Everyone got off safely. The crew managed to retrieve the cargo and transfer it to Ted's aircraft.

The Charlie Lake station crew worked out an ingenious solution to bring the plane onto dry land. They rounded up all the timber Red had available, and a lot of heavy planking. The plan involved feeding the planking under the plane until it floated on top of the jury-rigged raft. Once lines were well-secured and the makeshift raft in place, the crew brought in a local dynamite expert, known as a "powder monkey." Acting on his instructions, crews dug a series of holes in the ice in a straight, three-hundred yard line to shore.

The plan had been to create an ice-free channel through which the now raft-mounted plane could be pulled into shore.

A certain amount of dynamite would nicely break, or chip, rather than blow the ice apart.

The crews wanted good-size ice cakes which they could then break up to create their own channel. This beat sawing a channel by hand, and saved valuable time.

Additional men had been flown in from Edmonton to help remove the airplane from the water, change its engines and prepare an emergency dirt strip so it could be flown out and taken to the new airport which was under construction about five miles (8 km) away. Charlie Lake would then become history for commercial airline operations.

Many of these arrivals were newcomers, new to everything, and all were absolutely absorbed by the process of blasting an ice channel and hauling an aircraft to dry land. Their fertile minds had figured out just what to do to pay back the old-timers who hadn't exactly gone out of their way to make the newcomers' arrival a piece of cake.

The "Barkley Grow" was lifted to dry land and flown out. The powder monkey left to go elsewhere, and the young men were waiting to be returned to Edmonton.

Some time earlier, Red and Ma had built a small cabin about 75 feet (23 m) behind the bunkhouse; it had a couple of windows, a door and an airtight heater exhausted by a vertical stovepipe through the gabled roof.

Some of the old-timers overnighting this particular evening included Sheldon, Ted Field, Don Patry, Alex Dame, Glen Fenby and Ralph Marshall. Some suggested, as written in later publications that Sheldon has read, that Grant had been there too… but he wasn't, recalled Sheldon.

Sleeping arrangements had the boys in this new cabin while regular crews occupied the bunkhouse.

During the night something disturbed the bunkhouse crew.

A couple of them woke to stare at a small bundle of smoking dynamite sticks in the middle of the floor. Sheldon and two others hastily began waking their colleagues, all coming to the same conclusion: these damn young pups had seen the dynamiter at work, noticed the ice hadn't been severely damaged, and figured a bundle of dynamite wouldn't do much damage to a bunkhouse either!

"Fools!" thought Sheldon, "Those dumb city bastards!"

Don Patry made it to the door first.

Followed hard on his heels by Sheldon.

Red's 32-volt lighting plant lit the dim bulb in the bunkhouse.

Sheldon looked at Don's back, wondering why he was standing there at the door.

He seemed to be frozen to the door knob.

He was.

Sheldon reached out to help Don, or move him out of the way, when he felt himself being glued to Don.

The knob had been wired, in a slightly more powerful variant of the Winnipeg couch trick.

Both men were confused and did not know what to do next.

Sheldon and Don heard a scream.

It came from Alex Dame, who had just woken up, and lay there in his bunk, his eyes popping out, staring at the smoldering bundle on the floor.

A wonderful man, Alex was stocky, short and quite fond of sleeping naked in his sleeping bag. He made quite a sight trying to get out of the bag to make a bee-line for the door at the same time.

Then, another holler.

This time from Ralph Marshall, on a top bunk: "Jesus Christ! That's dynamite and it's going to blow. Let's get the hell out of here!"

Then Ted Field got into the act.

He and another man dove head-first for the bundle, coming from opposite directions.

They met head-on. One of them was going to have to toss the bundle through a window before it blew.

At no time had anyone taken note of one remarkable fact: quite a few minutes had elapsed since the first discovery of the smoking bundle, and it still hadn't blown them to smithereens.

Juice suddenly stopped flowing through the doorknob, releasing its hold of Don and Sheldon simultaneously.

But the door refused to budge.

No dummies, these young'uns.

Anticipating exactly what would take place, and what was in fact happening, they had earlier drilled a hole, at an angle, into the doorframe. After lighting their "dynamite", they backed off and quietly inserted a long, hard nail into the pre-made hole, effectively locking the door.

When they figured they'd had enough of a double-barrelled jolt on the door, they released the magneto crank which had been hidden outside and ran like blazes, quietly, to their cabin, pretending to be sound asleep.

Finally, within the bunkhouse, somebody had a stroke of genius!

Turn on a flashlight. Then shine the beam onto the bundle on the floor.

That dynamite bundle turned out to be nothing less than short lengths of red-coloured hose, attached to a still sputtering long-delay fuse.

Since the crew members realized they had all, to a man, been victimized by a bunch of wet-behind-the-ears youngsters, these young ones certainly had to be taught a lesson.

Hadn't they?

Certainly.

But later.

Without saying a word to anyone else, nor waking anybody else, they thought it all out, plotting their revenge. Sensing something was about to happen to them, the young soon-to-be-victims, supposedly asleep, had locked themselves into their cabin to avoid such anticipated reprisals.

Quietly making their way to the cabin, the seasoned crew members bound for revenge, found the door to the sleeping quarters locked.

This did not deter them one whit.

One went to fetch some of Ma's sulphur pots, used as a disinfecting smudge keeping things that bite out of harm's way. Others collected buckets of water and yet another came tooling along with a ladder.

First, up with the ladder.

Followed by a man with the sulphur compound, and the water - all destined to go down the stovepipe.

Still no stirrings from within.

Things were just too, too quiet.

From outside, came a hushed voice: "Hell, boys, it's only going to cost us a bit of money to replace a window, right?"

Right.

With the window glass so removed, the bucket brigade, earlier positioned, let loose. The boys gave up, unlocked the door and stumbled outside.

Within minutes all returned to Ma's kitchen for some hot rum and they verbally replayed the entire series of events with great spirit and gusto.

But Ma and Red weren't too thrilled about the situation, and Red sent a tersely worded note to Grant about it a few days later.

Sheldon is certain this was the straw which broke Grant's back and was in a large way responsible for his diminished sense of humour next time he saw him.

Grant eventually berated both Ted and Sheldon, reminding them that as his two senior officers, they should not have acted like juveniles and should have conducted themselves as responsible officers of the airline.

Grant had a long memory and wouldn't forget this incident for some time to come, especially when the public image of his company was at stake.

In the following incident, Grant was way out of line, totally misjudging the situation. But, as Sheldon admitted half a century later, who could have blamed him?

The setting: the famous Macdonald Hotel, Edmonton, 1942.

The occasion was a prestigious civic and business ceremony honouring Grant's achievements.

Present: The Mayor of Edmonton, Councillors, business men and women and other guests, such as Sheldon and his brother, Don.

It had all the trappings of an Edmonton-boy-makes-good celebration. Grant had just been appointed General Manager, Western Lines for Canadian Pacific Air Lines. Sheldon had earlier asked if he could bring his brother Don, because Isabel was at home in Vancouver, and Sheldon wanted some company. Grant agreed.

Sometime into the evening, Sheldon and Don heard noises outside the main entry of the two-room suite. Sheldon opened to see two young men down the hall, yanking yards of fire hose from the racks.

"Hey", yelled Sheldon, and ran out, with Don hard on his heels.

As they heard Sheldon and saw him dash out the door, they dropped the hose and took off in two directions. One made for the next floor up and the other ran down the stairs. Sheldon decided to go after the one headed downstairs, turned to tell Don only to see him reeling the hose back onto its rack.

Down those stairs he went, eight at a time using the hand rail for support. The man eluded him in the lobby, where Sheldon stopped dead in his tracks.

He didn't want to be seen chasing anyone while wearing the uniform of the Chief pilot of Canadian Pacific Air Lines!

He returned to the floor in time to help Don restore and secure the fire hose, and in time to see Grant open the door and ask what was going on.

Eyeballing Sheldon and Don, Grant roared: "What in the hell are you two guys up to?!"

"Grant," stammered Sheldon, "a couple of punks pulled this hose out and they were just about the open the door and let us have it."

"A likely story," snorted Grant, returning to the suite, shaking his head and scowling.

Sheldon spoke to Grant about this incident the following day, trying as best he could to explain all the circumstances.

Grant would have no part of it.

"As sure as I'm standing here Grant, it was not Don and me."

Grant dismissed Sheldon's attempt at any explanation. "Oh, we're not going to discuss it any further. Just forget it."

The event cropped up many times over the years and Sheldon is convinced that Grant never once believed him.

## Passenger disappears in flight – but never left the airplane

While an obvious gap in communications lay at the core of the above mis-understanding, the heart of the next one could be found only in linguistic shortcomings and culture shock.

It scared the daylights out of Sheldon nevertheless.

It took place nearly six years before the Macdonald Hotel incident, involving Sheldon and a middle-aged native male on a flight from the Omenica Mountains to Fort St. James, all of it spiced by a dead-stick landing. For those unfamiliar with aviation expressions, a *dead-stick landing* is one that is carried out when the engine of an incoming aircraft stops, forcing the pilot to land the plane without power.

As Sheldon headed the Fokker over the Manson Creek region, still 100 miles (161 km) north of Fort St. James, things only got worse along the flight path. A few miles north of "The Fort", as it is still known to the inhabitants, the engine gave up, finally starved of fuel.

Until now, his passenger was obviously enjoying his first plane ride. He sat in the cabin along with some cargo. Remember that little peephole behind the cockpit between the pilot and the passenger cabin?

Without sufficient engine power, Sheldon wanted as much weight as possible towards the rear of the aircraft so he could make his pending touch-down on water as tail-heavy as possible as the plane neared Battleship Islands.

He twisted around and opened the peephole to ask his passenger to move either himself or anything else towards the back… way, way back… to the back of the cabin.

The fellow barely spoke English, but he must have understood the essence of Sheldon's message as Sheldon caught a glimpse of him working his way to the far back of the cabin.

He returned his concentration to the cockpit.

The Fokker didn't behave on landing as he'd expected, but they were down anyway.

When the Fokker stopped its forward motion, Sheldon clambered down the ladder, walked back on the float and entered the cabin to invite his passenger outside.

He looked inside.

No passenger!

Surely he couldn't have misunderstood his request and opened the door and jumped! Nah! Sheldon would have sensed if the door had been opened in the air; besides, it would probably have damaged the fuselage. It was closed when he walked back to open it.

Well, where was he?

But for the cargo, the cabin was empty!

Something had to have happened to his passenger.

Sheldon climbed into the cabin, uncertainty deepening in his mind.

He couldn't have lost a passenger!

Looking towards to the very rear of the cabin, he noticed that one of the clips securing a canvas fabric had been unfastened.

The fabric moved, ever so slightly.

A head popped out from behind this fabric. Sheldon then saw the face of his passenger, eyes wider than saucers, as if to ask: "Can I come out now?"

Sheldon took one gulp and restrained himself from bursting out laughing, one of the most difficult things he had ever done in years, because suddenly he understood. The man had taken him literally, and had moved as far back "as possible".

Practical jokers were no respecters of gender.

Nor was Sheldon when it came to a good practical joke.

He pulled one on Elianne Roberge early in 1939. It phased her a bit, but didn't rattle her nerves too badly, and certainly didn't injure her reputation any.

She told me so when I interviewed her in a long-distance telephone call that I made to her in Vancouver before she died.

Elianne was one of the first seven women in Canada to obtain a commercial pilot's license, but in 1939, she hadn't been able to make the grade as a pilot for Grant. She would have loved to, but male chauvinism dominated airline companies where a pilot's gender was concerned, and there were a number of other social obstacles for her to overcome.

Elianne tripled as a stenographer, private secretary and also worked in traffic for YSAT. Too bad Grant didn't see fit to quadruple her services as she was an excellent pilot to boot, says Sheldon.

Known for her reliability and stability, she was always flexible. Management and colleagues grew fond of this perky, diminutive and attractive brunette. She normally worked the Vancouver office, but had often subbed in the Edmonton office, and had travelled the YSAT system extensively while carrying out her duties.

She certainly was no stranger to air crews.

Elianne's skills served Sheldon well during an earlier search and rescue mission for Len Waagen a year earlier. That search had come down to the wire without any results and Sheldon needed help, which she provided, in conducting the enquiries and preparing the company's final report on the lengthy mission.

Grant's private secretary was Kay McLean, his wife's sister. Kay was getting married and he needed a temporary secretary while she went on her honeymoon. Grant asked Elianne if she could help him out. Elianne accepted, but only if she received assurances from Grant that this was a temporary posting: her preference was Vancouver since she couldn't fly for him.

Assurances given and accepted, she flew up deadhead to Dawson Creek, where she bumped into Sheldon. The Fort St. John operation had been temporarily suspended, for reasons Sheldon has since forgotten, and had been moved to Dawson Creek between September 1939 and the spring of 1940. There, she boarded one of Sheldon's flights into Edmonton.

Elianne, knowing that Sheldon spent a good amount of time in Edmonton, sought his advice on a decent place for a young lady. Not a hotel room, mind you, but a family environment ... or even a roommate might be nice, if that could be arranged without any trouble on his part.

Sure thing. He had just the right place for her - the manager of an *exclusive* home for ladies.

Delighted at being told that no one, but absolutely no one, got into this *home* without a thorough screening, Elianne then learned that Sheldon would set it up, get her a taxi in Edmonton and be taken directly to the Beulah Home.

All she had to do then was ask for a Mrs. Finlay, saying Sheldon sent her.

If she needed references, she was to contact Grant immediately, and he'd take care of that little matter.

No one told anyone in Edmonton that Elianne was arriving, but a compassionate employee went to meet Elianne to escort her.

She asked where Elianne would be staying, only to be told that Sheldon had given Elianne the name of what she thought was a first-class home. The escorting employee, no stranger to the city, gasped when she heard the name.

The home was a refuge for unwed mothers.

Right about the same time, Grant came out of the office, heading for his car. He spotted the two women, engaged in animated conversation, and recognized them both. He ambled over to say hello to Elianne.

On learning what Sheldon had told her, he shook his head and muttered audibly: "That God-damned Sheldon Luck!"

A few weeks later a note showed up in Sheldon's mail basket in the Vancouver dispatch office. The note contained two words, one punctuation mark and two initials:

"You bastard! E.R."
Both shared this joke many times in years to come.

## Edmonton Bulletin's "Battling" Joe Dwyer was a classic example of just how easy it was to play practical jokes on reporters

Aside from employees and trusted customers, there was one more category of prime-sucker for a practical joke: newspaper reporters, especially the ones who flew the line regularly, either en route to assignments, or returning from them.

The more publicity the airline got, the better the chances of drumming up business. All air crews knew this, and knew how enthusiastically Grant responded to good publicity.

"Battling" Joe Dwyer got it twice from Grant's aircrews.

Ted Field pulled a good one, while in the air, on this intrepid Edmonton Bulletin journalist.

But first, Joe almost bought it in the air while on another flight, this one with Sheldon at the control of a Waco, southbound into Williams Lake from Prince George.

It was almost as if fate was setting him up, in a cruel fashion, for what Ted Field would soon do to him.

The incident with Sheldon gave Joe a good dose of the difficulties faced by pioneering pilots. He had been Sheldon's only passenger on an early airmail flight in 1938. About five minutes out of Williams Lake, something happened to the Waco's aileron controls.

The plane didn't feel right, and started doing things of its own accord. Sheldon happened to glance to the right hand top corner of the cockpit and saw what looked like upholstery tearing. He made out some movement along the top longeron of the cabin, indicating something drastic was taking place.

The sooner he landed the better.

Unknown to Sheldon, the upper front spar of the biplane was in fact free to warp in the turbulent air. The Waco was responding to inadvertent aileron action; expected behaviour in earlier aircraft which possessed designed warp features. The warp had been deliberate in earlier aircraft.

In this case, it was purely accidental and potentially very dangerous.

Simply put, it could kill both Sheldon and Joe.

It meant that the Waco was coming apart at its seams.

Sheldon, though frightened, had a pretty good idea of what was happening and suspected his wing would be ripped off from fuselage. He put the Waco into an easy turn back to Williams Lake, in clear but turbulent weather. He had to get it down as close to the ground as possible. Should the wing indeed separate from the fuselage, and should the plane be close enough to the ground if that did happen, then he was fairly certain that he and Joe could walk away from the resulting impact.

After landing, Sheldon tore into the upholstery to confirm his suspicions: the upper front fitting in the centre section had, in fact, broken. The wing's upper front spar should have been attached to this fitting.

The wing ribs were the only things holding the wings in place.

They overnighted in Williams Lake to await a new machine so they could resume their interrupted flight and airmail run.

Fate and a suspicious boy-type twinkle in Ted Field's eye were setting Joe up for a totally different sensation, that of being helplessly trapped, about a year later, when the company had changed its name and was now known as Yukon Southern.

Another Grant McConachie innovation – a long time before any other airline would do so – saw YSAT ships equipped with conventional AM broadcast radio receivers – on-board radios – to help relieve passenger boredom during long flights and to entertain them.

He thought it would be great public relations to have the pilots provide passengers with musical programs or with news reports during a flight.

Ted had been in Fort St. John on a routine flight, and was scheduled to return to Edmonton with a recaptured escaped convict on board. A man had been charged with murder, tried and found guilty and was sent to Saskatchewan to serve his time. He escaped but had been captured in a haystack on the outskirts of Fort St. John. Police were escorting him back to face more charges and resume his sentence.

Joe just happened to be in Fort St. John at the same time, and was quite excited about being the only reporter on board the same flight as the prisoner and his police escort.

What a scoop this could be for the Bulletin.

Ted had seen Joe milling about the airport and also overheard him talking to police. Joe saw Ted at about the same time, and asked if he could stop briefly at the telegraph office to send a news dispatch for his paper before the flight started.

One of the escorting police asked with barely concealed irony, but with a wink, if Joe could be trusted. The police didn't want any advance publicity before they arrived: they had their own promotional plans on this one and didn't want Joe botching up their plans for a top-notch publicity boost for the long arm of the law.

Joe acquired his "Battling" nickname by accidently getting trapped in a free-for-all slugfest with hoodlums in Edmonton. Police arrived moments after to give him a hand and dubbed him with his new nickname.

The policeman in Fort St. John, knowing Joe, had taken a good-natured poke at him with the wisecrack about trusting him.

Sorry, but no time to send that telegraph.

Ted caught the drift and brewed a plan of his own.

While Joe had no time to send his telegram, Ted however took the time to prepare his hand-written script, to be read, once he was airborne, over the internal broadcast system on board.

Once he made it up to the cockpit as a guest, and the plane was airborne, all Ted had to do was flick a switch, select a station, and with another control, override the announcer's voice from the ground. It would seem to listeners in the passenger cabin that the new voice was coming from the same radio station as the previous voice – if Joe handled the transmission skillfully.

While in the vicinity of Grande Prairie, Ted decided the moment of confusion had arrived.

He located the radio station frequency at Grande Prairie and piped in a classical music program - broadcast daily at the same time.

Slowly, with the volume dwindling, the music faded out in the passenger cabin loudspeakers, only to be replaced with a new voice and the following message:

"Ladies and gentlemen, we interrupt this program with a news item special to our listeners in the Peace River country..."

Through a view port in the cockpit door, Ted could see the passengers but they couldn't see him: all had stopped talking and were staring at the speakers in the passenger cabin ceiling.

With his best radio voice, Ted resumed:

"It had just been learned that a dangerous convict whom police had been trailing for weeks has just been captured near Fort St. John. The Edmonton Bulletin's Joe Dwyer played an important role in the final moments of the capture. If fact, it is thought that Joe's assistance probably brought the dangerous convict to earth earlier than what would have been possible without him."

Silence and the music volume swelled to replace the "new reporter's" voice.

Ted watched, chortling quietly to himself as he saw the stunned looks develop on Joe's face, on the faces of each policeman and on the prisoner's face.

Joe had nothing to do with the capture.

Wasn't even there when it happened.

One policeman got up, walked over to where Joe sat and shook his fist in front of Joe's face, bawling him out. Joe shrank from this display of pending violence, protesting that he had never sent a wire to his office, and besides he wasn't even there, so how could he have been involved?

No one believed him.

Ted decided to pour salt on the open wounds. Next thing the passengers knew, the same announcer was back on the air with a fresh news report that a civic reception had been planned for Joe on his arrival soon in Edmonton. The Edmonton mayor and the Royal Canadian Mounted Police superintendent in Edmonton were bringing Joe's eighty-three year old mother along to witness the honours which would be heaped on Joe!

Oh boy!

Ted peeked back to assess the reaction to this news item.

Each police officer on board had freaked right out, as had Joe. He sat cringing in his seat, in obvious agony, his head slowly turning, from side to another, his mouth mumbling something about his being the victim of some cruel, uncomprehending fate.

Although it took Ted quite a bit of diplomatic skill, he finally broke down and admitted everything before the plane landed in Edmonton, and the practical joke ended well.

### How high is the ceiling? Seven-six!

Quite often a slip of the tongue or a mis-understood message can result in a good, honest laugh. One such wrongly interpreted message made the rounds for several years.

Severe fog conditions around Lac la Biche, Alberta, presented bush pilots with problems, especially those who flew regularly between Edmonton and Fort McMurray, a distance of about 240 miles (386 km).

They would usually call the Edmonton railway office to receive weather reports at Fort McMurray. This was information gladly given, as well as for points along the railway, such as near Lac La Biche, which was about half way, and slightly to the east of the Edmonton-Fort McMurray direct line of flight.

One morning when the station operator had more on his mind than a weather report for a pilot, he stopped them dead in their tracks with his answer.

A growing family concerned him so much that the living quarters over the railway depot had become much too small. He had often complained to the railway division office for more space.

Months elapsed without any answer to his request.

Late one afternoon, he got word that someone from the construction department would arrive shortly to assess the problem with him.

The operator and his wife were elated.

Next morning, the telegraph key clicked out a request: "What's your ceiling? How high is it?"

He must have had the construction department on his mind, never realizing it was a pilot asking for weather information.

Without thinking, the operator pulsed back on the telegraph key:

"Beaverboard, seven-foot six."

## Two women, one man, one sleeping bag and a few mice do not comfort make

No one will ever know what their reactions were when two husbands learned that their wives invited Sheldon to share their bunk with them one night. At the time, one of the women was pregnant and the other had an inflamed appendix.

The interesting social event began as a simple flight out of Fort Nelson.

The company agent's wife, Mrs. Chris Christensen, needed to get to hospital fast because of her appendicitis, and Mrs. Harold (Anna) Engleson, the policeman's wife, was certain that her baby was coming sooner than expected.

She too had to get to Prince George hospital.

Sheldon and his charges left Fort Nelson under an overcast sky in the company Waco.

The ceiling lowered rapidly as they flew south to Fort St. John. By the time the Waco reached the height of land by the Beatton River region, the ceiling dropped even more and light snow began to fall, reducing forward visibility. Then the snow fell heavily.

Since there was no place to land and wait out the snow, he had to keep on flying south, and stay on track for Charlie Lake. First he had to try and find the Peace River to orient himself. The Peace flows in a northwesterly direction for about 30 miles (48 km) on either side of Fort St. John, and Sheldon had hoped to be able to be low enough to spot it as he crossed it.

Fort St. John radio told him the Charlie Lake landing facilities were socked right in. Since he had left the major mountains behind him, he felt more secure, trudging along at about 400 feet (122 m) above the rolling hills below.

As he flew into the Peace River Valley the Charlie Lake radio operator told him that according to the strength of Sheldon's transmissions that he couldn't be too far from the base.

But in which direction.

East? Or west?

Sheldon just didn't know.

If he headed to his left, he could try landing at Taylor Flats, a ferry crossing on the Peace. If he turned the other way, the hills rose higher and he risked plowing the plane into a hillside. To make matters worse he was flying in a blizzard.

As Luck would have it... and did... he chose correctly.

He took the Waco down as low as he dared and visibility improved to the point where he saw a cabin with a large snow-covered area immediately to front of it.

A perfect landing spot.

Without wasting any more time, he landed a couple of hundred yards from the cabin door. Sheldon got out first, asking the ladies to remain in the aircraft until he explored the cabin. He returned and carried each woman through the heavier and deeper snow drifts, and made a couple of trips back and forth to fetch emergency survival supplies from the Waco.

The cabin turned out to be quite a find, with a good supply of wood, plenty of provisions and an ultra-large bed. All the clues indicated this was a trapper's main cabin and not one of his line's cabins.

He quickly lit a fire on the stove and all were quite cozy and comfortable in short order. Time came to hit the sack. Sheldon laid out his sleeping bag on the floor and put two sleeping bags on that huge bed. The trapper had covered the entire thing with a canvas mattress stuffed with long grass which made it quite comfortable for the two ladies.

Things didn't stay quiet for long.

Mice had crawled out from every nook and cranny of that cabin, drawn by the soothing heat from the stove. Then they decided Sheldon's sleeping bag made an even neater gathering place for this impromptu convention.

The ladies watched Sheldon's mounting discomfort as the mice crawled all over his sleeping bag, his face and even into his sleeping bag.

Finally one of them said: "Well, for goodness sakes, there's plenty of room up here for you too, so bring your bag up."

Mrs. Engleson made a casual remark about him being in no danger of attack by either lady.

Sheldon enjoyed a mouse-free night.

Next morning the blizzard had passed by, and Sheldon walked out into clear and cold air. He worked the radio and learned that Alex Dame would come to his rescue with another aircraft and spare fuel tins for the Waco.

When Alex arrived, Sheldon learned just how right his decision had been in turning left, or to the east – they weren't 15 miles (24 km) from Taylor Flats.

### Something wicked this way came… and grounded a plane world-wide when it arrived

This closing incident in this chapter is best described by the phrase: "The fart that went 'round the world."

And, is believed to have grounded an airliner in the process.

As stated before, and explained in greater detail later, Yukon Southern boasted that it became the first airline in Canada to get its hands on the sleek, shiny Lockheed 18 Lodestar aircraft.

Lockheed rated this ship as the fastest twin-engine airliner in the world.

YSAT enjoyed much success in the short time the Canadian government allowed them to keep them.

Both were Grant's babies, his pride and joy.

He became touchy and sensitive about them. If anything more than a routine, minor snag developed at the Vancouver terminal, he'd want to know about every little detail and what was being done to fix it. Word was out that he'd give his eye teeth to fly one regularly, but flying a president's desk took up too much of his time to do anything more than get behind the cockpit for the occasional publicity shot.

On a southbound run, weather prompted Sheldon to remain overnight in Prince George with George Milne, his co-pilot, and passengers. While there, they made a social event out of it and spent the night with friends, enjoying a rather generously-sized baked bean supper.

By eight o'clock the next morning, Sheldon, George and the passengers were ready to resume their flight to Vancouver.

Air crews were still getting used to the quirks and qualms of a new airliner, and had limited experience in operating it in cold weather conditions.

The Lockheed had one quirk: if a pilot selected cabin heat during take-off, an unpleasant odour filled the passenger cockpit. This came about as a result of the engines drawing full power on take-off, generating considerable heat. If the cabin heat were applied on take-off the blowers would bellow the heat into the cabin all right, but the odour of the insulation would accompany it.

Not a serious thing in itself, but it was mildly uncomfortable to a sensitive nose. Pilots learned to "crack open" the fuselage heaters just a wee bit on take-off. When the plane reached cruise altitude, the pilot reduced the power demands on the engine and the cabin heaters were adjusted to normal heat levels.

Sheldon and George both knew this and proceeded according to routine.

Moments after take-off, George could no longer hold back the mounting internal pressure in his oh-so-human body.

He was a shy type of guy, the soul of sensitivity and discretion.

Therefore, he didn't even blush as a pungent aroma wafted heavily about the cockpit seconds later.

Sheldon began to fan his nostrils when the spark of an idea suddenly lit up in his mind.

He picked up the microphone, called the company frequency in Prince George and reported: "a bad odour in the cockpit."

George nearly jumped out of his seat, whispering loudly, shaking his head violently side to side: "No, Sheldon. No, don't do that!"

Prince George had no time to answer him.

Edmonton cut right in.

Unusual atmospheric conditions that morning made it possible for Hans

Broten to pick up the radio traffic from Prince George - just about 400 air miles (644 km) due west of Edmonton. This was a freak reception, nevertheless, but a fateful one for Sheldon.

And this had been the first time in months that the atmospheric conditions were just right to skip radio signals in this manner!

Hans had quickly alerted Grant about the unwelcome fragrance in the Lodestar cockpit.

Seconds after Sheldon's report of the bad odour, Hans was on the radio: "McConachie wants you to return to Prince George immediately and investigate the matter."

Sheldon had temporarily forgotten about Grant's fixation with any problems, real or imagined, on the Lodestars, but George hadn't.

Things had gotten out of hand already and the Lodestar hadn't flown five miles (8 km) from Prince George.

Desperately wishing he had kept his mouth shut, Sheldon radioed Hans, asking him to let Grant know that the problem was over, that the air had cleared itself, and could he please, please, cancel the order to return to Prince George and continue the flight to Vancouver.

No.

The Lodestar returned to Prince George.

Once inside the company office, Sheldon found another message from Grant: contact him right away on landing. Before he did so, Sheldon sought out George Campbell, the Pan-American Airlines mechanic, and his right-hand man, John Frederickson.

Pan-Am had the contract to supply ground services for YSAT, one of the best deals Grant had ever made. Sheldon told George and John about what had taken place and what had gone wrong with his little joke on George Milne.

Both roared with laughter.

Grant must have been in an ugly mood that day.

He wouldn't release the Lodestar until the problem was checked out thoroughly.

Had Sheldon told Grant what he had done, he knew Grant would come down on him like a hammer.

Feeling about as intelligent as a sackful of hammers at this stage, Sheldon waited the next question: "Did you activate the cabin heaters on take-off?"

"Well, it was a cool morning Grant, and I cracked them open just a bit. I was prepared to open the system more when I got to cruise."

He hoped, but knew it wouldn't smooth things out with Grant.

Grant wouldn't let it go.

Nor would he release the plane, saying he simply could not afford to take any chance, any chance, with a problem like that.

Those Lodestars were Yukon Southern's lifeblood.

Eventually, Lockheed officials were contacted in California. They were puzzled when asked about the odour problem in the cockpit, instead of the cabin.

They'd never heard of this one before. It was a new one on them.

Sheldon heard that Lockheed called other Lodestar operators around the world, a situation which is rumoured to have temporarily grounded the Lodestars while engineers investigated.

Sheldon later returned and told George and John about his call to Grant and the subsequent results.

In no time flat, this story came to be known as the "fart that was heard 'round the world."

## 5. Who Influenced Whom?

Robert William Service cremated Sam and shot Dan.

In the Arctic, that is, through the medium of great poetry.

Anyone asked to quote some of this great Canadian poet's epic works about the far and mysterious northern regions of Canada is quite likely to recall a line or two from one or two of his better known creations: the *Cremation of Sam McGee* or the *Shooting of Dan McGrew.*

Service, born in Preston, England in 1874, went to Whitehorse at the age of thirty, and spent from 1904 to 1912 there, and in Dawson as a humble bank clerk. He converted what he saw into literary masterpieces, some poems, verses, a novel and two auto-biographical works. His two most famous pieces are named above and have attained classic status.

Many famous Canadians have often asked, "Did Robert Service ever plan to return to the Yukon?" One reputed to have asked that question was noted Canadian author Pierre Berton, panelist on the popular CBC-TV quiz show, *Front Page Challenge.*

Sheldon answered that question when he appeared on the show in 1982.

Yes, Robert Service did plan to return to the land he loved so much, but never made it.

Sheldon knows, because he was the only pilot ever known to have had Robert Service as an airplane passenger, and that was on September 12$^{th}$, 1941, for a look-see flight over Vancouver.

Few knew that Service was supposed to have an aversion to flight. Not that he was afraid of flying, but preferred boats and trains over planes.

Sheldon and Yukon Southern changed this attitude, if indeed it was true.

Grant McConachie and Jack Meek of the Vancouver Sun had made arrangements for Sheldon to take Service over Vancouver and Vancouver Island in a familiarization flight before he went north.

Service had recently escaped from France, early in World War II, and made his way back to Canada, landing at Halifax, where he and his family took the train to Vancouver before the planned trip back to the Yukon.

This was one public relations bonanza which Grant didn't want his airline to miss, and for good reason – Service was popular and well known right to his death in 1958.

Sheldon attended the media conference which preceded Service's first-ever airplane ride. There, he met the man himself, along with his wife and daughter who were invited to go up with Sheldon. They declined the invitation for the flight and Service told Sheldon that he had no objection to going up alone with him.

He recalled Service as being a quiet, unassuming man, a complete contrast to the image Sheldon had created of him in reading his works. The man who graphically depicted such knock-'em-down, drag-'em-out scenes in poetry ought to be one whopper of a feller in real life, thought Sheldon.

Many news and publicity photographs were taken at the airport before boarding. Sheldon kept a special one for himself and his children, autographed by Service. The picture shows him and Sheldon, resplendent in his captain's uniform, under the nose of a Barkley Grow, the *Yukon King*. The photo caption quoted from the Vancouver Sun lends credibility to the rumours about Service's earlier aversions to flying.

From his stay in the far north, came the poem, *The Cremation of Sam McGee*.

Something went awry with his planned return to his beloved Yukon. A telephone call from the United States forced him to cancel his plans and take a train for California.

He never did return to the land he popularized in his writings, ending his days in France.

The Vancouver Sun caption under the photograph (facing page) reads:

> *Though Mr. Service has travelled in every country in Europe, through the United States and Canada, he had to return to Vancouver after 33-years absence for his first plane ride and now admits he is a confirmed air traveler. Questioned during the flight, Mr. Service ended a lively controversy of some years' standing when he said the shooting of Dan McGrew did not actually occur, but was the product of his own mind. He didn't know anyone by the name of McGrew, but there really was a lady named 'Lou'. Mr. Service said he knew Sam McGee only*

*slightly. When he was a teller in the bank in Dawson, the name McGee on his ledger impressed him... Mr. Service intends to stay only a short time in the Yukon, flying both ways with Yukon Southern. He is going to Hollywood in December.*

Robert Service serves well as a role model in depicting the many types of personalities who moved into and out of Sheldon Luck's life during his flying career.

There were truly memorable and remarkable characters worth noting.

Some of them greatly influenced Sheldon, others he influenced in return, and yet in many instances, meeting such a broad and diversified range of personality types simply came with the territory and left either pleasant memories, or, at times, memories best left forgotten.

These men and women came in every size, from every imaginable walk of life.

Some he treasured greatly, others became blots in his memory, and some flitted into and out of his life like so many swallows. They personify the men and women who worked Canada's northern reaches, giving it more than a veneer of civilization.

Frank Watson was one of those Sheldon recalls with fondness.

Watson Lake, Yukon, is named after him.

Frank settled in the Upper Liard River after World War I. Reputed to have been a Remittance Man, Frank could, with the help of a few hot rums, quote extensive poetry - especially Shakespeare, and some biblical passages. With each new rum his grammar and articulation took a turn to eloquence, suggesting to others there was more to Frank Watson than met the eye, or passed the car.

Frank and his native wife enjoyed a rather large family.

He loved nothing more than to bring culture and education to his adopted people, and when told by the Hudson Bay Factor at Lower Post that some aircraft would soon fly over, Frank figured that this was just the thing to make their day.

It was not known which aircraft would be coming by, but there were a number of American expeditions into the region during the early 1920s, including the First Alaska Air Expedition in the summer of 1920 and the United States Army Air Service round-the-world-flight of 1924 which visited Canada twice.

Many early bush pilots did a lot of pioneer charter flying in the region as well.

Frank, familiar with aircraft from the war, had expected the natives to be enthusiastic about seeing their first airplanes. When the appointed day arrived and they flew overhead, Frank tried patiently to explain that an airplane was only some type of metallic bird with a hard shiny skin, built and controlled by man.

Such information did not cut the mustard, at least as far as the native people were concerned.

His family and friends who gathered to watch the airplanes suddenly took off for the bush, in one great rush when these metallic air birds first appeared. It was rumoured that it took him nearly two weeks to round them all up.

So much for culture shock.

His family and native friends believed those metal birds were new angry gods, and they had enough of their own old gods to worry about, thank you.

In the winter of 1937-38, Frank was certain the airplane was here to stay. UAT had been operating from Lower Post, some 15 miles (24 km) south. Word reached him that UAT wanted to modernize the base, but he knew the lay of the land and knew full well that the terrain at Lower Post wouldn't sustain a good landing strip, not without considerable expense, and not when he had prime land available.

He also knew the Liard River was somewhat hazardous for float operations. Pilots took considerable risks taking off and landing close to rapids.

Frank had built some cabins and cultivated a respectable garden at a site north of the present airport. He contacted Grant advising him of a good stretch of land along the lake, close to his homestead and free of heavy timber. It was also level and sandy, with a forest cover of light aspen and birch brush.

Sheldon and Ted field stopped in at Watson Lake in 1938, acting on radioed instructions from Grant that they take a personal look at this Promised Land. It met the specifications as promoted by Frank and by late winter of 1938-39, company operations had moved to Watson Lake.

Fate had other plans for Frank, who would not live to see the transition stages of UAT becoming YSAT and eventually merging into Canadian Pacific Air Lines. During the in-between when spring thaws made landings and take offs impossible on the lake, UAT got a call from the Lower Post operator saying that Frank had taken ill and needed a mercy flight to transfer him to hospital.

UAT's Edmonton office made contact with a doctor. Based on symptoms of Frank's illness as relayed through UAT, he gave a basic set of instructions to help Frank until he could be flown to hospital. He diagnosed influenza. Sheldon picked up a specially-weighted package at Fort St. John on one of his scheduled flights to Whitehorse.

En route to Whitehorse, he passed by Watson Lake and dropped the brightly coloured, shock-proofed package containing Frank's medicine right into the clearing next to his home.

When the ice ran out the following week, permitting float operations, Ted flew in and evacuated Frank to the hospital in Fort St. John. He seemed to be recovering nicely and was seen walking along hospital corridors in what looked like improving health. However, one afternoon he went into shock and died soon after.

Some time later, Watson Lake radio operator Vic Johnston handed Sheldon a carefully wrapped package. It contained Frank's favourite rifle, a Lee-Enfield .303 from World War I. Mrs. Watson had brought it to the base, wrapped it in a moose hide scabbard and asked Vic to pass it on to Sheldon as a memento of Frank.

Sheldon still kept the rifle to the day he himself died.

Some characters were so colourful and interesting that they literally stood out among the crowd. Sheldon rated among these Tommy Clark, the Hudson Bay Factor at Fort Nelson and Andy Russell, his brother-in-law, who was a trapper and trader at Lower Post.

They were two among the few who had the savvy to take advantage of the growing technology which came with airline development in the north. By the winter of 1938-39, many ground radio stations had been put in place north by north-west between Edmonton, Alberta and Whitehorse, Yukon, and south to south-west between Prince George and Vancouver, both in B.C.

Admittedly these early stations were primitive by today's standards, offering line-of-sight voice contact between pilot and ground, and over-the-horizon for the more powerful larger bases.

But they did the job.

Tommy and Andy picked up on the voice contact part. Before UAT moved the base from Lower Post to Watson Lake, Andy and Tommy would ask special permission to have UAT radio operators relay messages between themselves at Lower Post and Fort Nelson.

In doing so, radio operators had to be careful to prevent unauthorized use of the airwaves. They weren't licensed for commercial radio traffic, but were there only to serve airline needs. The federal government's Department of Transport had set up a radio monitoring net with a station in the Peace River region. These monitors quickly became skilled at listening in for non-authorized traffic.

However, it was hard to say no to such men as Tommy and Andy, and besides, they were careful to limit their conversations to necessities and not abuse the privileges afforded them by UAT.

### "Kiss my what?" "For a sack of *what?*"

But sometimes they forgot themselves.

Tom walked over to the radio shack one night when he knew that flying operations were completed for that day. He began talking with Andy in Lower Post, on a pre-arranged schedule. Tom asked how things were going, and if Andy needed more supplies.

No. Not right away, not for a week at least, thank you.

Just about to end the conversation, Andy reached out and clicked the microphone switch once more. He had a special offer to make to Tom.

"Say, Tom, I'd kiss your arse for a sack of spuds."

Tom replied that he'd have the potatoes on the next flight in.

A sternly-worded letter from the DOT showed up on McConachie's desk a few days later.

It cautioned UAT about the illegal use of radio bases. McConachie noted the admonishment, but remembered also that his company played more than just an aviation role in the wilderness.

UAT was there to help itself all right, but by stretching the job description and authorized radio usage definitions just a little bit, it could also help the locals help themselves.

### Two masked raiders mar the good life in the wilderness but alert eyes a thousand miles (1,609 km) away helps trap robbers

Something quite sad happened to Tommy: he got robbed in June, 1936, affecting his family. It did something else - it cast unwarranted aspersions on his good-natured character, and in a way, provoked him into quitting his job at the Post.

Tommy's wife lived at home with their two children on the reservation. He took great personal pride and care of these children, sending them to the big city for an education. He took even greater pride and care of his wife, Mary-Ann.

The Hudson's Bay Company did not consider it in their best interests for the Factor to leave his Post at night, even if it was only to nestle into bed with his wife. If she was a native, this made matters more delicate and was frowned upon. Tommy wasn't up to sleeping alone at the Post when he had a family.

He never left the store untended however. Bob Gillard, a Scottish lad from Labrador, lived on the Post, and during the summer of that year, shared quarters with two carpenters.

One Thursday night, about 11 o'clock, Bob and the carpenters had gone to bed in their second-storey rooms. Tommy had gone home to his wife and family.

Two masked raiders broke into the Post.

They caught Bob and the carpenters by surprise, ordered them down into the office, as if they knew the layout of the building, bound their wrists and jostled them into a dugout cellar after having located and lifted a huge trap door in the floor.

The captive trio had to jump into the cellar since there were no stairs.

Looking up at their captives, one of them warned in a loud voice that if anyone dared move or try to get out of that cellar within the next half hour, they'd return and blow their heads off.

The raiders next piled empty fuel cans over the trap door and went about their business: stealing furs, estimated later by the HBC as being worth $150,000.

Some time passed and the captives heard no sound; certainly more than half an hour had passed. Mustering their courage, they released each other's bonds and commented on the extreme quiet on the main floor. They hadn't known about the empty fuel cans above their heads, other than having heard some commotion when the trap was shut. By and by, their courage rebuilt, they stood on one another's shoulders and forced open the trapdoor. The robbers were long gone.

A massive police search began within a few days.

Throughout the autumn of 1936, over the winter and spring and summer of the following year, police made extensive use of Sheldon and other UAT pilots to track them down. Police hadn't a clue as to where the crooks disappeared to, but they did have some suspects in mind.

One was a well-known fur trader who might have been involved at some stage of this theft.

He had been associated with a large fur buying establishment, which had once been accused of shady deals. This trader had previously chartered a Fairchild Pilgrim aircraft - forerunner of the Fairchild 82 - in the Fairbanks region of Alaska.

Police had reason to believe the crooks loaded the stolen furs onto an aircraft.

Regional tribes reported sighting unusual markings on a Muskwa River sandbar, and police thought they might be tracks left by a float plane which had been hauled up onto the sandbar and then hidden in the bush. A river boat survey failed to uncover any additional evidence of these markings, so police tried an air search.

Game officials from Prince George called on Sheldon to fly them to Fort Nelson. From there he flew them over and around rivers in the area, including the Muskwa, until finally the strange looking marks were located.

Nobody knew what they were. They certainly weren't made by any floats that Sheldon had ever seen before.

Tommy was under severe pressure. He estimated that he paid about $28,000 for the furs, but the HBC evaluation of the missing furs, conducted in London, England set the value at $150,000, the price they would fetch in

England. News of this exaggerated amount shattered him.

The final blow came when the HBC saddled Tommy with responsibility for the missing furs.

He quit his job.

All this time the furs lay safely hidden in a cache a few miles south of Fort Nelson.

It took an alert trapper near Fort Nelson and an avid detective magazine fan in the Coutts, Alberta and Sweetgrass, Montana, border region to help catch the crooks and bring them to justice.

This was an interesting long distance amateur detective scoop, given that Fort Nelson is nearly a thousand miles (1,609 km) north of the Canadian – American border that separates those two communities.

The first clue came from fur trapper, Archie Gardner. He was nearing Fort Nelson in his riverboat, and had to stop to fix a minor engine problem. He worked his boat to shore and set out on foot when he realized the problem was worse than he originally thought.

He only had four miles (6.4 km) to go to reach Fort Nelson.

An unusual-looking and large pile of something which seemed to be covered with canvas caught his attention when he was less than a mile from the river. It was a few feet off the path on which he travelled. As no one was known to be living, trapping or trading in this vicinity, his natural curiosity overcame his usual instincts to leave strange things alone.

He edged over to take a closer look.

The crooks had chosen this precise moment in time to return to their booty, checking it out one more time before retrieving it that very night. One of the pair had Archie in his rifle sights but his partner, as it turned out during court testimony, had talked him out of shooting him. Robbery was bad enough, but murder was another thing.

Once Archie saw what lay below the covering, he remembered the news about the robbery and quickly made his way to Fort Nelson, unaware that he'd been sighted, to notify the police and the Post.

Back at the cache, the thieves decided to scrub their night retrieval mission, and hightail it away from there immediately, leaving the furs behind. Their boat was going to take them and the furs to a waiting pack train, which would then transfer them a long distance towards the interior of the province to their camp on Henry Lake.

Soon after Archie arrived in Fort Nelson, B.C. Provincial Police officer George Clark, no relation to Tommy, boarded a police boat with Archie and headed to Archie's boat.

When they got to where Archie spotted the pile, it was on fire. Furs don't burn too well during the early stages of a fire. But still, an estimated $12,000 of furs had burned by the time Archie and Constable Clark arrived and salvaged the remainder.

They knew the crooks had to be nearby.

Constable Clark called on the services of Provincial policeman Frank Cook from Fort St. James to help in the nearly province-wide search.

Clark followed their trail across the top of British Columbia with horses, always two to three days behind the elusive pair. He knew by then who they were, and tracked them all the way south to Hudson's Hope, only to lose their trail.

Constable Cook had in the meantime issued the equivalent of today's APB – an All Points Bulletin, which went to police offices and detective magazines throughout North America.

The second clue that helped nail the thieves came from very far away, from a young but alert mechanic who owned his own garage near the Coutts, Alberta / Sweetgrass, Montana border crossing between Canada and the USA.

He was pulling himself out from under a car which he was servicing when he saw two pairs of legs walk towards his garage.

He heard them ask if the border crossing was open at night.

It wasn't, he told them, but added that they could cross over early in the morning, reminding them that he'd be open to sell gas by eight o'clock.

He continued his genial banter with them, when something about their faces struck him. Over the next few seconds, he recognized their faces from sketches which had been drawn, and printed in a number of his favourite detective magazines, which he kept in both the garage office and in his home.

He had something exciting on his hands, and was careful not to let the cat out of the bag. Finally, after all these years of fantasizing what he'd do if ever confronted in real-life by crooks, he did exactly what most would recommend, let the police handle it. He directed them to a small community about 10 miles (16 km) up the road, and when they were out of sight he called the police.

Before midnight that day, the pair was behind bars.

In addition to choosing the right equipment for the job, it took the careful selection of hard-working and, above all, reliable men and women to complete the crazy jig-saw of pioneering a successful airline.

Sometimes it took somebody doing contract work for the company, to give it a boost when the going got tough; somebody who could move mountains, such as Vic Johnston.

Well, if not move mountains, would moving an Allis-Chalmers tractor do?

Big and powerful, Vic arrived in Watson Lake to help build the company's new base. A good logger, he also knew how to put log buildings together and he could build an airport.

An Allis-Chalmers tractor and a compactor machine for the runway were flown in piece-by-piece during the winter. The original plan called for an ice runway at first, then followed by gravel runways later. The compactor would be used after a snowfall, to compress the air out of the snow and harden the surface. This provided an excellent surface for planes on wheels or skis.

Vic operated the tractor-compactor combination with uncanny skill, through frequently adverse weather producing well-packed runways, even if it meant working 18 hours a day for several days straight.

Spring had sprung and the ice began to melt.

Shore ice is treacherous tending to weaken first and melt faster.

The safest ice is found toward the centre of a lake in early and mid-spring.

Vic had been working with the machine out on the runway and brought it back to shore one night. As the crew was moving the tractor back to the runway next morning, the left wheel broke through the thinning shore ice.

Sweating and swearing, they tried to pull the heavy tractor out of the ice.

It wouldn't budge. All they got for their efforts was a rapidly expanding pool of water around the partially submerged wheel. Vic soon tired of their futile efforts and took charge.

He ordered planks made ready, and then prepared to slip them into place. He entered the shallow water, surrounded the wheel with his body, embraced it in one huge bear hug, grabbed it by the spokes and lifted it clear off of the water.

The men quickly slipped the planking under the wheel. The planks straddled the open water between ice and shore and within minutes Vic had the tractor freed and operational once again.

Few could match wits with Vic, a self-educated, highly articulate man. He excelled in mathematics but was especially gifted in calculus and astronomy.

Not bad assets for a man to have.

McConachie's genius was that he knew how to spot and pick his good people, even contractors.

Grant first met Vic while he was working for the railroad before he got his start in aviation, and remembered him all this time.

### It took a special woman to be a bush pilot's wife in a $20-a-month cabin home on her husband's $80-a-month salary

Not many women had what it took to be a bush pilot's wife.

Their husbands tended to boot about the country leaving their families behind for long, lonely periods. At least it was one way to give their children an opportunity for a sustained education in the larger cities. But an absentee husband was tough to take.

It wasn't any easier following your husband from place to place either, packing up a household, unpacking and thinking you'd be settling in, only to have to pack again and hustle somewhere else once more.

When businesses called for the services of bush pilots, bush pilots just had to go.

On August 8, 1936, Sheldon and Isabel celebrated the birth of their second child, Nancy. Three days later Sheldon had to report for duty in Edmonton.

He wouldn't see Isabel, Nancy or their first-born, Jamie, for another three months. It took a special woman to build a bond which would last over the years between herself, her children and her man who was always in search of adventure, yet never wanting to be too far apart from his family for too long.

Few wives would tolerate that kind of nonsense today, claimed Sheldon.

Strong pilots' associations exist to try and provide better lifestyles for their members, including such things as a decent amount of time spent with loved ones.

During their early married years, Sheldon spent a lot of time away from home at any possible job trying to build up money for his necessary air time. One of these jobs included operating a threshing machine; good money could be had with one of those units. Sheldon took a 10-day course at International Harvester in Calgary on such a machine. Soon he was able to contract out his services, feed his family and buy some airtime to build up to his commercial pilot's license.

A teamster could earn between 50 and 60 cents an hour, while a combine operator could pull down as much as $10 a day, including whatever food he could pack into his stomach.

Isabel became Sheldon's mainstay at home during these lean years, searching for any work she could do to help out. She even got a part-time job in the public library.

Fortunately for them, she was also a first-class gardener and loved to do canning. She and Sheldon would shop at fanners' markets late Saturday nights when they'd stay open until about eleven o'clock. Those without refrigeration had to sell off their remaining meat at near distress prices. Sheldon recalls a sample price: 70 cents for a quarter of a lamb.

Often, late in the evenings, Sheldon later admitted, he selfishly asked a lot of Isabel without realizing it.

His imagination would take to the skies as she sat and watched him sit on the bed, hand wrapped around the top of his grandfather's cane, positioned vertically on the floor. To Sheldon, his eyes closed, the cane had become the control stick of an aircraft and he was visualizing the plane's responses to different maneuvers... lost in a world of his own making, completely oblivious of Isabel's presence.

Grant sent Sheldon to Fort St. James in May 1937. Isabel, Nancy and Jamie joined him later, making the trip by train from Edmonton to Vanderhoof. A friend, W.D. Fraser picked up the family and brought them into their new home in Fort St. James, often affectionately known as "The Fort."

Home.

A $20 a month cabin.

A typical cabin had what were known as "beaverboard" partitions – most likely an early term for of particleboard – which divided it into two bedrooms and a kitchen. It usually it came with its own Winnipeg couch, but not much else. In Winnipeg this same couch was known as a Toronto couch.

Bathrooms were luxury items unless you were in a big city; here it was the time-honoured outside facility – the outhouse – some distance from the hand-operated water pump.

Their new home's previous bachelor occupants kept the crude plank flooring clean by frequent applications of used cylinder oil. This made life miserable for Isabel, while Jamie and Nancy had a whale of a time getting themselves and their clothes dirty on it. The oil may have helped the bachelors keep dust levels down to a minimum but it seemed to develop a permanent affinity for the children.

The Fort offered a lot to Sheldon.

Besides the sheer thrill of flying for a living over a land he loved so much, there were always the good, kindly neighbours at hand, solid men and women, most of them living off the land. Nature provided plenty of fish, moose and deer, and Isabel brought her vast gardening skills with her to augment the family larder.

Little wonder they could get by on as little as $80 a month.

This was the figure which Isabel decided would be the minimum salary which she knew the family would need to provide for themselves after Grant flew in especially to see them about the issue of money.

On top of it all, Grant passionately pleaded with Sheldon to accept a deferred salary, as things were really tough in Edmonton.

Seeing Grant's financial plight, Isabel came up with the $80 a month figure as a salary.

As to the deferred part of the salary, Grant made good on this promise in the fall when business picked up. He had also promised other strong financial rewards for their good faith, rewards Sheldon never did see – such as shares in the company.

By then, Grant had acquired quite an internal reputation for making promises and was having a hell of a hard time keeping them.

Sheldon's loyalty to the man and the company went far beyond expecting a promise to be kept when it was made under duress, as he figures Grant must have been that night in their cabin.

Bush flying may have fed Sheldon's appetite for adventure, the unknown and excitement but it did little for his pocket-book.

One of the truly great unknowns of early bush pilots was when they'd get their next pay cheque. And would it bounce?

A blustery evening in August 1937 and high waves on Stuart Lake and The Fort (St. James) provided the background for a meeting between two dynamic and energetic personalities - Sheldon and Russell Baker, the founder of Pacific Western Airlines.

When two people meet for the first time a certain kind of spell, or gut feeling, known as body chemistry mingles between them and takes over.

Either it works or it doesn't, and nobody in the world seems to know how it works.

If this elusive chemistry is good, the result is often a long-lasting firm friendship; if the chemistry is neutral or bad, it can result in long-lasting resentment – either way, this chemistry rarely changes over time.

The chemistry between Sheldon and Russ? It usually lay somewhere between neutral and simply unpleasant.

Sheldon and friends were on the government dock watching the wind-driven waves breaking out on the lake when a Fox Moth on floats came into view. As they watched, Sheldon realized the pilot was coming in for a landing.

He couldn't help himself being curious about a pilot who would try such a landing in turbulent water conditions.

Winds had reduced considerably from their previous afternoon force, but they were still strong enough to make a water landing right now hard and quite impractical. Normally pilots can take advantage of a stiff wind in the final seconds before let down in rough water, but these winds weren't there to *help* this young pilot.

Sheldon couldn't understand why he hadn't gone around to the calmer waters behind the dock; certainly he must have seen the group of men on the dock, and the calm water behind them? If he did, it didn't matter to him.

The Fox Moth landed. If the aircraft breaks up, thought Sheldon, the fool lad will drown because there wasn't a large enough boat to head into the swells to rescue him.

Many bobs and bounces later, the plane closed in on dock-side. Astonished, Sheldon and his friends walked over. As they neared where the plane would reach dock, they saw it turn to one side, and begin to list with the pilot tacking it into the dock. It had taken such a pounding that rigging had loosened. It should have been in bits and pieces, but miraculously, it wasn't.

Once secured, a chap bounced out and introduced himself as Russ Baker, of Ginger Coote Airways. Grant wouldn't be making a bid for Ginger Coote's company for some time yet.

Russ said he'd just completed a charter out of Wells, about 75 miles (121 km) south of Prince George, and had flown in to The Fort looking for work purely on speculation.

Some introduction.

Spunky to say the least and indicative of the nature of the man whose name became synonymous with that of Pacific Western Airlines.

A local newspaper article from The Fort many years later described him as "...a legendary giant among a small corps of hard, tough bush pilots, who steered their flimsy aircraft into the uncharted wilderness of northern British Columbia in the middle 1930s..."

Russ had never been to The Fort before. This "legendary" giant of later years failed to impress Sheldon or his friends that evening. All this would change in coming years, as many at The Fort got to know Russ a lot better: he could be a persuasive charmer when he turned it on, and he too was a man of great vision, not unlike Grant McConachie and his dreams.

Maybe Sheldon had spotted too many McConachie-type characteristics in Russ Baker during that first meeting to be truly comfortable with the Baker from that point on.

Since Russ was hungry and Molly Forfar's hotel dining room had closed for the night, Sheldon invited him into their home. Once there, Isabel gave Russ a decent supper. Sheldon then walked Russ over to Molly's where Russ stayed the night.

Russ arrived at The Fort with the impression that work was to be had for the taking. Ginger had heard that Grant's outfit had been operating successfully for some time now and discussed the prospects with Russ before he sent him north.

Ginger and Russ wanted a piece of McConachie's action.

Sheldon wasn't about to yield any corporate secrets... besides, there was just enough work around to pay for the plane and his and Isabel's meager salary, let alone sharing the slim pickings with a newcomer.

He made it appear to Russ that there was hardly any work at all:

"Look Russ, we have two aircraft sitting here and we haven't turned a wheel in over two days."

The implications were obvious and clear-cut. Whatever he and Ginger had heard about the great amount of work out here was exaggerated by a large amount. Also it was late in the season and the big charter contracts had just about expired. He tried to leave the impression that UAT and Sheldon were just sitting here, hoping for work.

Naturally Sheldon wouldn't admit that no aircraft had taken off in the last two days because of severe winds, but hinted that a lack of work was the only reason the plans were sitting there, idle.

Somehow Sheldon did not think that he had impressed Russ too much, but Russ seemed to accept the information and took off the next day, resolved to return there someday to work with Sheldon, despite what Sheldon had told him.

Russ did return a few months later, as an employee of United Air Transport, working under Sheldon, doubtless another minor irritant in their relationship - at least from Russ's point of view.

Sheldon is convinced that if Ginger and Grant hadn't gotten together when they did, Russ would have made a bid to take over Ginger's operation, something he was quite capable of doing, as later deals over the years would prove.

After Grant had negotiated his deal with Ginger Coote making Grant area manager for UAT's Pacific District, Russ had become part of the expanded organization as one of Ginger's employees.

On paper, Sheldon too had a new boss, Ginger, and really enjoyed working with him. Grant in the meantime had pulled Sheldon out of The Fort into Prince George to take over there, and replaced him with Russ Baker.

Eventually Russ quit the company and contacted Punch Dickins at Canadian Airways Limited in Winnipeg, Manitoba. s

Russ soon returned to The Fort as a CAL pilot, in direct competition against UAT.

## Overweight was the norm in the cut-throat business of bush-flying ...overweight in cargo, that is

To this day Sheldon is convinced that Russ orchestrated the events which led to the one and only time he lost his license over an infraction.

Competition between CAL and UAT was as fierce as could be imagined and Russ and Sheldon weren't getting along too well personally before Russ quit to join CAL.

Just before Sheldon was to move down to Vancouver, a telegram arrived at lunchtime from UAT's head office. It told him that Grant had received an order from Ottawa grounding Sheldon for ninety days for having carried excess weigh on a charter.

The telegram said Grant was keeping him on staff in that time, on full pay. It was said that Grant went to Tom Cowley, who, it was also said, royally chewed out the unsuspecting McConachie with such choice words as, "How do you expect us to deal with these pilots who break regulations if you operators are going to protect them all?!"

This triggered a verbal barrage best left to a fertile imagination.

Canada's Department of Transport took a dictatorial approach to anyone breaking its rules. Given no chance to defend himself Sheldon had no choice but to accept the grounding.

A stream of orders issued from Edmonton to Prince George: stop flying and go bill collecting instead. The company had a lot of unpaid bills in the district, which if collected, could go a long way to improve its overall financial picture and pay some of its own bills in the process.

Quite successful as a bill-collector, Sheldon had no idea Grant was going to bat for him with every ounce of energy he could muster, trying to gather all the details on the overloading charge laid against his best pilot.

Evidence gathered revealed that a Prince Rupert law firm, representing a competing air service, had filed an overload complaint against Sheldon with Inspector Carter Guest, the man who endorsed Sheldon's first Air Engineer Certificate in 1937.

The law firm had an exact date, a precise location and the weight, nearly to an ounce, of the amount overloaded on Sheldon's aircraft.

Years later, Grant told Sheldon that he learned Guest tried his best to soft-pedal this accusation, despite his reputation in the business as being a tough guy to deal with. Guest was no stranger to some of the nearly impossible conditions bush pilots had to deal with on extended charters, and was more sympathetic to struggling operators than he was originally given credit for.

He knew overloading was a way of life.

As Sheldon went on collecting more bills, Grant kept on collecting more information on the infraction.

It had taken place all right, during a camp move from a gold mining operation at Humphrey Lake, 45 miles (72 km) northwest of Fort St. James, on the west flanks of the Omenica Mountains. Everything had to be airlifted and it took two flights. On the last trip out, a small Chinese cook stood looking forlorn and abandoned on shore.

Despite the fact that the cook was surplus weight for the second flight, he was visibly frightened at the prospect of overnighting alone, without equipment. Sheldon didn't have the heart or intention of leaving him behind to wait for a third flight the following day.

He had left Fort St. James with full tanks and topped them off from the cache at the mining camp. Of course he had room to spare for the man who probably tipped the scales, dripping wet, at a hundred and twenty-seven pounds. It merely meant one passenger more than the aircraft was licensed to carry.

But then, UAT wasn't using seats in those days.

The overloading charge against Sheldon came to almost exactly 127 pounds (57 kg), on the same date and for the same charter flight.

On the average, Sheldon recalls that government inspectors tried their best to be fair, understanding and sympathetic to remote operators. Inspectors often played confessor roles to pilots and operators alike. If a pilot did something wrong, such as overloading, and was reasonably certain he would be reported by a competitor, he would do the wise thing and turned himself in voluntarily.

In this manner the offending pilot could get what amounted to a "pre-hearing". Sheldon had no warning or any suspicions that the relationship with Russ would turn sour over this manner. At this unofficial pre-hearing, the pilot could explain the mitigating circumstances – and there were plenty – which led to the infraction.

If the inspector were of the same calibre as the late Howard T. Ingram, or T.G. Stephens, the offence would be allowed to go officially unnoticed and the pilot would receive a verbal caution.

Someone had to have it in for Sheldon to do such a thing. Why?

Kenneth Molson, in his book *Pioneering in Canadian Air Transport* (1974, James Richardson & Sons Limited, Winnipeg) offers a glimpse at the answer:

> ...*While overloading of aircraft was against air regulations and pilots were reprimanded if found doing it, in practice if was very difficult to enforce as the flying was done from small towns far from the major centres where aviation inspectors were located. Since Canadian Airways had adopted a policy of abiding by the regulations and their competitors chose not to, it naturally disturbed Canadian Airways to see others getting away with it. The company would report offences that came to their attention, to the Civil Aviation authorities which did not make them popular with their competitors. On the other side, the competing pilots and operating staffs would sometimes taunt the Canadian Airways pilots about the small loads they carried, which would irritate them...*

Canadian Airways had one of its bases at Fort St. James, managed by Russ Baker.

Where there's a will, there's a way, even if it takes tragic circumstances to alter a course.

Grant was going to get Sheldon's license back, come hell or high water.

A tragedy claiming the lives of a pilot and his three passengers unfortunately became the catalyst which put Sheldon back into the cockpit.

On Friday, May 27th, 1938, Len Waagen had taken off from Zeballos in a UAT aircraft with Ginger Coote markings. It was a routine flight into Vancouver with Mrs. George Nicholson and H. Boyd, Stevetson, both from BC, and Charles Rumsey from Ontario as its only passengers.

Their failure to arrive triggered a massive search and rescue mission.

Grant stressed the need for an experienced pilot to help check out the many reports and sightings. UAT aircrews, equipment and facilities were extensively used throughout this search for one of their own, along with facilities and personnel from Ginger's former company.

Canadian Airways, under circumstances such as these, dropped all pretext of animosity, discarded competition, and pitched in with all the resources and personnel it could muster.

However, Grant's most experienced pilot was grounded. He threatened to hire an inexperienced pilot if he couldn't get Luck back, right away. An inexperienced pilot is one with less than one hours' commercial hours of air time, far less than what professionals need in a SAR mission.

He went one step further, and threatened that the Civil Aviation branch would be held personally liable if anything were to happen to this inexperienced pilot. McConachie could always more easily replace a good aircraft that an experienced pilot.

Len's disappearance had altered the rules of the game; Grant was right, he would need his most experienced man to help search for Len and his passengers. All SAR missions are conducted as rapidly as possible on the assumption that all have survived a crash and are in need of prompt medical help. Any delay could result in death, if there are any survivors.

Grant had touched a sensitive nerve with the government.

They would give in to him under two conditions: that neither he nor Sheldon say anything about the restoring of Sheldon's license, and to keep the lifting of the suspension as quiet as possible.

Of course Sheldon had to agree to sin no more.

Word did leak out to the media, but not from Sheldon.

Given the media attention focused on the search, it was just a matter of time before some enterprising reporter discovered from sources that Sheldon had been grounded and that Grant had been instrumental in exerting pressure in the right places to get him airborne once again. A newspaper report read in part:

> ...accompanying Coote is Sheldon Luck ... (who) had been grounded for a technical infringement of flying rules, but he had been granted permission to fly in the search by C.G. Upson, Director of Civil Aviation in Vancouver. Ginger is tiring from the unremitting strain and Luck is spelling him at the controls.

Many SAR missions are plagued with numerous reports and sightings from different regions, and SAR Waagen was no exception: reports came in from along the hundreds of shoreline miles where he might have gone down. Even though many reports originated miles from each other, all had to be checked out.

Earlier a bit has been written about those who met Sheldon and influenced his life in return, such as Elianne Roberge, a pioneer women pilot in Canada. Sheldon first met Elianne on the search for Len Waagen. (Nine months after the accident, a timber cruiser found Len Waagen's missing aircraft. An exhaust valve had blown, forcing him to the ground. A "timber cruiser" is a forestry term for a person whose profession is to assess, among other criteria by air or on foot, the accessibility, quality and potential value of timber in a given stand of harvestable forest.)

A newspaper took note of Elianne's arrival, describing her as one of few Canadian women to hold a commercial pilot's license. She flew regularly with Sheldon, checking out reports and hunches from others. She made an invaluable contribution to the search effort, especially when it came time to assess, analyse and type up each and every report for the final UAT mission report.

But there was a lot more to Elianne than her ability to analyse and type up each and every report for the final UAT mission report.

During the seven years in which I followed Sheldon across Canada and interviewed him both at his BC home and in my home office in Lachine, Québec where I lived at the time of the key interview about Elianne, Sheldon never did mention the second woman in our interviews about the Len Waagen accident, other than give a passing reference – Margaret Fane Rutledge.

By the time Elianne had met Sheldon, during the SAR mission for Len, Elianne and Margaret were already members of a pioneering group of remarkable Canadian women pilots known as "The Flying Seven."

Quoting the website (with some minor grammatical and other necessary corrections):

> B.C.'s famous Flying Seven women pilots charted unknown territory.
>
> Back in 1936, when aviation was still in its infancy a group of women flyers got together to form The Flying Seven. The idea for the Flying Seven group in Canada sprang from a 1935 visit Margaret Fane made to California.
>
> At the Burbank Airport she met Lauretta Schimoler with whom she had been corresponding to exchange Canadian and U.S. information on women pilots. Schimoler introduced Fane to Amelia Earhart who was getting ready to leave on a flight from Los Angeles to Mexico.
>
> They all went for lunch and discussed the possibility of the Canadian women pilots joining the American group called the 99s. This group had started some time before with 99 members, with Earhart as president. It was suggested that the Canadian women form a chapter of the American group. With the size of Canada and the few women pilots there, spread across the county, that idea was thrown out.
>
> In July of 1936, Fane had left Edmonton where she had been the only woman member of the Edmonton and Northern Aero Club.
>
> Upon arrival in Vancouver she was pleased to find there were other women with licences. Some had learned to fly in the Vancouver area and, with the addition of herself and Elianne Roberge who had trained in Montréal, there were a total of seven.

*So, the "Flying Seven" Canadian Women Pilots became an active group.*

*In November 1936, to give the club a good start, they held a "Dawn to Dusk" flight.*

*One member of the group took off at dawn and before that plane landed, another took off. This went on until official sunset when the last landing was made. The imperial Oil Company donated the oil and the fellows at the airport came out at dawn to help get the planes ready. They stayed until sunset to*

*make sure the women were okay. This was the only Dawn to Dusk flight ever held at Vancouver Airport.*

*The Flying Seven went on helping out at air shows, holding flying and spot landings as well as competitions among themselves for trophies and other prizes.*

*When WWII broke out, the group offered their services but were not accepted as pilots by the Royal Canadian Air Force. So, they took part in fund-raising to buy aircraft for #8 Flying Training School in Vancouver.*

*Management of the Orpheum Theatre offered the theatre for a big night and the Cave Supper Club acted as venue for the show.*

*Jack Wasserman of the Vancouver Sun provided publicity in his newspaper column. In addition, the Flying Seven borrowed a couple of airplanes from which they dropped advertising leaflets; they ended up raising $100,000, which at the time paid for eight training planes.*

*To further assist the war effort, the club organized ground school training. These classes were a great success. The school board lent classroom facilities and several qualified flight instructors volunteered their time. Many graduates joined the Women's Air Force while others went to the Boeing plant where their skills were needed.*

*During the war private flying was not allowed. After the war the members of the Flying Seven were scattered. Some had married and had children. Some had moved to other areas. Those left decided their dreams of a Canadian organization to match the American 99s would be impossible to manage. By now there were a greater number of Canadian women pilots, so it seemed more practical to form chapters of the American 99s. This was done with a great deal of success and the co-operation between the two countries has worked well.*

More information, thanks to the internet, has since surfaced about Elianne, information that was not available to me when I produced the original book, *Walking on Air*, which gave birth to this expanded version.

*The Flying Seven, left to right: Jean Pike, Tosca Trasolini, Betsy Flaherty, Alma Gilbert, Elianne Roberge, Margaret (Fane) Rutledge, and Rolie Moore.*

Here, I reproduce information from the following web site: The History of Metropolitan Vancouver

> ...in 1980, the *Province's* Chuck Davis interviewed Elianne Roberge. She was Elianne Schlageter by then, and she and her husband Fred lived in South Vancouver.
> "I got interested in flying in Prince Rupert back in 1921," Elianne said. "We'd seen a plane flying over the town once, but one day a man who was going from Mexico to Siberia brought his plane through on a train. It was a biplane and everyone was just fascinated by it. Well, he had it tethered down that night, but a high wind came along and started knocking it around, and by the morning it was in bad shape. Kids were taking pieces of the fabric from the wings and I wanted some, too, but I was in school in the convent. So I put up my hand and said I needed to leave the room, and they let me go, but instead I ran outside and down to where the plane was and got a big chunk of the fabric."
> She laughs at the memory. "That night, I cut the fabric into one-inch squares and wrote my name and the date on each piece in ink. I sold them next day for a penny apiece. It was September 13, 1921."
> [We just Googled for that Mexico-to-Siberia trip and found

this: "*Polar Bear 1921 = 2pOB. Built by Morton Bach in his backyard with design help from Clarence Prest. Used for an attempted flight from Mexico to Siberia, which ended short in northwest Canada.*" *The 'Polar Bear' referred to is likely the name of the plane.]*

"The first time my mother ever saw me fly," Elianne says, "I crashed."

To join the Flying Seven, you had to have a flying licence. "We wouldn't take learners," Elianne explains. "All the girls were experienced. I started flying in 1929 and stopped in 1963. My licence is No. 678, and I still have it. You won't find many people in Canada with a lower number."

In 1980 all the club members, with the exception of Betsy Flaherty, who had died a few years earlier, were alive. "And the Flying Seven still exists," Elianne says in this 1980 interview. "We never disbanded. We still have a little bank account. We still get together now and again. Tosca flew up from California on a commercial flight to see us at the Abbotsford Air Show last weekend. We're still around."

Margaret Fane Rutledge also helped during the search, participating on many flights as an air observer. She went on to become Ginger's personal secretary when his previous office manager, another talented woman, left to devote more time to her family. Margaret not only replaced her but assumed duties as a spare co-pilot whenever necessary. Sheldon said that she kept Ginger's office running smoothly and efficiently whenever she wasn't airborne herself during the search.

According to the web site, Margaret was born in Edmonton, Alberta, and became interested in flying at an early age. She obtained her private licence in 1933 and her commercial licence in 1935. She was a charter member of the Flying Seven, a group of Canadian women pilots, based in Vancouver. She worked for Ginger Coote Airways as a co-pilot, radio operator and dispatcher. She was later a reservations supervisor for CPA.

*Margaret Fane Rutledge*
*1914 - 2004*
*Photo: Margaret Rutledge Collection*

## Fan dancer Fay Baker fans Calgary headlines

Special flights set aviators apart from other professionals. Perhaps this is because aviators tended to be parts of the headlines and parts of the news-making process by participating in adventurous and exciting developments ... if only just by being there when news was being made.

Sometimes a pilot would make headlines because he unknowingly became part of a publicity scheme.

One can never be certain these weren't the circumstances when Bill May, one of Sheldon's close friends, flew into the history books with a beautiful, shapely and popular fan dancer of the mid-1930s.

The background: Sheldon worked periodically at the Grand Theatre in Calgary, sometimes on stage, other times as a house detective, or even in the cloakroom – anything to make a buck to build airtime.

Isabel's father, Jimmy, had hooked Sheldon into the theatre business for a brief period of time. Jimmy had been a maintenance man and carpenter for the Lougheed family estate, one of the largest holdings in the Calgary area. Included among these holdings was the Grand Theatre where Jimmy spent a lot of time, and where Jimmy became well-known and well-liked. When Jimmy put in a good word for Sheldon, it was enough to land him part-time work.

The Grand Theatre booked only stage plays and performing artists that drew large crowds. Sheldon could make as much as three dollars a night, which beat hauling manure around.

Studying the advance booking notices one day, Sheldon saw that the famous fan dancer, Fay Baker, was coming to town. He read every single word which described her many charming and spectacular talents. This was one performance he wouldn't miss for the world!

He did.

She failed to show.

Following her last Winnipeg performance, she got into an aircraft piloted by Bill May.

Something had happened.

They went missing in the woods of northern Manitoba.

Of course nobody knew that's where they were; her fans and other interested newspaper readers only knew she was missing, along with the pilot.

In what seemed like a perfectly staged performance, the first news report indicated that a bush pilot was down.

The second news story gave his name.

A third news article told of a passenger, a lady.

The fourth news item burst the bubble, giving her name.

The fifth major news story dealt with their miraculous discovery, with both unharmed, but supposedly feeling "out of sorts" from the experience and allegedly needing a few days of rest to recover from the ordeal.

Her date at the Grand was rebooked for another time.

This story aroused the interest and blood pressure of every red-blooded young man who no doubt conjured up magnificent fantasies of what he would have done had he been that unfortunate pilot.

The entire thing was believed to have been a well-rehearsed hoax by her press agent. A cabin had been chosen, food flown in, and a good sunny day selected for the take-off for what should have been a day or two of rest. It seems that the pilot, Bill, had no knowledge that the whole search was nothing more than a publicity stunt.

Bad weather really did set in shortly after take-off, and Bill found himself flying into an endless supply of tennis-ball size snowflakes. Bill was supposed to have flown her in to the cabin, stay with her and return on a certain date.

The unofficial story has it that Bill got cabin fever after a few days, got into the aircraft with Fay and flew her out.

Eventually Fay kept her date at the Grand Theatre, and performed every night for one week, much to the delight of her packed-house audiences.

### Pioneers made of sturdy stuff

Canada's northern pioneers were sturdy, memorable types with interesting personality traits and characteristics. Most pioneers left indelible etchings on the memories of those who were exposed to them for more than a chance encounter.

Those who worked with and for primitive air services were pioneers; so were most of their clients who came from the same basic mold.

Not everyone got along. The clash of strong personalities caught in the pot-pourri of pioneering life sometimes resulted in awkward, irritating and explosive combinations.

When opposites met, and the meeting did not breed outright hostile feelings, the results were often exasperating, leaving one or the other nonplussed.

This happened to Sheldon when he first met top bush pilot Ernie Kubicek in Fort St. James.

Ernie had arrived in a Fokker, G-CAHE. Grant wanted Sheldon to use the Fokker while Ernie flew the Waco back to Edmonton for work which could only be done there.

In no time flat, Ernie broadcast more than a tinge of professional jealousy that Sheldon had flown the Waco first. Sheldon couldn't understand where the hard feelings were coming from; that was just the way things worked out in the scheduling of planes and pilots. All the senior pilots were out on charters the day Sheldon first reported for duty. He wound up with the only available aircraft, the Waco.

It had nothing to do with Grant not giving his senior employees a first crack at new equipment in favour of a newcomer.

Since Sheldon was alone in the cabin - Isabel and the family wouldn't arrive for some months yet - he invited Ernie to overnight with him along with mechanic Red Rose.

Ernie refused.

He tromped off in a huff to stay at Ed and Molly's hotel.

The resentment displayed by Ernie was completely out of character with the image Sheldon had of him. He had based his projections of what Ernie would be like from stories of Ernie's skill and courage relayed by others who had befriended him when he joined the company.

Another incident had begun one morning when Ernie and a mechanic were tinkering with a Fokker Universal's engine before taking it up for a test flight at Takla Landing on Babine Lake.

Ernie had invited a couple of men along for the flight. They had been on a scow at the same dock watching him and the mechanic at work. They were part of scowman David Hoy's crew and included David's son, Bob. David declined the invitation, but Bob and one or two of the younger lads eagerly accepted on the Fokker, C-GAHJ.

As the plane cleared the water, the left rear float fitting snapped.

Heavy and long, it visibly sagged several inches as seen from below, and by those in the passenger cabin. They immediately told Ernie what happened by means of the peephole in the bulkhead. Unknown to them, Ernie already suspected exactly what happened.

If the float had let go completely, the situation could have become much worse than it was.

As long as it was a rear fitting cluster, Ernie could maintain flight with the float hanging on, trailing, assuming a water-ski angle of attack into the wind.

Cool and methodical, Ernie brought HJ around, ever so slightly to prevent the ship from drifting sideways, and let it settle, gently kissing the water so the float could ease back into its broken socket.

It took a pilot with exceptional skill and a calm head to handle such an emergency. Ernie displayed consummate skill and was a fine example of the calibre of pilots required to routinely and safely conduct air services to and from remote areas.

What made aviation pioneers different from the other types of pioneers found in great numbers elsewhere in Canada? Three things basically: the weather – probably the most unpredictable and potentially lethal of all things in Canada's mountainous and remote regions; really dangerous large carnivorous

*What the intrepid airborne letter carrier of the far north, and his airplane, used to wear in winter. Photo from Sheldon's personal collection and saved for posterity in the Public Archives of Canada in Ottawa, ON, shows Sheldon just before take-off on January 26th, 1938, for the first airmail flight to Germansen Landing in central-northern BC.*

and predatory animals; and the isolation factor. Other than this, there were no great differences between pioneers in the far north and elsewhere in Canada. Pioneers everywhere had to face daily problems unique to their respective locations.

Male bush pioneers, like most pioneers elsewhere, leaned toward toughness. It's called "macho" these days, meaning manliness, ruggedness, and courage… all coupled with a large amount of sex appeal.

Trappers and prospectors ranked among some of the toughest and ornery pioneers. If they were "macho", the one thing they lacked was scent-appeal.

They were a pretty dirty batch, emitting strong odours acquired and embedded in the pores of their skins from camp fires, handling furs, dogs and what-nots in their wilderness treks lasting months at a stretch.

Few ever even had a chance to take a bath for months, until they arrived at such places as Red's and Ma's at Charlie Lake.

Trappers usually ran their lines in winter, making their way out with catches in the spring to Charlie Lake. There they waited for the first plane to take them into the big city where they could make money selling their goods.

Sometimes they'd have to wait a day or two for the plane. Invariably they dipped into the last of their supplies, which included, more often than not, a bottle of over-proof rum. They would start telling tales which grew longer as alcohol shaded the truth about events experienced the previous winter.

They really were characters of the finest cut.

One was known as Tough Tom, an excellent paying customer. Once, he went to Edmonton, all cleaned and spiffed up, on his annual supply trip. Grant happened to be in town at the same time, saw Tom and decided to throw a party in Tom's honour, inviting air and ground crews to join in the fun.

Not used to the rich food that Grant had lavishly laid on, Tom became ill late that night. He looked around, and no one seemed to notice just how sickly he had become; they were too busy having a good time.

Tom made for the bathroom. Somebody else was on the throne.

In sheer desperation, he found an empty closet. Still no one took notice of his whereabouts. He dove in, not wanting to embarrass himself nor his friends. Once inside the closet, he found a large overcoat, opened the pocket and filled it.

The party broke up soon after.

Grant made his way home, not feeling any pain. He tried to sneak into the house without waking his wife. He got the key into the lock, opened the door and just nicely made it inside thinking he'd gotten away with it when the lights blazed on.

Taken aback, he began to take off his overcoat.

Standing there, not quite teetering nor tottering, he slowly shoved his hand into a pocket. Instantly he knew something was very wrong. He lifted his arm, took one look at his hand and charged for the bathroom.

Grant told this story on himself with great gusto and good humour over the years.

Queasy stomachs didn't last long in the bush, where the conventional niceties did little to keep one alive. To be fair, not all pioneer types in bush regions participated in or condoned the events such as the one related above.

Most "bush folk" were fine men in their own right – trappers, hunters, traders and prospectors, who all displayed, and appreciated, high degrees of respect for civilities and courtesies common to larger centres.

Many of them could teach "civilized" folks the true meaning of civilization and quality of life.

Western and northwestern Canadian mountain sides and valleys were speckled with prospectors in the '20s and '30s, looking for rich mineral deposits. Placer gold operations accounted for a large part of UAT's charters.

Being a prospector entailed spending or owing a lot of money. Flights, equipment and grub had to be paid for. Furthermore, registering each and every claim they staked could put quite a dint in their pocketbooks.

Prospectors usually tried to secure a large area first and prove out their finds before incurring the expense of protecting their claims by registering them at the nearest gold commissioner's office.

Periodically, prospecting friends would pool their money for grubstakes, equipment and aircraft charters.

Prospecting was a dog-eat-dog world. If claim jumpers were busy at work, competitors were snooping around trying to find out what was happening. For good reason prospectors were naturally suspicious of strangers or inquisitive acquaintances and often seemed to go to extremes to prevent detection of their exploration areas.

Many of Sheldon's prospecting clients insisted he create the most roundabout way of getting to their sites. He'd never heard other pilots speak of similar requests, but attributes their silence on the matter to a pilot-client trust relation, similar in many respects to a lawyer-client relationship. Few prospectors he ever knew wanted direct flight to their claims. They'd rather pay the extra cash to confuse onlookers.

The manner in which this might work would involve a prospector planning to explore south of the Whitehorse area. He'd make arrangements with UAT's Edmonton offices for him and his equipment to be picked up hundreds of miles south, say at Burns Lake. A contract condition prevented the pilot from flying on to Whitehorse to refuel there.

He could easily have chartered George Simmons's Northern Airways out of Carcross, Yukon Territory, to make the flight at better rates, but he'd prefer to pay the extra cash for security reasons.

Part of the reason for such stringent deception measures lay in the fact that another good prospector, or competitor, could often tell what kind or kinds of mineral were being explored simply by looking at the equipment being loaded onto an aircraft.

Bush pilots were frequently subject to intense, but often amateurish and patently obvious interrogation techniques in bars about where certain charter flights went when they involved prospectors. No doubt everybody has a price, but most bush pilots were proud of the fact that their client relationship was nobody else's business.

Rounding out the truly interesting character types who laid the foundation for progress in the north are last, but not least, the pack train operators - mountain men in the truest sense of the word. Their work horses and mules provided yeoman service in moving thousands upon thousands of tons of a wide variety of cargo into remote northern regions.

This could include equipment, machinery, luxury items such as grand pianos, staples, farm goods, and an incredible range of supplies - not everything moved by air or could move by air as a number of places were simply inaccessible to an aircraft.

### Meeting the legendary, one-off, Skook Davidson

Before Grant sent Sheldon to Fort St. James, he'd taken time to advise him about one such mountain man and pack train operator, the legendary Skook Davidson. Grant had met him when he flew out of The Fort in the early '30s, and told Sheldon that he'd better prepare himself to meet a man who could out-Wayne John Wayne.

He'd never met anyone like Skook in his life before, nor did he ever meet another one after.

Skook had but one known peer of the same calibre: Cataline, known far and wide as "The Great Horse Trader."

Named Jean-Jacques Caux at birth, Cataline lived in the 1860s and made his living with pack trains. He earned a reputation as a notable eccentric by, among other things, rubbing cognac into his long flowing hair to give it vitality.

Cataline built a reputation for honesty, reliability and integrity during the famous Cariboo Gold Rush Days.

It's been said that at Cataline's death they broke the mold.

But apparently not, for Spook was made of the same mold.

One fine Saturday afternoon in September, Sheldon had been trying to complete his monthly statement for Grant when a loud voice and noise at the door interrupted him.

He went to investigate. Fronting him stood an image which had leapt from the pages of some wild adventure book, a very large and tall man, with a bottle of rum in one hand and the other almost extended in greeting.

Sheldon couldn't say anything at first.

Skook did:

"You're Sheldon Luck, the new pilot!"

Skook always seemed to speak with at least one exclamation point punctuating the end of each phrase.

Sheldon blinked and barely nodded in agreement.

"Have a drink!" barked Skook.

This was more than a mere encounter from an adventure book... this two-legged creature was from the fringes of some other dimension.

Sheldon, still unresponsive, the hulk spoke again.

"I'm Skook Davidson!"

Sheldon replied with a quote: "Mr. Davidson..."

"I'm Skook Davidson, not Mr. Davidson."

Sensing that this was going nowhere fast, Sheldon collected his wits and politely tried to decline the offer of a drink. After all he could be offered a charter any time and he certainly couldn't very well have a drink right now. Could he?

"I want a God damned charter! I'll give you a charter right now! We'll go to Prince George and have a party!"

It didn't take much longer for Sheldon to make the connection between this immense character, the name and Grant's previous advisory.

Of course, this was Skook, in the flesh.

And rarin' to go.

In no time flat the charter was on. A wild one it promised to be, but a cash paying customer shouldn't be denied. Skook seemed to be bent on consuming vast quantities of alcohol and Sheldon wasn't about to try and stop him.

Skook led Sheldon by the arm and both went over to Ed's and Molly's. Sheldon soon learned that Ed, Molly and Skook were the best of friends. They rounded up Molly and Sally Redman, Molly's assistant.

What good was a party without women?!

Skook made a telephone call to Bert Coughlin in Prince George and placed an order for nearly $700 worth of booze and asked Bert to book him some party rooms at the Prince George Hotel.

Less than an hour-and-a-half from that initial meeting, Sheldon found himself landing by the junction of the Nechako and Fraser Rivers below the CN Railway bridge near McLean's Auto Court.

Then, to the hotel where the party began on their arrival.

Similar in some respects to a well-heeled bash of any establishment in any large city, everybody who was anybody was there.

He met, among others, Bruce Parker, one of the few haberdashers in the north... Alex Moffat - whose son Harold would become a mayor of Prince George in later years, and Ivor Guest, a senior pioneer in the area.

They partied long into the night, but Sheldon left early, not knowing what the morrow would bring from his charter.

Another flight.

This time, south 150 miles (241 km) into Williams Lake, so Skook could re-propose to the love of his life, Lilly.

For the third, fourth or fifth time, Skook couldn't remember too well.

He wasn't feeling any pain that Sunday morning.

Skook and Lilly had met before World War I.

Their parents were both ranchers, but her parents also had a trading post, which has since been converted to a museum. Reports indicated Lilly had been a strikingly-beautiful teenager, who retained her natural good looks and shape over the years.

Apparently in 1914, Lilly and Skook attended a dance at 150 Mile House. Skook loved to drink and would back down for no man, even as a youngster. He and another lad went at it in a spirited manner over some silly argument.

Lilly strongly disapproved of both drinking and fighting.

Then Skook and Lilly went at it. After a brief, loud flurry of words, he stormed out of the dance hall, went south to Ashcroft, caught the first eastbound train into Kamloops and signed up as an army recruit.

He'd rather fight than give up drinking, so he went to war. A world war. The first one.

Home by 1918 as a wounded veteran, he tried vainly to resume his love affair with Lilly.

She'd be pleased to accommodate him, provided he drank no more.

That was one thing he just couldn't do, so he and Lilly split.

There had been brief and terse meetings in the intervening years, always resulting in Skook remaining a bachelor.

Now, he was going to give it another try. Talk about tenacity. Skook had called ahead and made arrangements for Lilly to meet him at the dock at Williams Lake. When they arrived, sure enough she was there, as beautiful a woman as Sheldon had ever laid eyes on.

Sheldon had invited Bruce Parker to accompany them, not knowing what might happen en route, either there, or on the way back, and Bruce was a pretty large man in his own right. Grant wasn't the only one who had warned Sheldon about some of Skook's outbursts and his potential in a donneybrook.

Between Bruce and himself – Sheldon was also a tall and strong individual – he figured they could handle Skook if anything happened.

Sheldon and Bruce busied themselves securing the Fokker to the dock, and winced as they heard Skook roar from inside the cabin, "Lilly me darlin! I've come to get you. We're going to get married!"

He had to have Irish blood in him somewhere, thought Sheldon, to break out into this accent and carry it off quite well.

However, his words were also quite slurred and Lilly got the message. She let Skook approach. Sheldon overheard her, clear as a bell, "Skook, you were drinking the last time I saw you. As far as I'm concerned, you haven't stopped drinking since the last time we saw each other!" That had been about five years before.

Sheldon and Bruce both reasoned that from the dejected look on Skook's face, he wouldn't be seeing her again for some time. He was whipped.

Returning to the cabin, and his bottle – he knew better than to let Lilly see it – he resumed quenching his unending thirst and sat there sulking.

The Fokker took off to return to Prince George, and en route Skook tried several times to jump from the plane. It took everything Bruce could muster to keep him on board. As Sheldon taxied to McLean's Auto Court, Skook tried to jump again, hoping to drown, but Bruce was successful once more in restraining him.

A lopsided walk back to the Prince George Hotel, Skook supported by Sheldon and Bruce, and they were back partying. It hadn't stopped just because some people went to bed. Sheldon cornered Dr. Lyons and after a brief consultation, they shepherded Skook into a bedroom.

As the Muskwa-Kechika management commission wrote on the website, outfitting in north-eastern British Columbia took on an active role in the early 1930s, when Skook showed up on the scene. The commission cites from Leo Rutledge's book, *That Some May Follow*, that Skook had been working with a survey crew when he became enamoured with the Rocky Mountain Trench and the Kechika River valley and subsequently became a permanent resident and guide outfitter in 1939. He set himself up at Terminus Mountain and named his place Diamond J. Ranch. A plaque commemorates Skook. Dr. Lyons poured a small amount of sedative into a stiff drink of moose milk – a northern concoction consisting of seven per cent butterfat, skimmed milk and very strong rum. Skook either fell asleep or passed out.

Sunday continued peacefully and Skook slept through the day and night. Monday morning. Skook, Molly, Sally and Sheldon returned to Fort St. James, with Skook quiet as a church mouse all the way back.

This "quiet as a church mouse" type of man influenced many more people than Sheldon… he moved provincial historians to name a British Columbia mountain in his honour: "Mount Skook Davidson," and earned a commemorative plaque which pays tribute to his remarkable career as a packer and frontiersman. Canada's version of a historical Daniel Boone in some respects.

## 6. Visions in Conflict

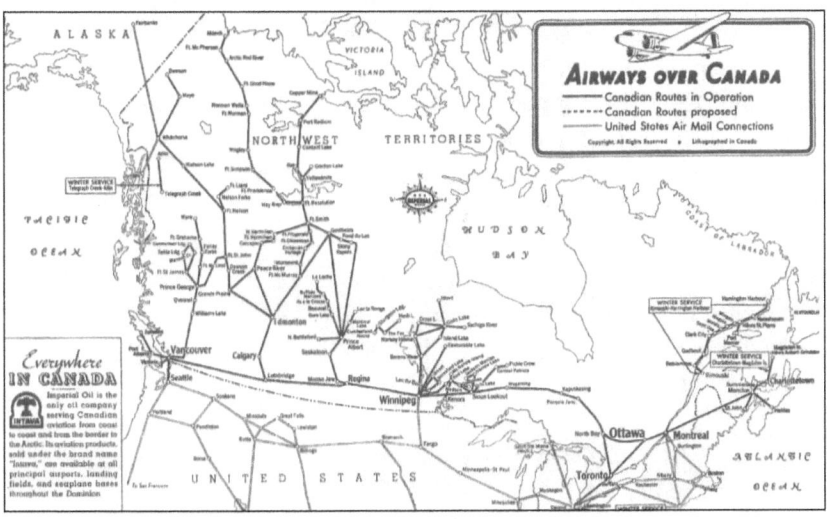

Just how important and relevant was Yukon Southern Air Transport in the development and growth of commercial and military aviation and of Canada as a nation... and was it really a threat to the one that got the political nod to become Canada's national airline, Trans-Canada Air Lines (TCAL)?

Evidence of YSAT's contribution is clearly seen in a brief analysis of an Imperial Oil map issued in 1941, titled "Airways over Canada."

The legend shows solid lines as being Canadian air routes in operation. Dashed lines represent proposed routes in Canada – there aren't any dashed lines anywhere on the map except in the legend – and solid double lines depict

United States Air Mail connections.

A quick glance at the map is very telling. Hardly anything is shown in the way of regional air services in Eastern Canada, yet there were many small and efficient carriers operating throughout Ontario, Quebec, the Maritime Provinces and into Newfoundland, which wouldn't join the Canadian Confederation for another eight years after the map was printed.

There are only two air route clusters on the map; one small, the other extremely large by comparison.

The small cluster leads from Winnipeg, north and east into northern Ontario.

The only other cluster, more widespread than anyplace on the map, covers as many air miles in a northern orientation, if not more, as are shown in the east-west direction.

The map doesn't identify the airline operators on these routes, but one can safely assume Trans-Canada Air Lines operated the trans-continental routes linking the major cities. The clusters had to represent key routes flown by smaller regional airlines, such as Yukon Southern Air Transport, because TCAL operations were non-existent in the northern and northwestern regions of the country.

While Canadian Airways Limited captured most of the regional network elsewhere on the map, including some portion of the northern and northwestern routes; YSAT had the lion's share of the western and northwestern routes, ample evidence that this was no small league bush line.

World War II forced Canada to push back its frontiers and develop those incredibly large and unpopulated areas on the map.

TCAL faced an unusual problem in its first few years, one never quite encountered by YSAT: public acceptance of air travel.

Philip Smith, author of *It Seems Like Only Yesterday - Air Canada: The First 50 Years* (Spring, 1986 - McClelland and Stewart), notes in the opening paragraph of Chapter 1:

> *Trans-Canada Airlines was established to carry the mail. Passengers, it was hoped, would be forthcoming, but there was some question about that. "Air-mindedness", as a Member of Parliament said during the debate on the matter, "is a state of mind brought about through dismissal of fear." There were still plenty of people around in 1937 who would no more have set foot on an aeroplane than they would willingly have stepped into a bear trap. And there were those on both sides of the Atlantic who felt that no matter how intrepid the potential airline passenger might be, he had no place aboard a machine designed to speed the mail. "Mails may be lost but must never be delayed," wrote C.G. Grey, the influential editor of the British Aviation*

journal *The Aeroplane*, to a friend in Ottawa, and "passengers may be delayed but must never be lost."

Note his reference to passengers as being of secondary importance to the creation of Canada's national airline, and the observed reluctance of men and women to board a flying machine.

YSAT – McConachie's dream child – had chutzpah, was taking wing and assuming potentially giant proportions. It had air mail, cargo and passengers. It offered customers the most modern equipment, complete with first-class air and ground crews with innovative ground support operations along with an administration, all of which were second-to-none in Canada.

It truly was in the business of frontier-busting, YSAT style!

Few men and women were ever afraid to step aboard a YSAT aircraft. Passengers made a big to-do about flying with YSAT, clustering around their pilot like flies around honey for picture taking at almost every stop, grinning like little children.

Having your picture taken with your pilot was something you could show your grandchildren, and allow you to brag that you were part of the pioneering era in Canadian aviation.

It gave YSAT an aura which McConachie used to great advantage in his ceaseless hustle to promote his company and to support his vision to capture his share of the global air market which he knew to be just around the corner.

The significance of that 1941 map? The major population areas of Eastern Canada needed room for their growing populations to expand; the nation needed the resource-rich regions; and YSAT was there, if not first, then probably as the best.

Independent Airways had given way to United Air Transport, and after that, it was known as Yukon Southern. This was known to have been a young company which had cut its teeth in pioneering and was evolving into an airline of some note. As it grew, it undoubtedly-had financial teething pains. McConachie tried every trick in the book to keep the financial bloodhounds at bay. Most employees worked for a pittance; few today would consider even working under similar conditions unless they knew there was a big fat cash bonus coming down the pike, and soon.

The company's major weakness had been well-noted by historians and popular writers: a constant lack of cash flow. There always seemed to be more accounts payable than receivable, forcing everybody on the payroll to make do.

Comments such as the following were daily routine:

"Yes, well that part should really be changed, but, you know, if you really take a good look at it, it can last for a few more days. Don't you agree?"

The answer, of course, could only be, "Sure, now that you mention it."

This philosophy had to work.

There simply was no money to do otherwise.

To a large degree, it did work.

Proof of this can he seen in the Wright Whirlwind J5 engine. It was basically a fine engine which did more than its share of work, but had nowhere near the life expectancy of today's modern engines. Many engines today can operate for a couple of thousand hours between major overhauls.

J5s powered UAT / YSAT's Fokker aircraft, and were designed to operate an average of eight hundred hours before a major overhaul. Most were checked long before that eight-hundred-hour mark. Pilots, mechanics and engineers kept a close watch on its performance when it started pushing past four hundred hours.

Overhaul centres in the 1930s were rare; those that did exist were much too rich for UAT / YSAT's blood, so the company carried out most of its overhauls in its own shop. Many make-do overhauls came from there.

Excessive demands naturally resulted in many engine failures, but had little to do with the rumours that they nearly broke McConachie.

Since the company fleet operated over so many mountain ranges, pilots were always coaxing them to climb on every flight, to gain space between them and the jagged peaks below. An engine on a loaded aircraft works harder on a long climb than it does if it only has to take off and spend half a day running smoothly under normal cruise at an average altitude which rarely varies, as is most of the case east of the Canadian Rockies.

This in no way is meant to belittle the value and importance of other air service operations across the nation, but is truly a reflection of a geographical fact of life. Many of UTA / YSAT's detractors overlooked this critical element in their jibes against the company, its equipment and personnel UTA / YSAT pilots had no choice but to trust their engines and ground support crews. An engine failure between two points over the mountains, hundreds of miles from the nearest landing strip, as stated earlier, could spell certain death for a pilot and his passengers, as in the Len Waagen case earlier.

Pilots were on constant alert to prevent such incidents which could lead to disaster.

Many pilots today boast of an accident-free record.

Perhaps the reader will remember McConachie's comment on seeing Sheldon's Boeing 40H4 lying as a burned-out metal skeleton on Peerless Lake in March 1936.

Some time before the accident, during one of the many occasions when Sheldon had asked him for work, McConachie fired back: "Have you ever had an accident?"

"No."

"If you've never had an accident, then that's one experience you still have to go through before you can qualify to know all about flying."

After Sheldon told him about the close calls with the Whacky Waco and the open fields, McConachie retorted: "Very well then, but what would have happened if your engine quit while you were flying over trees and mountains?"

### Accident-free flying record nothing to brag about

Neither Sheldon nor McConachie enjoyed listening to anyone who bragged about an accident-free record. And not on superstitious grounds either. If an engine failed over the more open areas of Canada, a pilot could keep it airborne and glide a long way to a relatively safe, if crumpled, forced landing.

Sheldon's experience with the Fleet 50 Freighter is a perfect example of an unsafe landing condition. In this situation, the forest cover was considered generally light, but he and his passengers could have become mere statistics had he been flying over a vast fir or spruce-dominated area where trees soar hundreds of feet above the ground, and are more than a yard or so wide at their bases.

With the exception of Len Waagen's tragic crash, and the Driscoll family show dog, anyone involved in a UAT / YSAT incident or accident walked or limped away.

Maybe some of the company's critics did have a point in referring to the operation as minor league, but their comments have to be viewed in the light of the undeniable fact that the company and its crews opened up for development one of the toughest corners of the world, without the sophisticated help and modern technology one can call on today.

A media-generated myth about McConachie suggested very strongly he had a vast amount of flying experience. He awed so many writers that they unwillingly started a trend which made it look to their readers that McConachie was the entire company and that he alone did most of the flying.

In fact, he was about the only pilot in the organization to rarely experience an engine failure, simply because he had so little spare time in which to fly.

Front-running a growing and money-gobbling organization kept him out of the cockpit.

That same magnetic charm of his, which melted writers and editors hearts, also worked on his employees.

That UST / YSAT overcame scads of adversity is a tribute not only to his perseverance, but to the roster of pilots and personnel which he gathered about him. He was a great man all right, with an uncanny ability to pick equally great men and women to back him from within.

His people ranked among the best to be found in any one air line in Canada. Yet the company and its personnel often recoiled under the onslaught of a malicious whispering campaign making the rounds within the industry which tried to give the impression that McConachie was surrounded by a bunch of crackpot pilots.

A strong camaraderie dominated relationships within the company. Employees tolerated many of McConachie's peculiarities, taking his promises of better times just around the corner with a large dose of skeptical and good-humoured faith.

An example of McConachie's ability to extract the nearly impossible from employees is best seen in the following two examples. The first refers to his impassioned plea to Sheldon and Isabel in Fort St. James. The second is a pay cut which he somehow convinced Stan Emery into taking.

McConachie had taken stock of the situation, flew in to visit Sheldon and Isabel, and prefaced his plea, which Sheldon remembers with great clarity, in these words:

> *We're in dire straits. I'm trying to hold off creditors, and our Board of Directors is trying to advise me to declare bankruptcy. I think though that if we can tighten our belts and really dig in, then we can gel through until winter. The fish hauling business will start up again, and that's a steady flow of cash in itself.*

Thereupon, within the confines of the $20-a-month cabin Sheldon and Isabel called home, he asked them frankly and openly how much money they'd need to live on.

Isabel, in charge of family finances, had anticipated such a request and had her answer ready: rent, food and clothing for herself, for Sheldon and for the children:

"Eighty dollars a month would do nicely, but only for the rest of the summer and the early fall. Then, Sheldon and the children will need heavier winter clothing and we'll need more money."

Once he had a figure to work with, McConachie next asked them to draw exactly that amount for a short while, until UAT got back on its feet.

He assured them of his gratefulness, and promised to see what he could do about getting them better money in the future.

### "Better pay cheque" promise fails to materialise

Sheldon's regular pay cheque, accumulated over the last few months, awaited him when he went to Edmonton in the fall but there wasn't an extra penny more in it.

McConachie knew the importance of meeting a payroll, even a delayed one.

That Fort St. James promise of "better money" for Sheldon and Isabel failed to materialize. But then, thought Sheldon, he did have a job, and enough cash to take care of the needs of his growing family, and he too, shared McConachie's visions that the company would soon become an important factor in Canadian aviation. It would be worth sticking around to be part of its happening.

Only a few ground personnel and two pilots refused to, or could not, take him up on his plea that summer.

One pilot, with an additional source of income from a heritage family fund, offered to work without any kind of salary for the duration, and in fact, asked for nothing more than nominal expenses until things improved.

The second incident involved Stan Emery, before he learned to fly and while he was with ground support operations. Just about to write his air engineer's license, he asked McConachie for a small raise.

Nothing elaborate, mind you, say $20 a month more.

He'd been getting about $60 a month.

McConachie took Stan into the inner sanctum, an office high in the control tower at the Edmonton airport.

Stan came out with a grin spreading from ear to ear.

He'd agreed to take a $15 cut in his monthly pay was now reduced to $45.

Stan remained with the company to become one of its senior jetliner captains.

On August 28, 1940, McConachie sent a letter to Sheldon covering working conditions, anticipated work loads and salary levels. As of September 1, 1940, he would earn $350 a month, and $5 an hour extra for any flying hours above sixty-five a month. In the letter, McConachie promised to boost his salary by $25 a month on September, 1941, which would have to do Sheldon until August 1942, at which time, "... we will discuss further raise, if any."

He also guaranteed Sheldon two weeks holidays with full pay for the period, and the following year, in addition to the standard compensation package in vogue at the time, two weeks with pay for sick leave and additional time, negotiable with management.

McConachie always did have the best interests of his staff at heart. At no time, insists Sheldon, did he ever seek the continued support of his employees for personal gain. He had a lot of salaries to protect and many families whose lives were directly under his charge. He never let his vision of a global airline overshadow this reality.

Few outsiders then could understand such fierce and intense loyalty to a man and his company.

Stepping up from the bush leagues into the majors brought a new set of problems, especially for Sheldon as Chief pilot of Yukon Southern Air Transport.

On Wednesday, August 6th, 1941, McConachie wrote a letter to Sheldon, typical of the way he handled business decisions. He instructed him to "take over operation of the line."

McConachie had already promoted him to Chief pilot and Ted Field to General Manager some time before.

His directive for Sheldon to take over the line was accompanied by a description of what McConachie and Field were about to do:

> *Ted Field and I are going to Winnipeg to pick up the other Lockheed 14 and will be back here next Monday. In the meantime I would like you to take over the operation of the line. It is not necessary to tell you to operate as conservatively as possible. An accident now would be absolutely ruinous.*
>
> *You can contact me at the Royal Alexander Hotel, Winnipeg, in the event you require me for anything. I would be pleased if you would send me a telegram Thursday night on your arrival in Vancouver letting me know how the trips ran for that day. I believe that is all for now, Sheldon. Regards.*

The letters speak volumes for the degree of informality and trust which had been built up over the years between these three men - Grant McConachie, Ted Field and Sheldon.

They were the triumvirate who ran YSAT.

The trio agreed verbally that all operational planning within the company be done by all three sitting as one – no new pilots were to be brought on board without the unanimous concurrence of the other two, and this agreement extended to the screening of all new applicants.

### Some hard command decisions had to be made as chief pilot

As chief pilot, Sheldon had to make decisions about colleagues and friends he'd flown with for years in the bush. When it came to sitting in the command, or left-hand, seat of an airliner and being responsible for the safety and lives of the passengers, Sheldon had to undergo a serious re-appraisal of his professional relationships with men who befriended him, and who he respected during those critical foundation-laying years for just this type of airline operation. However, some of his friends he'd known for years just didn't have what it took to handle command of an airliner.

He had to draw an extremely well-defined line between personal and professional relationships between himself and these men.

It hurt to turn down the command seat of an airliner to men he had known for years as being exceptional bush pilots. There weren't many, but the few to whom he had to deny left-hand seat responsibilities caused him a lot of anguish. Some took his decisions with maturity, returning to regional air services and rounding out their careers with dignity. Others didn't take his decisions so well, quickly snuffing friendships which had taken years to nurture.

The period between the early bush services and the turboprop saw aircraft become larger. With every passing month they became bigger and more complex to operate, demanding new pilot skills bordering on what has become a new job in an airplane – that of cockpit management.

Many superb bush pilots couldn't handle this quantum jump, but yet retained their competency and skills in bush operations. Airliner handling characteristics were dynamically different from the smaller and more agile bush planes which could respond almost immediately to a pilot's decision.

The sizes and speeds of airliners imposed completely different and new emergency response procedures under a wide variety of conditions. Drastically different flying habits had to be learned by seasoned bush and other air service veterans.

Instinct still played a major factor in cockpit decisions, but it shared a seat with new flying and management skills. Operational systems and airline operating procedures evolved, removing from pilots many decisions which once were routine in bush and regional air services.

Instrument Flight Rules (IFR) were taking over all airline operations, which more and more were penetrating adverse weather conditions which bush lines and smaller lines would avoid at all costs. Dependability despite adverse weather conditions became the norm; passengers and cargo clients demanded more flights and larger and more comfortable airliners.

During the autumn of 1941, Yukon Southern had become a full-fledged airline, regional only in the geographic definition of the word, but no less polished, refined and accomplished, than its corporate nemesis, Trans-Canada Air Lines. In its scope of operations and services throughout much of western and northwestern Canada, however, Yukon Southern was just as professional as TCAL!

Sheldon didn't know it then, but Grant had a well-established pipeline running throughout the intricate corporate network, and knew someone was monitoring his company's progress with an eagle eye.

Punch Dickins, considered the Dean of Canadian Aviation, wrote to Sheldon in 1980:

> *I knew that CP (Canadian Pacific Railway) was becoming interested in some of the bush operations, but did not know about their buying into them.*

In the last few months of 1941, Sheldon knew something was happening within the company, and not just from a sudden improvement in its cash flow, although he admits this was a pleasantly surprising hint that something was happening, fast.

He went out on the Whitehorse run one morning as a Yukon Southern captain, and returned the next day as first Chief pilot of Canadian Pacific Air Lines, still in his YSAT uniform.

Towards the end of 1941, pay cheques were coming from the Canadian Pacific Railway and no longer from the Edmonton YSAT head office. According to many sources, CPR had begun its take over of the company as early as late 1940, but Sheldon doesn't recall this happening until late 1941. A moot point half a century later, but of interest nevertheless, which CPR historians can correct if necessary.

Still the public wasn't all that familiar with the fact CPR had taken over YSAT; the official announcement was still some months away.

Obviously a lot of corporate change was taking place without his knowledge, almost, but not quite in direct contravention to the verbal agreement between himself, Ted and Grant, had dealing with operations ... but unsettling for himself nevertheless.

As 1941 gave way to 1942, Sheldon grew increasingly more uncomfortable; many more decisions were being made which bypassed his authority by administrative newcomers McConachie had brought into the company.

Whenever he tried to bring up these inconsistencies and dichotomies with McConachie, McConachie kept reassuring him that everything was all right, but that because he, McConachie was now involved in heavy corporate infighting, he couldn't tell Sheldon everything that was going on. McConachie repeatedly urged Sheldon to be patient, that all would soon be well and taken care of.

Pioneering unexplored wilderness bred one type of sturdy character.

Pioneering big business bred another.

The advent of a new thing on the horizon called the corporate giant spawned a new creature called the "corporate man".

Pioneering often bent a person one way or another.

These new corporate types Sheldon had to deal with were bending his mind.

Sheldon thought that many of the newcomers which McConachie brought on board resembled corporate undertakers more than empire builders.

However, for now, Sheldon took Grant's advice to heart, suppressed his emotions, took his time, and stuck it out with the emerging giant.

Gordon Sinclair, writing in a *Toronto Star* article, wrote glowingly about both McConachie and Sheldon, telling his readers that Sheldon's "charmed life is the talk of the north."

The late Ron Keith, author of the popular biographic sketch on McConachie, *Bush Pilot With a Briefcase: The happy-go-lucky story of Grant McCo-*

*nachie,* wrote a major article for *Maclean's Magazine* on January 1st, 1942, about a flight which was to have been flown by McConachie but wound up with Sheldon at the controls.

Ron described the state of the art in modern airline development. In his report, he gave an extensive view of the new airport construction program between Kamloops and Alaska, by way of the interior of B.C., and on through the Yukon. The work loads imposed on McConachie by this program prevented him from taking the flight, and he passed it on to Sheldon.

Dubbed "The Bomber Road" by another writer, Charles L. Shaw, this program alone accelerated the development of modern navigation techniques which helped expedite American bombers to staging points in Alaska, then on into Russia.

As corporate interests had been watching the growth of YSAT from a distance so were foreign editors.

In March, 1942, the *Saturday Evening Post* ran a feature article on the company, taking its audience back to McConachie's first commercial flight.

Millions of Americans read Mark and Maxine Finley's article, accompanied by colour and black-and-white photographs. One of these photographs, on the lead page of the article (p. 16) shows Sheldon with a pipe in his right hand, and a smiling McConachie on the far right, in front of a large air route wall map.

The caption reads:

> *Chief pilot Luck and President McConachie of Yukon Southern, now a Canadian Pacific property; they built it up from baling wire.*

The Finleys reported on McConachie's vision:

> *He saw a chain of fog-free airports forming an arrow to the north between the folds of Canada's inland mountain ranges – a year-round route which would bypass the tempestuous coastal weather which had blocked regular air travel to the Far North.*
>
> *The materialization of that dream is Yukon Southern Air Transport, which operates over an inverted Y-shaped route northward from Vancouver and Edmonton to join at Fort St. John and continue on to White-horse, key city of the Yukon, and Dawson, near the Alaskan border. At Whitehorse, the route joins the line of Pan American Airways Division and terminates abruptly - and suggestively - at the edge of the narrow Bering Strait. Just beyond is Russia. And down over the horizon lies Japan.*

> As an airline, Yukon Southern has been Canada's hardy orphan. She grew up with finance, nature and logic as her enemies. But the upstart was tough, resourceful and resolute. She got vitamins out of the void, and the results have astonished the monied interests at whom she made eyes only two years ago.
>
> It took the current co-defense program of the United States and Canada with a $9,000,000 appropriation for a string of airports surveyed and selected by McConachie and his men, finally to vindicate the Scotman's judgment.
>
> Alaska-bound United States Army bomber pilots, nosing into Whitehorse sometime during the sparse two-and-half hours of winter daylight, are in a position to appreciate just how practical his faith in the clear weather of the inland route really was. And although the line still has international limitations, the toughest part of the conquest of nature is over. Maps show that Chicago is 4,000 miles (6,437 km) closer to Shanghai by the new northern route than by the southern one, and Tokyo only thirty-six hours' flying time from Edmonton, Alberta, next door to the United States. Potentialities of the short-cut to Alaska, to Russia, to the Orient are obvious.

The article goes on to pay more tribute to McConachie, and his men:

> Without benefit of airports or lighted runways or radio beams, they carried mining machinery, sawmills and their working crews, trappers, miners and Indians and their dogs into isolated spots where gasoline was three dollars a gallon – when there was gasoline to be had...
>
> ...He and his pilots mapped the country correctly, and learned it by heart – a vital necessity for later air-line contact flying. Together the boys played a game of financial and aerial chess. They learned to pull round-trip payloads out of the hat, to fly fish and furs back to city markets after a charter trip, and to get the last mile out of a tankful of gasoline.
>
> It was through competitive bidding over one of these charter freight trips that McConachie first met Capt. Sheldon Luck, called the luckiest flier in the world. Luck is now Yukon Southern's chief pilot.
>
> Luck and McConachie were competitive bidders on a season's haul of chilled fresh fish from the lakes of Northern British Columbia

Note: a small geographical error in the province name above. The above should have read northern Alberta and not British Columbia.

*Knowing Grant's reputation as a businessman, Luck deliberately cut down his own profit margin and was given the job. McConachie's wrath shook the Northwest timbers. But out of the incident grew a mutual respect, and today the two are coworkers.*

*The other two members of what is now known as Yukon Southern's Four Horseman are Bernard ("Barney") Phillips, vice-president in charge of traffic, and Ted Field, operations manager. Through the four, the company became known as the young men's air line. Their average age is thirty-one.*

The Finleys go on to review some of the flying skills acquired and problems experienced - as seen earlier - and close off their well-written and interesting article with the following few paragraphs which answer, in part, the query posed at the start of this chapter: *was* Yukon Southern a real threat to Trans Canada Air Lines, and if so, how?

**Luck on Wings**

Yukon Southern's first big break came in 1940, when the Canadian Pacific Railway bought a controlling interest in the line, retaining the entire administrative staff.

With the purchase of the two Lockheed Lodestars allocated to the line under the 1940 defense priorities,

Note: The Finleys didn't quite get the story 100 % correct; those Lodestars weren't allocated.

*...(it made possible) flying the 600 miles (966 km) from Fort St. John to Whitehorse nonstop. The company had already installed two-way radio, and our own Pan American Airways, which operates its service to Alaska over this route by international agreement, shared its maintenance and weather-reporting systems at Prince George and Whitehorse with the struggling youngster.*

*When Yukon Southern released its Lodestars to the Canadian government last summer for defense purposes and received in turn the smaller Lockheed 14's, the company was awarded a third weekly round-trip airmail contract.*

> *Good fortune's second payment to Yukon Southern came last spring with the Defense Airport Building Program. Its completion this summer will see improved airports at Edmonton and Whitehorse and entirely new ones at Prince George, Grande Prairie, Watson Lake, Fort Nelson and Fort St. John. ...*
>
> *... As the new air chief of Canadian Pacific, McConachie will continue to concentrate his efforts on Yukon Southern, since it is by far the most important of C.P.R.'s six air lines.*
>
> *For all this rosy future, Grant McConachie's fight for his air line may not yet be over. The industry's grapevine has sounded a repeated warning that government-owned Trans-Canada Air Lines wants to take over Yukon Southern following the completion of the airport chain. If this is true, the government has three weapons: one, cancellation of the air-mail contracts that represent 40 to 50 per cent of Yukon Southern's income; two, the duplication of administrative personnel in Yukon Southern line and Canadian government transport offices; three, the fact that the government can not be sued without its permission.*
>
> *One thing is certain, Grant McConachie, who claims a vested interest in the Canadian Northwest, would not give up his pioneered air line without a knock-down, drag-out fight.*

Alone, Yukon Southern did not pose a direct threat to the security of the newly formed national airline, TCAL.

By analyzing the works of various authors who have written about the 1919-1937 period, one can deduce that selected cabinet members and senior postal officials bullied and bashed CPR in its natural ambitions to extend its ground and sea transportation services into the air.

In 1919, Canadian Pacific Railway received a permit to purchase aircraft, an option historians claim CPR wouldn't exercise until 1939.

By 1926 James Richardson, president of James Richardson & Sons, put up $200,000 to create Western Canada Airways Limited, later becoming Canadian Airways Limited, a top contender for the national airline flag.

But for a series of unfortunate misunderstandings and confusions that linked him, his directorship on the board of the Canadian Pacific Railway and Clarence Decatur Howe, Prime Minister Mackenzie King's powerful and resourceful Minister of Transport, the history of today's national airline could have been quite different.

What in all likelihood bothered King and Howe specifically seemed to be the apparent motives behind CPR's take over of not only YSAT but nine other airlines in Canada.

Inference suggests they viewed this takeover as a sort of corporate revenge move by Richardson and the CPR, a direct threat to the safety and security of the national airline to which they had so painfully given birth, and which received Royal Assent on April 10th, 1937.

The integration of air services into CPAL* brought together a team of skilled, competent and proficient air and ground crews, supported by powerful and highly successful CPR administrative know-how; all in all, a business operating machine which could have, if left unchecked politically, become Canada's key national flag carrier.

This likely bothered the Canadian government at the time.

The struggle continued with deregulation processes started at the time of writing, but with all current politicians wary and hopeful - a situation not too unlike that of the late 1930s when Canada did not want to miss out on expansion and aviation opportunities.

Authors who have written extensively and interestingly on the struggle between CPR and the Canadian government over who should have control of a national airline – such as Kenneth Molson in his book on CAL and Philip Smith's TCAL history – give little credit to the important foundations laid by companies other than CAL, such as YSAT.

These two companies, combined with the solid financial support of CPR, could have resulted in a national airline of as much note as Air Canada has become.

While their comments, especially Smith's, were far from disparaging about CAL and other air services, they barely scratched the surface and relegated the importance of their pioneering work to a back seat.

That TCAL was a political creation, sired by politicians without a whit or an iota of airline experience, there is no doubt.

McConachie would have groaned in disbelief had he read a comment made by John Wilson, Canada's first Controller of Civil Aviation (1927), quoted from Smith's book:

> One of the weaknesses of the operating firms is that they are run almost entirely by men whose experience is limited to flying. They have no experience in transportation as a business and its many ramifications.

McConachie may have been a weak sister on the financial end of things, but there was no weakness in his knowledge and understanding all of the ramifications of the airline industry.

Undoubtedly, there were financial problems, a large measure of them

*See Author's Note, page 168

stemming from the search and rescue mercy missions: some were flown by him, most of them by his pilots, as demonstrated earlier, and many of them resulting in costs exceeding $20,000, which YSAT had to write off.

Grant was absolutely brilliant in business, and supplemented whatever natural weaknesses he possessed by adroit manipulation, incredible charm, wit and a stunning imagination which never left the realm of reality.

Take how he pulled a publicity coup over TCAL in the summer of 1941, for an example.

Many TCAL / Air Canada pilots used to comment on the fact that their airline was the first in Canada to take possession of the world's fastest twin-engine airliner, the Lockheed Lodestar.

Canada had been at war since 1939. New airliner purchases could only be done if the airlines had procured a priority position with the joint Canadian-American agency.

TCAL had in fact done this and took delivery of its first Lodestars, CF-TCR and CF-TCS, on August 14th, 1939.

In the spring of 1941, McConachie bypassed bureaucracy, scoring a valuable publicity first for Yukon Southern, as it was still known, and also scoring a few points for himself in the CPR boardroom in Montreal, whose directors watched every move this young man made and calculated his increasing value to their corporate plans.

McConachie had developed a close personal and working relationship with Juan Trippe, President of Pan American (Pan Am). It had a number of Lodestars already approved by the agency for delivery to its subsidiaries, Chinese National and Pan Alaska.

McConachie had made a deal with Trippe, with Ottawa's blessings, to let Pan Am, through Pan Alaska, operate from Seattle through to Prince George, Whitehorse and on into Alaska. The Finlays had the right substance in their Saturday Evening Post article.

What they didn't write about however, likely because McConachie kept a lot of his plans close to his chest, was that Pan Alaska would take advantage of the YSAT routes and land on the airfields being built at Fort St. John, Fort Nelson and Watson Lake as alternate airports.

In brief, Pan Am was the holding company for Pan Alaska and was to service YSAT routes wholly in everything but traffic services in Prince George and Whitehorse.

But most important, Trippe would sell YSAT its first two Lodestars.

Yukon Southern got its Lodestars in May 1941, and had them in operation by June.

A direct snub at TCAL?

No doubt.

The Vancouver Sun ran a two-column photograph showing McConachie and Sheldon under the nose of a Lodestar, named *Yukon Emperor*. McConachie certainly had no pretenses about the empire he was building.

*First Lodestar on Vancouver-Yukon Run.*

*A large Sunday (June 1st, 1941) afternoon crowd of people witnessed the inaugural trip of a Lockheed Lodestar plane, of Yukon Southern Air Transport, at the Vancouver airport on Sunday. The plane landed from Whitehorse at 5:45 p.m., two hours after taking off from Prince George, the last stop made on the south bound trip.*

*Among passengers on the plane was Grant McConachie, Yukon Southern president, shown at left above, chatting with Captain Sheldon Luck, chief pilot for Yukon Southern, who was at the controls of the ship.*

> The *Yukon Emperor* and its sister ship, *Yukon Empress*, augment the company's fleet of three twin-engine Barkley Grows and other planes. The fastest commercial transport planes in the world, the Lodestars will run out of Vancouver and Edmonton for Whitehorse three times weekly, going north one day and returning the next.
>
> The fact that Mr. McConachie and Captain Luck are both over six feet (1.83 m) tall gives an idea of the size of the plane.
>
> Mr. McConachie stated more people are flying to and from the north than ever before and he looks for exceptionally heavy traffic in and out of Vancouver this summer.

## Where civilian airlines' Captain stripes came from… Cheaper to give them two, three or four stripes than a $50-a-month salary increase

That photograph, incidentally, is believed to be the first in Canada showing any chief pilot wearing stripes on his sleeves, as Sheldon had done. They were McConachie's brainchild, borrowed from another airline great in the USA.

On a visit to another airline in the States, he noted a Lodestar captain on a New Orleans flight with three stripes on his uniform. He asked the airline president to comment on them, as twin stripes were the conventional way to signal a civilian flying rank.

The president told McConachie of his decision to put senior line pilots, and operational managers who were still flying, into a uniform with three stripes. McConachie thought this was a great idea, worth more in public relations value than adding $50 a month raise to a man for being a senior pilot.

McConachie knew how to play up to a man's vanity where image was involved, and generally his tactics worked.

Of interest is the fact that Pan Am had its senior captains wear dark plain suits, with black stockings, black shoes, black tie, and a plain white shirt.

Whenever they removed their airline caps they looked more like undertakers than airline pilots, so as a public image improvement, Pan Am is reputed to have switched to the more distinctive and stylized captain's uniform.

But someone in Ottawa didn't like the Lodestar deal at all, and in no time flat, an order came down that YSAT immediately return its Lodestars to their California manufacturer, Lockheed, so they could undergo reconfiguration and engine changes – from Pratt and Whitney to the Wrights favoured by TCAL.

In exchange for the Lodestars, TCAL sold YSAT two Lockheed 14H-2 Electra aircraft.

Nothing of note happened to the Lodestars for more than two years after they were returned to Lockheed, nor did anything further develop on the YSAT

/ Pan Am agreement.

McConachie wasn't the only one to cultivate a friendship with Juan Trippe.

C. D. Howe, in the two years before creating TCAL travelled extensively throughout North America trying to get a first-hand appraisal of the airline business as it was in the States and as it could be in Canada. During these forays, he cultivated a close relationship with Trippe, and the famous Eddie Rickenbacker of Eastern Airlines.

At some stage, Trippe must have spoken widely about his growing relationship with McConachie, and Howe quite likely found out about the Lodestar deal on a first-hand basis, rather than relying solely on informed government sources within Canada. Knowing his earlier antipathy towards having CPR in any way involved with a national airline, it is little wonder the order to return the Lodestars came down from Ottawa.

For a brief two-month period, YSAT took full advantage of its Lodestars, registered as CT-BTY and CT-BTZ, before being given the order to return them to Lockheed.

At late as 1943, BTY and BTZ were photographed sitting on the Lockheed tarmac in Burbank, California, still sporting their original Canadian registry letters, but ignominiously stripped of the titles *Yukon Emperor* and *Yukon Princess* which YSAT so proudly displayed on their shiny aluminum skins.

The federal government's intention for many years had been to link both the CNR and the CPR in a national airline operation.

The difficulties inherent in this kind of corporate fabric and desired government control, direction, and future protection of the new airline from voracious private interests is very well documented in a number of books.

Two have already been cited, and a third is W. Kaye Lamb's *Canadian Pacific Railway* (1977, Macmillan Publishing Co. Inc. and Collier Macmillan Canada Ltd.)

Kenneth Molson, in his book *Canadian Airways*, offers a similar perspective on just what kind of an organization Sheldon had become part of, overnight:

> ...a kind of monster of a far-reaching network ... (it) represented a nightmarish hodge-podge, far from the tailor-made routes of TCAL ... with 14 different types of aircraft, not to mention engines, and most of it (them) outdated.

The other companies brought into the new corporate fold included, in addition to CAL and YSAT were Mackenzie Air Services, Prairie Airways, Starratt Airways, Wings Limited, Quebec Airways Limited, Dominion Skyways Limited and Arrow Airways Limited.

Although not listed anywhere, the tenth company is presumed to be White

Pass and Yukon Air Service, which had been absorbed by YSAT when it had been taken over by CPR.

Of those companies, many believe that Yukon Southern indeed was the most advanced in many, many respects, and the one which dominated headlines, especially throughout western Canada. It had the best established route structure, believed at the time to be the longest single route structure served by any regional airline in North America.

Sheldon was aware of all of these rapid changes which were taking place within the organization, but not their details nor how they would affect the future of the new company.

That he had been so inexorably linked to McConachie in the last couple of years prior to the spring of 1942, by the media, and by McConachie's own admissions to Sheldon, and yet passed over in so many corporate decisions just made life that much tougher and harder to understand for Sheldon.

*Author's Note:

Which companies went into the makeup of Canadian Pacific Air Lines, and when did it officially come into being?

According to the May 1982 edition of CP Air News, the company's employee newspaper, the commemorative date to keep in mind is July 1$^{st}$, 1942, when CPAL officially came into being, even though individual air services companies had been in the process of being acquired during the previous two years.

The company publication lists differ slightly from mine, which does match lists in other publications. My list does not contain Ginger Coote Airways, which is in the CP Air News' list.

The reader may recall that YSAT, according to Sheldon, had absorbed Ginger Coote's company during the air mail trials between Vancouver and Whitehorse, and had already been part of YSAT when it was taken over by the CPR.

Sheldon also recalls that another company was in the process of being purchased by Grant McConachie in the 1939-41 period, that of George Simmons' White Pass and Yukon Air Service, but this is still subject to confirmation.

I have tried, along with a few officials in CPAL's public relations offices in Vancouver, to locate corporate records dating back to pre-CPR takeover days, but they just couldn't be found.

## Building an airline business not remotely anything like building the airline alone

McConachie made excellent use of Sheldon.

No other man in his outfit had ever generated as much ink as Sheldon.

Readers in the late '30s and early '40s cannot be blamed for getting the distinct impression that all was well between Sheldon and YSAT / CPAL.

Everything pointed to a long and successful airline career for him.

As stated in the introduction, Sheldon was a different type of personality than McConachie and the new corporate types who dominated almost every aspect of CPAL.

He found himself trapped in a whirlwind of activity and development, surrounded by problems so vastly different from those encountered in building Yukon Southern into an airline of note.

These were problems of a corporate nature, not the ones associated with frontier bashing.

As Lamb so succinctly put it, independently-minded personalities and the newcomers probably made life miserable for each other in the restructured organization.

Sheldon would have nothing to do with being a desk jockey.

The best place for him, he thought, would be in helping out in the war effort.

Until now he had been on an essential services list.

One pleasant morning in Whitehorse, he decided to quit, rather than risk further confrontation and embarrass McConachie, who still remained fiercely loyal to his Chief pilot, but was himself enmeshed in things about which he could not yet confide in Sheldon.

Sheldon could no longer do as McConachie kept urging him to do, which was essentially... "wait until later, trust me."

Sheldon couldn't any longer.

He quit Canadian Pacific Air Lines in May, 1942.

The world of aviation that Sheldon entered on December 24th, 1930, when he first soloed, had vaulted from the primitive to the complicated in less than a decade. He was Chief Pilot of an airline which had been at the centre of a controversy, and the victim of intense political infighting which had ranged from mid-summer 1933 through to early 1937.

He wouldn't be the only personal victim of the scramble which saw American know-how and technology steal the thunder they had worked so hard to pioneer, side by side in spirit with their collegial air service companies.

If ever an injustice had been done to a group of men and women, and businesses in the past, it was the one which saw, at the stroke of one man's pen, the formation of Trans Canada Air Lines – without the participation of any

Canadian airman.

Canadian aviation had left the diaper stage, learned to walk, and communicate well when World War I broke out in 1914 – a scant five years after J.A.D. McCurdy first flew Alexander Graham Bell's *Silver Dart* on Feb. 23rd, 1909, in Baddeck, Nova Scotia.

In another four years, Canadian military aviation interests skyrocketed – between 1914 and 1918 more than 3,000 Canadians had answered the patriotic call to duty, and, no doubt a daring adventure, to take part in the aerial dogfights over Europe.

In those four years aviation underwent a growth period which surpassed by an incredible measure the wildest dreams of its few pioneers, converts and advocates. To them, the only way humanity would progress would be if it took to the air, with a flair.

Business interests around the world had taken note and air services were springing up like wildflowers in the mechanized countries on the planet.

The Canadian Pacific Railway even got into the act as early as 1919, acquiring its first permit to purchase an aircraft, although it wouldn't exercise this right for another decade. Also in 1919, the first air mail between London, England and Paris, France, crossed the English Channel.

Air mail would be a powerful moving force behind the development of Canada's first national air line, but not for a generation or so down the road.

Right from the end of World War I many visionaries, both in government and in business, were seriously concerned that Canada would be left miles behind the world if it didn't take to the air seriously.

And soon.

Prior to 1927, Winston Churchill is quoted as saying that civilian aviation must fly by itself in the United Kingdom.

What hope did civilian aviation have in Canada?

Little.

The Canadian government had enough problems forking over railway subsidies to the CPR, and to the deficit-ridden Canadian National Railways, created in 1924 with the integration of many little financially-deprived railways into one national network.

If a national airline were to be developed, Ottawa decided it would, by golly, be without the heavy subsidies already being dished out to both national railways. If, indeed a national airline were to evolve, the Government would, of course, assist in regulations and safety considerations, but there would not be any free lunch.

### Air mail, not public demand for air service, main force behind national airline service... Passengers? A mere afterthought... not wanted on board, thank you!

Politicians decided there was no need to concern themselves with a new, generally unproven, form of transportation. Public demand for a national air service didn't exist.

Canadian civilian aviation between 1919 and 1929 flew it alone. Many air veterans of World War 1 saw the commercial potential of their military wings, and tried to set up air services wherever and whenever they could. Some would make it, barely; most were destined to fail.

Pulp and paper, and other large forestry companies, were the first to lock onto the distinct advantages of the airplane, for timber cruises over vast forest reaches, fire spotting and mapping. Almost concurrent with forestry interests in aviation, mining companies took to the air to survey and expand their interests throughout the vast regions of Ontario and Quebec.

Their involvement in aviation however was by and large limited to suit their own corporate interests and not directed towards public service as such.

It had been noted, in fact, that most primitive air service companies which had surfaced in England, for example, where the population densities were greater than those in Canada, and the geography was relatively kinder, constantly had to be bailed out by governments.

Civilian aviation didn't seem to be a good business investment.

Britain, tired of bailing-out these starving operators since 1921, found it didn't work and formed Imperial Airways in 1924, predecessor of British Overseas Airways Corporation (BOAC), now British Airways. The government also backed it with financial guarantees to help it out during its formative years.

The Americans were ahead of everyone in a number of respects: in 1925, US air mail services were full-blown across its share of the North American continent.

Air mail would also kick-start commercial and civil aviation in Canada and be the prime motivating factor for the creation of Canada's first national airline.

In 1926, the acknowledged founder of Canadian commercial aviation, James A. Richardson, invested $200,000 to create Western Canada Airways Ltd. His drive and leadership helped it flourish over the years, as he routinely went about salvaging smaller operators. By 1928, his company had become the largest in Canada, offering air services from Ontario to the Pacific coast.

Although he initially remained out of Québec and Maritime operations, he learned that many American interests wanted to buy out failing operators reeling under cut-throat competition.

He stepped into the breach, became a director of the Aviation Corporation of Canada and helped purchase four leading eastern-Canadian operators in a successful bid to keep control in Canadian hands.

Two events took place in 1927 which would help commercial aviation strengthen its wings in Canada.

The first came with the appointment of John A. Wilson, as the first Controller of Civilian Aviation.

The second saw the post office allocate $75,000 a year for air mail services, and issuing the first air mail contracts.

Wilson noted in 1929 that most air mail services were carried out by flying boats or planes on floats. He correctly predicted the need for aircraft operating on wheels if anything significant were to happen to improve air mail service.

Passengers really were an afterthought in those days.

Preliminary surveys had begun in the Prairies as they were obviously the best starting place for wheeled aircraft, given the nature of open land as against the geography and forest cover of the eastern or western provinces.

Most aviation activities in that year were centered throughout the remote bush regions, carried out by dozens of small operators and WCAL. Experience in other countries clearly indicated most small operators were doomed to failure.

Late in the year, Wilson suggested the CNR and CPR co-operate in setting up a national air service. CNR president Sir Henry Thornton visited Richardson in Winnipeg suggesting the time had arrived for a national airline.

Richardson, also a director of the CPR, consulted chairman Edward Beatty, and both agreed there was no room in Canada for two competing large aviation companies. Since the indications were that both railways would form the new national service, Richardson planned to merge WCAL with Aviation Corporation, then, along with the CNR and the CPR as minority partners, create a new company to be called Canadian Airways Limited, which actually came into being in 1930.

Liberals and Progressive Conservatives gave their blessing to this new company. Each railway chipped in $250,000 for 10,000 shares of CAL.

Richardson became its president and Thornton and Beatty (later, Sir Edward) acted as vice presidents. When R.B. Bennett's Progressive Conservative party came to power in 1930, CAL received a four-year air mail contract.

This strongly hinted at much more to come.

When the British press reported this, Sir Eric Geddes, chairman of Imperial Airways (IA) immediately wrote to Thornton and Beatty, offering in no uncertain terms the complete cooperation of Imperial Airways in the formation of a trans-Canada air service.

Both evaded confirmation of the offer suggesting press reports were exaggerated.

Geddes can't be blamed for concluding that Canadian businessmen had little or no interest in helping develop trans-Atlantic air mail services. Wilson shared his concerns, worried that Pan Am would be the first to cooperate with IA in offering trans-Atlantic air mail out of Newfoundland.

Two major CAL air mail routes existed in western Canada at the time.

One was an overnight service between Winnipeg and Calgary.

The other was a day service westward, from Regina, in the central Canadian prairie province of Saskatchewan, to Edmonton, via Saskatoon and North Battleford, both in Saskatchewan, arriving in Calgary, Alberta, the following day.

Passengers wanted on board, but this delayed the experimental nature of the flights, and the post office tried hard, and successfully, to curtail passengers from participating in this venture.

Caught in the second year of a strangling depression, the federal government cancelled all inter-city air mail contracts in 1932, justifying the move as an economic measure.

This put CAL in a major bind, as Richardson and his backers had injected nearly $3,000,000 into developing what they were certain would become Canada's first national air service, only to have the rug pulled out from under them.

Bennett didn't limit his economic scissors to commercial aviation; he reduced the budget allocation to what would become the Royal Canadian Air Force by 70 per cent.

Wilson came to the rescue by diverting funds from work camps for the unemployed, putting hundreds of men to work building landing strips across the Prairies, at the princely sum of 20 cents an hour.

In mid-summer 1933, still confident things would turn around, Wilson wrote Richardson, urging him not to give up hope, that a nation-wide, Halifax, NS, to Vancouver, BC, air route could be in operation as early as 1934. He asked if CAL would be interested in being selected to carry the air mail on this trans-continental route, hinting strongly that the government wanted to give the contract to one large and strong air service company.

From this point, until March 17$^{th}$, 1937, when Sir Edward Beatty asked the then Transport Minister, the Hon. C. D. Howe to "....omit any reference to this company..." from Bill 74, the act which created Trans-Canada Airlines, things went from bad to worse for Richardson and CPR. Any realistic hopes they may have nurtured about being first at bat for a national airline were systematically bashed around the political arena as one curve after another came their way from a waffling Liberal government and a post office which did business on a "divide and conquer" basis.

A yo-yo game had begun between the mighty CPR and the post office, with the post office pulling all the strings, leaving CPR bobbing up and down, getting nowhere fast in its natural ambitions and desires to form Canada's first national airline.

Assistant Deputy Postmaster General Peter Coolican teeter-tottered over Richardson.

He, Wilson and Major-General A.G.L. McNaughton were members of a government inter-departmental committee looking into the formation of a national air mail service.

It met in July 1933, but Wilson was away in Newfoundland pressing his point to keep Canada in the running for participation in a trans-Atlantic air mail service.

McNaughton and Coolican conveyed the message to Richardson that if his company wanted the contract, then he'd best shed his "bush" operations; that running a national air mail service was a big enough job for one company.

As Philip Smith wrote, this was an outright slur against CAL, the aviation company which was perhaps the only bright spot in a gloomy economy.

Richardson countered with a suggestion he split his bush operations into a separate subsidiary, but Coolican would have nothing of it, inferring that the interests of a national air mail service could not be subordinate to the interests of a large private company.

He obviously feared a monopolistic situation which would edge the smaller operators out of the bidding picture, a situation which he held to be untenable. In fact many smaller operators took huge cuts in their bids to carry air mail, banking on making up the losses by the potential additional business an air mail contract was bound to bring in.

This certainly didn't serve the case for expeditious and businesslike delivery of the air mail.

Over the next year, Richardson and his backers worked at refining their proposal for a national air mail service.

Once again, the Post Office threw another curve from out of left field: Coolican had earlier specified air mail should be carried at high speeds, up to 160 miles an hour (258 km/hr), but now boosted that to a 200 mph (322 km/hr) specification, with an 800-mile (1,288 km) range carrying a 600-pound (272 kg) payload.

Still no contract from the government to CAL which now had to revise its plans to meet new government specifications.

When the Liberals thumped the Bennett regime on October 17th, 1935, Richardson and company were certain a new policy in aviation would be handed down soon by Liberal leader Mackenzie King. To this end Richardson visited King late in the month, waving a red herring about a university appointment for someone else, all the while yearning for some positive indication from him on a national air mail service during what Richardson had hoped would appear to be idle chit-chat after they'd dispensed with the appointment issue.

Unknown to Richardson, King had already considered the establishment of one strong Department of Transport which would link air, ground and marine services.

His staunch transport minister, C. D. Howe, for example, strongly recommended the government either do something positive about the financially plagued CNR or just dump it.

In February 1936, Richardson still plugged away at his dream and wrote to both King and Howe reminding them that CAL was the only company which had everything necessary, and in place, to do the job, with his understanding that both railways could cough up with the necessary financing.

Responding in the same month, Howe wrote both railway heads (S.J. Hungerford had replaced Sir Thornton) concerning Richardson's proposal, assuring them that the government would keep CAL's experience in mind, and would support both railways being on the national air service's board of directors.

Then, in April 1936, the federal government publicly announced its intention to establish a national air service, but warned that it wouldn't tolerate runaway cut-throat competition from smaller operators.

Still, no word about the strong hints that CAL was in the driver's seat for the job. Something had gone quite wrong, because Howe had a reputation as a straight-shooter and had never been known to double-deal.

Somebody highly placed in the post office had taken a dislike to Richardson and his plan, and subtle antagonism had reared its ugly head.

For example, since 1932, CAL had been carrying out the Winnipeg-Pembina, North Dakota air mail contract for the Post Office, quite satisfactorily. Suddenly, word got direct to Richardson that the Post Office was complaining that CAL's deHavilland Dragon Rapide's 157 miles an hour (253 km/hr) was too slow, compared to the Boeing 247's speed, the airliner used by United Airlines in the States.

The antipathy could only be radiating from Coolican, who evidenced some distress about Richardson's word when he learned about two different per-mile cost rates about moving the mails west across the Prairies. The earlier, lesser cost projections had been based on incomplete studies, which when completed, did not significantly alter the final figures given by Richardson to Coolican.

Richardson sent his top man, World War I ace Don MacLaren to Ottawa to try and use his valuable military and political contacts to see if he could learn what was happening. MacLaren reported the formation of a Liberal-backed new aviation company, British North American Airways (BNAA), whose Liberal founders felt they had reason to believe would be the chosen one for the national air service.

A BNAA representative visited Woods Humphrey, Imperial Airways' managing director, suggesting his company appeared to be the political favourite to get the contract, and not CAL, but did admit that the Canadian government had some money in CAL.

Another competitor surfaced in the form of the Molson-family backed Dominion Skyways, but represented no serious threat to CAL.

However, various cabinet ministers supported Richardson, including Postmaster General J.C. Elliott, but King never quite made up his mind. When Howe asked Richardson to participate in a pioneering experiment with radio operations on the Prairies, and asked him to purchase a new Lockheed Electra for $60,000, Richardson went along with the idea.

He seemed to be getting better vibrations about Howe.

But, after spending the summer overseas on business, Richardson realized his support from Howe was mostly illusionary. Howe effectively held Richardson at bay, telling him there was no point in coming to Ottawa to discuss the national air service until cabinet had made up its mind.

Howe came up with a concept in mid-1936, a sort of crown corporation, 40 per cent government-owned national air service, with the balance held by all aviation interests in Canada.

The federal cabinet rejected this proposal in September 1936, and Richardson renewed his strong suspicions that the transport department and the post office were bedfellows in this matter.

Coolican constantly complained about CAL's Vancouver-Seattle, Washington air mail service, in addition to allegedly having been overheard casting aspersions on Richardson's good word.

At this stage of proceedings, Howe had switched most of his communications from Richardson to Beatty at the CPR.

Never one to say die, CAL, by September 1936, had completed the blueprints for a trans-Canada air service, and gave a final quote to Ottawa ... 70 cents an air mile for air mail.

The national service had a fleet of aircraft and schedules drafted for 3,445 miles (4,828 km) across the nation, and pilots and ground crews were at the ready.

CAL would hold 25 per cent of the shares with the balance of control split evenly between CNR and the CPR.

And it looked like Howe favoured this plan in October 1936.

A month later the cabinet appointed a sub-committee to review the plan, and members all agreed that the new national air service should be partly privately owned and partly government owned, with the right of public ownership.

In December of that year, Howe sent Beatty a memorandum, with the name "Trans-Canada Airline Co.", indicating that ownership would be equally shared by the two railways and such private aviation interests as it may nominate.

The government appeared reluctant to give the CPR full control of the new air service, and word was out that Ottawa wanted the CNR to nominate British North American Airways.

The fly in the ointment was the board of directors. Ottawa wanted CNR and CPR to appoint four directors each, with the government appointing one. This would give a 5-4 override against the CPR in key decisions, a position quite untenable to the CPR.

By February 1937, Howe had sent a draft of the proposed Bill 74 to Beatty. Effectively, Beatty said, the CNR *was* the government. He balked at the notion that the CPR was being invited to put up half the action without the inherent authority which should accompany an investment of this scope.

To further rub it in the government offered to buy the company at any time, at book value, completely ignoring any goodwill the new air service would have generated.

Beatty naturally took great umbrage at Howe's suggestion that goodwill would only come from the generous route structure which the new air service would be given by the government, and not from any efforts by his company's part in developing the business naturally.

Howe would try to justify his actions in years to come by loudly and frequently stating that the CPR had been offered a share in the new national air service, and refused - without once revealing why, making CPR come across, undeservedly, as the bad apple in the basket.

The government wasn't finished rubbing the salt into CAL's and CPR's wounds: it counter-proposed a revised board of directors structure, suggesting the CNR and CPR each appoint three members of the board and the government would appoint three of its own.

This would give the government a 6-3 edge over the CPR, which was supposed to be a full half financial partner!

Little wonder that Beatty refused the option in his letter of March 17th, 1937.

Bill 74 passed its first reading on March 22, and received Royal Assent on April 10th, 1937.

Answering the question which opened this chapter: no, by itself, Yukon Southern did not constitute an active threat: against TCAL.

But soon, however, Yukon Southern would no longer be alone.

## 7. Spooling up for Ferry Command

In the late 30s, passengers were thought of as being of secondary importance to the creation of Canada's national airline, and politicians made hay with what they claimed was an observed reluctance of men and women to board a flying machine.

What would take place after 1937, when England had no choice but to step in and try to stem the Japanese and Nazi military machines from further savagely marauding the planet, would mesmerize ordinary mortals.

But it took ordinary mortals – mere civilians for that matter – to do the job, largely from Canada and the United States, a job which is the subject of this chapter, and one in which Sheldon would be deeply involved.

Even as early as 1937, it had become painfully obvious that the massive manufacturing and shipping of warplanes – fighters and bombers – would have to take even greater importance than moving passengers around the planet.

But there was no organization in place to do the job which in a few short years would have to be done to try and shorten what was about to become yet another world war – the second one on the planet: WWII.

Sheldon was about to join such an organization which was made possible by the contribution of thousands of civilians who came to the rescue of the Allied Armed Forces starting as early as 1939.

What exactly was this organization? What was its background, and how did it come to be?

The only known public document in Canada in which Sheldon is credited for having been the first Chief pilot of Canadian Pacific Air Lines is a news release which was published on January 26, 1943, nearly eight months after word got out that Sheldon had left the company – when he had quit in May, 1942.

It also served as the first notice that he had joined a remarkable operation that at the time was little known to but a handful of men and women in three countries: England, the U.S.A. and Canada.

The news release about his departure was accompanied by a photograph and caption in the Tuesday, May 19th, 1942, edition of the *Vancouver Sun*, under the headline:

> *To ferry bombers across the Atlantic*
>
> *...He has been given a leave of absence for the duration of the war by Canadian Pacific Air Lines, which controls Yukon Southern, to join the Royal Air Force Bomber Command.*
>
> *Captain Luck is one of the most popular pilots operating out of Vancouver, with some 6,000 hours to his credit, he had experience all through the west, starting with his early training around Calgary and Edmonton. Later he hauled fish by plane from northern Alberta into Edmonton, to be shipped to Chicago (Illinois, USA)*
>
> *Then he spent much time operating around Fort St. James, Prince George and other British Columbia points before coming to Vancouver to operate on the Zeballos run when that town was booming...*

The article went on to briefly highlight the extent of YSAT / CPAL services, listing the addition of new Lockheed aircraft, and ends,

> *...Captain Luck had travelled between Whitehorse and Vancouver more than any other man alive, running close to 1,000 hours a year on the route in the last two years, at least. The Bomber Command will be a new experience but will serve him well in the tremendous commercial aviation department to follow the war. He will be accompanied east by Mrs. Luck.*

Variations of this release appeared throughout other Canadian newspapers, a standard airline practice on releasing their highly experienced and trained crews to the growing war effort. The military certainly didn't have enough trained pilots to fly the large multi-engine bombers to where they were needed most, in England, during the early years of what was rapidly becoming a global war.

Then, when his long-time friend Don Patry left to join Ferry Command, came the news release in which Sheldon is first publicly referred to as CPAL's first Chief pilot.

The article states that Don had been promoted to Chief Pilot for CPAL, "...since last May, when Sheldon left." Don had also been granted an extended leave of absence, and the article states that Don became Chief pilot when Luck, "...former Chief pilot, left to enter Ferry Command, along with North Sawle, Ralph Oakes and pilots from other airlines."

### The organization – Ferry Command

Philip Smith, author of *It Seems Like Only Yesterday – Air Canada: The First 50 Years* (Spring, 1986 – McClelland and Stewart, Canada), notes in the opening paragraph of Chapter 1:

> ... *Trans-Canada Airlines was established to carry the mail. Passengers, it was hoped, would be forthcoming, but there was some question about that. "Air-mindedness", as a member of Parliament said during the debate on the matter, "is a state of mind brought about through dismissal of fear." There were still plenty of people around in 1937 who would no more have set foot on an aeroplane than they would willingly have stepped into a bear trap. And there were those on both sides of the Atlantic who felt that no matter how intrepid the potential airline passenger might be, he had no place aboard a machine designed to speed the mail. "Mails may be lost but must never be delayed," wrote C.G. Grey, the influential editor of the British Aviation journal The Aeroplane, to a friend in Ottawa, and "passengers may be delayed but must never be lost..."*

Obviously air transport wasn't looked upon very favourably on either side of the Atlantic Ocean, neither for mails nor for passengers, let alone the mass movement of airplanes from one part of the world to another – the key subject of this chapter, and Sheldon's involvement in this new operation.

The organization which Sheldon joined was well on its way to being the world's first truly international airline, in every meaning of the word. It would be larger in scope and operations than Pan Am, which as early as 1934 already had a route structure in excess of 40,000 miles (64,374 km), and was well-established in 39 countries of the world.

Unlike Pan Am, it was only meant to last until the war ended, and with its creation, would help shorten the war considerably.

What Sheldon joined in 1942 it was more commonly known as "Ferry Command."

This was, in the most simplest of words possible, an incredible operation, a highly secretive one... a first in the recorded history of humanity.

A similar operation is likely not to be seen again on the face of the earth unless another world-wide war breaks out and is fought only with and by conventional weapons.

By war's end, in 1945, international air and ground support crews in this organization had undergone several official name changes and ferried more than 18,000 aircraft from Canada to all war theatres across the world's oceans - the North and South Atlantic, the Arctic, the Indian, the North Pacific and South Pacific, with an incredible safety record given its scale and scope of operations.

Ferry Command was separate, but similar to three other military transport commands – those of Canada, the United Kingdom and the United States. These also ferried large numbers of aircraft across the Atlantic, but usually with single crews who remained with their aircraft when they arrived overseas, or who were assigned to other areas.

Veteran and civilian employees alike often refer to the organization today as "Ferry Command" for simplicity, although it had at least three official names, which were changed as growth and circumstances dictated.

Ferry Command began in 1939 as part of a railway operation within the Canadian Pacific Railways Air Services Department, which carried through until late May 1941, when the Canadian Pacific Railway and the British Government agreed to officially terminate the name and the agreement at midnight, July 14, 1941.

A week later, on July 20, the Royal Air Force Ferry Command came into being.

While under CPR's bailiwick, it was also known by two other names: the Atlantic Ferry Command Organization, shortened to the then popular acronym of ATFERO.

This name stuck until March 11, 1943, when British Secretary of State for Air, Sir Archibald Sinclair, told the British House of Commons about the newest organization and its structural changes: it would from then on be known as the Royal Air Force Transport Command, with appropriate squadrons to serve its more diversified interests.

One of these included the RAF 231 Flight Communications Squadron, which Sheldon transferred to as a civilian captain on one of its three giant Coronado flying boats.

From the day he joined Ferry Command, Sheldon would cross the Atlantic Ocean seventy-seven times, flying four of the five spans of the bridge: the Arctic, the direct line from Newfoundland, the Florida/Bermuda/Azores connection and the South America / South Atlantic route, into the English and African theatres of war.

While Sheldon and McConachie's other pilots were doing their pioneering work in north western Canada in the mid-to-late 1930s, a different kind of pioneering work was underway at the same time in north eastern Canada, opening the vast and wicked expanse of the North Atlantic, from the eastern coast of Labrador and Newfoundland, across to the United Kingdom, and on to aerial warfare over Europe and Africa.

The lack of reliable weather information for flying across the North Atlantic was the single, biggest stumbling block to regular trans-Atlantic flights in the mid 1930s. Prior to World War II, up to one hundred and fifty, or more, of all kinds of commercial and military ships were used to send reliable weather reports to Canada, as well as to other weather stations in the United Kingdom, Greenland, Iceland and Europe.

It is important today, when we take international air travel so much for granted like hot and cold running water, that from the day the Wright brothers first took to the air at Kill Devil Hill in the state of North Carolina on Dec. 17$^{th}$, 1903, a scant 36 years had elapsed – not even a complete generation – before World War II had begun. By 1939, less than 100 successful crossings had been made of any ocean by any type of aircraft, let alone giant commercial or bomber aircraft – an average of less than three such crossings a year. These were truly pioneering days where fledgling airlines were concerned.

Weather reports from the United Kingdom and Europe dried up the moment war broke out; shortly after that, reports ceased coming from Greenland and Iceland as well. The Azores, hundreds of miles to the south, and too far off the North Atlantic track to be reliable, continued to send weather reports.

This eventuality had been foreseen as early as 1935, and an agreement provided some assistance for Canada's Department of Transport to establish a meteorological group to handle the needs of pre-war flights over the Atlantic.

By 1939, postal authorities in the United States, the United Kingdom and Canada reviewed what it would take to improve air mail flights over the ocean. Already impractical in winter because of the severity of North Atlantic storms, war made them almost impossible along the conventional routes. German marauders would pounce swiftly, dealing death to any vessel which risked breaking radio silence to report weather conditions.

An experimental weather forecasting unit moved from Newfoundland to a main weather station in Montreal, led by Patrick D. McTaggart-Cowan. With the formation of the Canadian Pacific Air Services Department, the actual work of weather forecasting could now be transferred to the ferry service and given to pilots who would undertake those perilous flights.

According to a 75-page booklet, *Atlantic Bridge,* published in 1945 by His Majesty's Stationery Office and the British Ministry of Information in London, England:

> ...*the greatest single contribution to the accuracy and safety of met forecasts was the excellent co-operation of the pilots in*

*keeping accurate records of weather encountered in flight. These reports constituted the only source of Atlantic data.*

The United Kingdom began buying Hudson bombers from the United States in early 1940, shipping them initially by sea – a process which meant a three-month lapse between an aircraft's release from a manufacturer and its first operational use as a bomber. To make matters worse, the bombers took up valuable cargo space which could have been consigned to other desperately needed war supplies.

German submarines kept a watchful eye on most of those transport vessels, and exacted an alarming toll on Allied shipping during the early war years.

The only way to make certain the bombers got to England where they were badly needed was to fly them over. But who would fly them?

While boardroom negotiations were quietly being conducted to acquire new aviation properties for CPR, a high-level political recommendation had been made that the CPR would indeed be the best agency to operate a ferry service. Its pilots could fly the bombers Britain was buying from Canada direct to Scotland, where other air crews would ferry them onwards to operational headquarters in England.

Several publications and documents credit Canadian-born newspaper baron Lord Beaverbrook – Sir William Maxwell "Max" Aitken, 1st Baron Beaverbrook – England's Minister of Aircraft Production in 1940, as one of the prime movers behind the spirit and body of what was first known as Ferry Command. At his urging, his best friend and personal representative, Morris Wilson - then president of the Royal Bank of Canada – wrote to the Canadian Pacific Railway's Sir Edward Beatty in July 1940, asking him for assistance in forming what led up to this massive once-in-a-history aircraft ferry service.

The intent would be for CPR to provide administrative and clerical space in Windsor Station headquarters in downtown Montreal, and the British Overseas Airways Corporation (BOAC) to provide technical help and co-operation with the Canadian Department of Transport.

But what of the pilots?

Where would they come from?

Most pilots would have to be civilians, and among the very best. There were just not enough military pilots around anywhere to be freed to do the mass-ferry job. In short order, professional airline crews from the United States of America made up over half of the complement of Ferry Command pilots, and the balance came from Canada, other Commonwealth countries and allied nations.

C.H. "Punch" Dickins joined CPASD as vice president, also becoming Deputy Director General of the British Air Commission in Washington, D.C., so he could have full access to the delivery policy then in force. In the meantime, plans were underway to turn Dorval into a major base and airfield.

When Sheldon had decided to quit in Whitehorse in the spring of 1942, he knew that Punch had joined ATFERO, and had sent him a 151-word telegram from Whitehorse asking him if he needed any good pilots.

Punch wasted no time in accepting Sheldon's offer, but expressed some concern about Sheldon's future with CPAL.

Punch planned the large-scale Newfoundland expansion for the organization, from which came the construction of the Goose Bay airfield in Labrador.

BOAC officers arrived in Canada by end of July, 1940, and the Royal Canadian Air Force loaned Squadron Leader (S/L) G.F. "Taffy" Powell to the organization. By August, the CPR and the British Government had signed their first agreement.

Of Dickins, former Air Commodore "Taffy" Powell writes in his book *Ferryman* (Airlife Publishing Ltd., Shrewsbury, England, 1982), he was:

> ...primarily a servant of the Canadian Pacific Railway... and made excellent use of the assistance of other men to help overcome the monumental engineering, supply and financial control problems inherent in setting up the organization. Morris Wilson, paymaster acting for the British Ministry of Aircraft Production, secured "...the highest level of impartial assistance to implement quick planning decisions and to safeguard the very large amounts of British funds that were being used..."

Punch recruited, among others, H.M. Long, from the heavy steel industry as his executive assistant and virtual managing director for the ferry group; John Schofield from the CNR as head architect; J.H. Norris, a building contractor to lead the construction program; B.W. Roberts, CPR, purchasing control, F B. Walls, general manager of the T. Eaton Company, in charge of supplies and J.G. McConnell, newspaper owner and publisher, to tend to public relations needs.

All these prominent men, and others later appointed, shared two things in common: they worked hard and did so without pay; they later numbered eleven in all and became known as "dollar-a-year-men."

It was the only way to handle a dangerous, yet diplomatic dilemma that needed a speedy solution.

Now!

The bombers destined for the United Kingdom were made in the United States and had to be brought across a border of a country at war with Germany, which Canada was by then. Under these conditions, American pilots could not fly the planes across the US / Canada border as this would clearly violate the

American neutrality act which was in force and would stay that way until the USA joined the allies in war on Dec. 8th, 1941.

When England and France badly needed Allied bomber and fighter aircraft support, the United States was not at war and could not violate its neutrality and risk being thrown into the war prematurely.

An ingenious solution respected the technical details of neutrality - the first bombers were flown to Pembina, North Dakota, by American airmen. From there, about 60 miles (97 km) south of Winnipeg, they were towed across the American / Canadian border by horses. Canadian and Commonwealth pilots flew them from there into Montreal, and other points. While stretching the point a lot, it was apparent that the Americans did not violate the technical aspects of their neutrality.

From *Atlantic Bridge:*

> Work began with the arrival, at the end of July 1940, of the British Overseas Airways Corporation Captains A.S. Wilcockson, D.C.T. Bennett, R.H. Page and I.G. Ross, and with the loan of Squadron Leader G.F. Powell, a former Atlantic captain of Imperial Airways, from the R.C.A.F. These men were famous flyers with years of experience ...they brought an airman's vision and unequalled practical experience. The organization was created. All depended on men with courage, brains and flying skill for the building of the Bridge.
> 
> The immediate tasks during the end of that summer of 1940 were to marshal the bombers and equip them for the crossing, and to find pilot-navigators and radio operators, train them and equip them for this specialized work. A hazardous adventure had to be reduced to routine enterprise of war. The British authorities expected losses. The men with experience, on the other hand, aimed at delivery without loss. That faith went through everybody.
> 
> All professions of the sky were needed and more ground-based professions as well to strike the foundations for this Atlantic Bridge, and get it and its cargo to start crossing.
> 
> While bombers were being ordered, built and brought over the border by horses, men to fly them were being assembled in Montreal with the help of two stenographers, two male clerks at Windsor Station and two ground engineers at St. Hubert airport, a few miles south of Montreal.
> 
> The men came from many countries and walks of life. For pilots, there was a nucleus in the famous captains of British

*Overseas Airways. The R.A.F. was too occupied with the Battle of the Atlantic to supply pilots. It was a case of passing word around that men were needed; and all the professions of the sky were soon sending their candidates.*

*There were bush pilots – men who were opening up the lonely northern territories of Canada, skillful, instinctive fliers who rode unmapped territory for trade and development, remote from the crises of Europe. There were barnstormers, men who would fly you for a dollar, thrill-makers, spell-binders, or taxi-men who from belief in flying and for bread and butter were teaching the men in the street the ways of the air. There were crop dusters, those whose job was to fly low, spraying crops by contract to counteract blights. There were sky-writers. They were amateur pilots who flew, business men who piloted themselves, pilots who worked for companies or commercial magnates. These and many others came. They came in the fall of 1940 and 1941 from the United States, Canada and Britain. They wanted to do a flying job. They wanted to help the war.*

*First and foremost their desire is to fly. Their belief in the future of their craft is unbounded...*

The same radio advances which helped Sheldon and his friends pioneer new air routes in north western and western Canada also helped make trans-Atlantic flying safer. The need wasn't just for pilots – but for good radio operators and the call went out. Experienced radio operators were few and far between then, as most trans-continental flying was being done by "riding the ranges", or by following clearly defined radio beacons audible to a pilot. R.A.F. Transport Command sought the necessary aircrew and ground support personnel, working almost entirely out of Montreal and reaching into every nook and cranny of the world.

Outposts had to be built for the many spans of the Bridge. The first such remote pillar for the span began to rise out of Gander, on the eastern tip of Newfoundland about 950 air miles (1,539 km) east of Montreal. It became the first of two eastern launching points to cross the North Atlantic.

Aircraft delivery data note: *Every attempt has been made to zero in on the exact number of bombers and fighter aircraft which were delivered through Ferry Command operations. Currently, the numbers available to me vary from a low of 10,000 to a high of 20,000. The actual figure of delivered aircraft probably lies within this range. Either way, it is a BIG number. It is known, for example, that about 8,000 bombers and fighter aircraft were also delivered to Russia in the same WW II period, with aircraft flying north from the*

*United States over Canada along what was known as the Northwest Staging Route, above the province of British Columbia, up over into Alaska, across the Bering Strait and into Russia. It is also known that more than 10,000 bombers and fighter aircraft were dispatched to theatres of war through the Canadian headquarters of Ferry Command at Dorval, Québec -, under the direction of the Royal Air Force Air Transport Command. Very little information is known about the civilian aspect of Ferry Command. While the information is not a secret, attempts were made to keep it hush-hush until the United States of America officially and legally joined the Allies on December 8th, 1941, the day after Pearl Harbor.*

By November 10th, 1940, the first flight of seven Hudson bombers took off from Gander. Next morning, Remembrance Day, they all landed in Scotland with the lead pilot observing the occasion by presenting a poppy purchased the day before in Montréal.

Nine days later, November 29, seven more Hudson aircraft took off, followed by a third flight of seven more bombers on December 17th.

The first of an incredibly low number of accidents in Ferry Command took place in these early flights. A public relations and morale cover-up came with one particular prang – a cover-up that has lasted until the publication of this book.

Records indicate that the fourth and last group of ferry flights in 1940 took off on December 29th. These same records say four of the seven made it safely, that one crashed on take-off, one returned with engine trouble and the third returned because of radio difficulties.

According to official versions, the lead aircraft of that seven-plane flight was an important one, dubbed the "Spirit of Lockheed-Vega Employees" clearly written under its nose. It was a gift from the workers at the American Lockheed and Vega plants to the people of Britain. It did arrive in Montreal on Christmas day and according to published documents, made it to Scotland four days later, on December 29th, exactly seven days after leaving the factory.

When *Walking on Air* was first published, 77-year old Ivan Harman was living in Westbank, in the Okanagan region of BC. He told me though his son, Gerry, that the original "Spirit of Lockheed-Vega Employees" airplane could NOT have arrived in Scotland.

Mr. Harman said that he was right there on the spot, in Gander the night that particular flight of seven Hudson aircraft took off and that he saw it – the "Spirit of Lockheed-Vega Employees" – crash on the snow-packed runway.

It wasn't the lead aircraft either, according to Mr. Harman, but third in the line-up.

He had first arrived in Gander earlier, on November 10 and had seen for himself the first, second and third groups of bombers leave for overseas.

On this fateful day, according to Gerry, his father told him that he was out on the airfield and distinctively recalled seeing the "Spirit of Lockheed-Vega Employees" lift from the runway, then hit the snow-packed surface with its undercarriage, and cartwheel tail-over-nose into a crumpled wreck. The crew escaped without serious injury before it exploded. All other aircraft of this flight continued their take offs and flew over the crashed bomber in orderly succession, finally arriving overseas.

Mr. Harman said that he went out the next day with a tractor to haul the wreckage away. Before he did that, however, he took out a hacksaw and cut a tip from one of the two propellers – keeping it as a souvenir. He gave me the propeller tip during the final production stage of the original book, *Walking on Air*.

I had let Gerry read the completed manuscript – the seventh one in the series of manuscript for the original book, after Sheldon had approved it and signed it off.

Gerry told me personally that his father was so moved by Sheldon's recollections that he asked Gerry to offer me the broken tip as a souvenir.

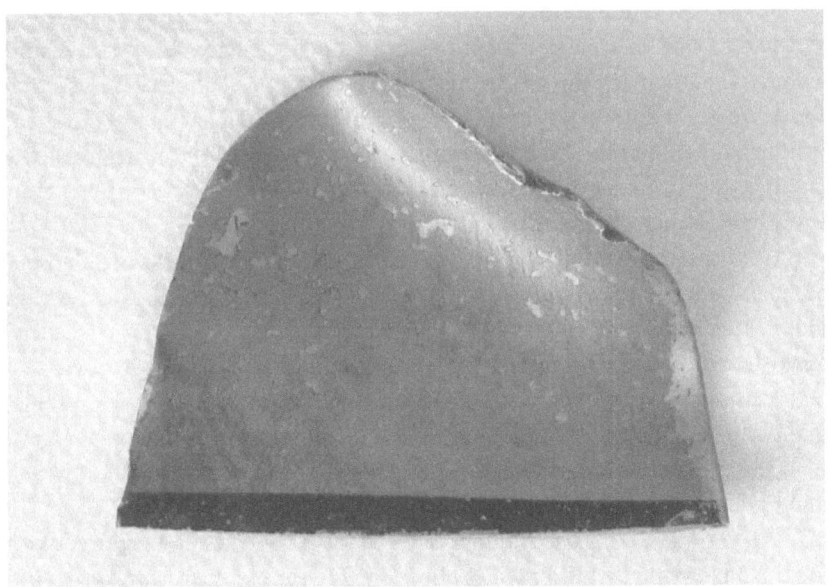

*The broken propeller tip from "Spirit of Lockheed-Vega Employees" is in my possession. It is always within sight, beside my keyboard, It is a reminder of what it took for others to earn for me the free life style I enjoy today in Canada when I completed the manuscript for this book – nearly 68 years after the accident that brought me the black-and-yellow, pock-marked propeller tip. A number of reproductions will be made of this prop tip - with a suitable plaque briefly describing this incident. Should all go well after the book is published, I want to donate the original propeller tip to the Mayor of the City of London, England, so that at least, a small piece of the original "Spirit of Lockheed-Vega Employees" actually*

makes it to the descendants of the intended recipients. Then I will have considered the gift delivered, with the prop tip representing all of the airplanes which did make it overseas. I will then donate the reproductions of this prop tip to various public and private aviation museums wherever they may be, if they so wish to retain a copy. My original plan had been to retain the original propeller tip for my former wife and our three sons as part of their heritage. However, I think they will understand my reasons for delivering the original article to London, and that they will be happy with their copy of a reproduction. While new information surfaced sporadically during the closing stages of research and completion of the final manuscript for this book, it had been exceedingly difficult to obtain any new information from today's Lockheed corporation headquartered in Texas, USA. But I continue my efforts until I close off the manuscript and live with the information available to me.

Through Gerry, Mr. Harman told me, that he appreciated why official records say nothing of this crash, even back in 1945 when the official documents were first published. The morale of the Lockheed and Vega workers would have been hit a hard blow had they known of this, he suggested.

That the Hudson wasn't the lead bomber in the flight, he said simply: "What the hell, it doesn't matter now."

He insisted that he was convinced that the descendants of the men and women who presented this gift to the people of Britain will not feel overly upset about the new information coming to light this more than half-a-century later. It in no way undermines the value of the work and effort their ancestors put into it, and the massive contribution they and their co-workers made to the war effort in assembling these bombers.

Over the years, there has been conflicting information, because a Hudson bomber, with the words "Spirit of Lockheed-Vega Employees" painted on it, did, in fact, arrive in England and was photographed and cited in newspapers for memorable service in the northeast of England. I have been unable, for this manuscript, to confirm this report of a replacement aircraft, but I have been able to prove that particular Hudson bomber did, in fact, crash in Gander that night.

This proof came from Richard Goff, who was the weatherman on duty the night the bomber crashed.

He told me during the summer of 2008 from his home in Gander, Newfoundland - where he lived then as a spunky 92-year old man, that he was on night duty in the weather office when he heard of the crash. He would not learn which aircraft it was until later the next day, however.

Obviously a Hudson bomber had been found somewhere, and quickly re-painted, given new registration numbers, and flown over to England for delivery to the people of London.

Since publication of the original *Walking on Air*, and through to the final manuscript for this expanded version of the original book, new information has surfaced, information which was not available to me until recent years, thanks

*This airport, in the northwest corner of Burbank, was built in 1930. By 1934 the airport had become Los Angeles' primary airport known as Union Air Terminal. During the 1930s Lockheed Aircraft Company, adjacent to the field, evolved into one the nation's largest aircraft manufacturers, and in 1940 Lockheed purchased the airport. It was then renamed Lockheed Air Terminal and used to test and deliver Lockheed aircraft. It also remained Los Angeles' primary civil airport and remained the area's only civil airport throughout the war.*

*During the war Lockheed built P-38 fighters, Hudson and B-17 bombers. The Royal Air Force's Air Technical Services Command and US Army Air Forces Western Technical Training Command had operations at the field. The airport and the Lockheed plant were extensively camouflaged during the war. The main Lockheed plant and runways were made to appear as grain fields and houses, and the parking lot was covered over with netting to appear as alfalfa fields. In addition, an extensive smoke screen system was installed to hide the plant under smoke.*

*Photos from the California State Military Department, California State Military Museum.*

to the incredible resources now available at my fingertips through the internet and its incredible search engines.

For example, I now know the name of one of the workers who donated his time on what was officially known as the Hudson Mk 111, T9465, "The Spirit of Lockheed-Vega Employees." The aircraft was in fact originally assigned to 269 Squadron, Royal Air Force and delivered to Wick, with a plaque commemorating the gift. Wick Harbour is on the northeast coast of Scotland.

That it was a gift, there can be no doubt, as evidenced by the following brief *Time* magazine article of Monday, Dec. 9th, 1940:

> Short, blond, athletic-looking, 21-year-old Burton Griffin works by night in the stock room of Vega's Burbank (Calif.) plant, goes to bed with the dawn. One morning last week young Griffin couldn't sleep; a wild idea chased through his mind.
> 
> Finally it drove him to put on his clothes, hustle off to the plant to tell his boss. Soon 1,500 questioned employees of Lockheed-Vega voted to put it in practice. The idea: "I got to thinkin' about Christmas and about all those bombers we're making for the British... And I got this idea about making them a Christmas present of one of the bombers."
> 
> Lockheed Hudson bombers cost $90,000, take 24,000 man-hours apiece to build. From its 20,000 employees (average pay: 75¢ an hour) Lockheed-Vega solicited voluntary pledges of two or more hours of pay per man, planned to make up the difference itself (expected to be almost 50% of the cost, despite an estimated 100% subscription). Proclaimed the Brothers Gross (Robert E., president of Lockheed, and Courtland S., president of Vega) after querying the State Department on procedure: "We will be very glad to transfer the funds so raised ... to Lord Lothian with the employees' instructions that the Ambassador use this money toward the purchase of a Lockheed Hudson for the people of England... " \*
> 
> Three days before Christmas, at Burbank's Union Air Terminal, workers will trundle out the plane, done up in cellophane and red ribbons. They will be disappointed if Lord Lothian is not there to see their gift christened *The Spirit of Lockheed-Vega* with two bottles of champagne (one for Lockheed, one for Vega).

\*Under the Neutrality Act, implements of war cannot be donated directly to a belligerent.

*Photograph of Lockheed Vega T9465 "The Spirit of Lockheed-Vega Employees" flying over Iceland where it was stationed with 269 squadron, RAF, after its presentation to the British people. Does this photograph make a liar out of Mr. Harman? I think not, but only further research will eventually win out. Was it a cover up to spare the feelings of the Lockheed employees or simply a case of mistaken identity?*

In 1947, when Mines Field was expanded to become Los Angeles' primary airport, this facility became a secondary airport. In 1975 the cities of Burbank, Glendale and Pasadena bought the airport and renamed it Burbank Glendale-Pasadena Airport. Lockheed continued in operation at the field for many years.

And who attended this ceremony? According to the web log of 269 Squadron, dated Dec. 22nd, 1940:

> *An estimated crowd of 20,000 people was present at the Union Air Terminal, Burbank, California to witness the presentation of the Hudson aircraft "Spirit of Lockheed-Vega Employees" to the people of Great Britain. This gift was made possible by the spontaneous and voluntary donation of two hours or more time on the part of each of some 18,000 of the Lockheed and Vega employees.*

Also of interest is another memory of Mr. Harman's - the two other aircraft which the official publication says returned to Gander didn't show up there; they may have gone elsewhere, but there was no such thing as an elsewhere at the time. He insists he would have known about their return because of his contacts at the base.

I found one and only one photograph – thanks to Google images search - which shows "Spirit of Lockheed-Vega Employees" in flight - over what looks like Greenland. Once again, this photo is copied from 269 Squadron's website.

Formation flights often had to be cancelled.

Prevailing North Atlantic weather conditions were so bad that they would have forced pilots to maintain extensive radio contact to stay in formation. And all flights had to operate under strict radio silence lest the Germans learn of their position by radio direction finders, and try to blow them out of the skies before they got to Britain.

From then on aircraft were usually separated by fifteen-minute intervals, and generally maintained this separation time on arrival. The planes flew similar headings, tried to maintain standard speeds, and were in little danger of closing in as pilots weren't interested in catching up to each other.

The first span was strictly a one-way affair. At first, aircrews returned by ocean liner, but a RFS (Return Ferry Service) was in the planning stages. It took a long time to return pilots by boat and the air crew training program in Montréal still had teething problems

Other steps were being taken in December 1940 to boost the number of crossings. Ocean warfare called for long-range seaplanes to monitor convoys and hunt submarines. PBY (Catalina) flying boats could be delivered quite readily from American assembly lines to the British possession of Bermuda, about 700 miles (1,127 km) from North America in the Atlantic, and 3,400 miles (4,828 km) from the United Kingdom.

Early in 1941, S/L Powell mobilized Bermuda's resources. The first seven PBYs in the expanded air bridge left the U.S.A. for the new base on Darrell Island, on the outskirts of Hamilton, Bermuda. Almost overnight, S/L Powell had set up an organization to receive ships, prepare an office, obtain maintenance crews and have every-thing ready for pilots to fly.

Thus, the UK began receiving more air patrol and anti-submarine warfare help from its second pillar of the Atlantic Bridge.

This paved the way for putting up the third and fourth spans. The third would be Goose Bay on the northern Labrador peninsula, and the fourth would be known as the South Atlantic span, using Caribbean and South American way points, over the South Atlantic to Ascension Island and up along the west coast of Africa. The fifth, across the Pacific, was yet to come.

As the Battle of the Atlantic raged on in 1941, Germany began to take great interest in the Ferry Command terminus in Scotland. Early ferry pilots had reported favourable landing conditions in the western regions of Scotland, especially at Prestwick, which had until now been a civilian airfield.

The Bridge was built. The air delivery plan was tested and successful - from Gander to Bermuda. The UK's need for more aircraft became urgent, imposing more and more demands on the rapidly expanding ferry service. Skills had to be mastered on a daily basis, despite the remaining single largest problem: that of accurately forecasting winter weather on a regular basis.

More bomber types were added to the delivery list: B-17 Flying Fortresses and B-24 Liberators.

By February 1941, twenty-four complete RAF delivery crews flew to Dayton, Ohio, to collect more aircraft – they were still operating under the wing of the Canadian Pacific Air Services Department. After special training there, the crews flew the Forts and Liberators to Montreal for staging through to Gander and Prestwick.

In that same month, the Bermuda span delivered fifteen flying boats.

One flying boat left San Diego in March 1941, arriving in Manila four days later via Honolulu, Midway, Wake and Guam – adding the fifth span of the ferry service, and the first across the Pacific Ocean. Also in March, 25 pilots received various levels of instruction, and 50 navigators and 50 radio operators were in training in Montreal.

Then the Arctic Circle span started taking shape. On April 22$^{nd}$, 1941, a Liberator took off from Gander to Greenland, and back to St. Hubert, for a 14-hour, 44-minute long survey flight to locate possible base sights and marker points along the new route.

Allied leaders had long since viewed the possibilities of ferrying bombers and fighter aircraft, up over the Arctic Circle, across Greenland and into Iceland. Stepping stones such as these giant land masses made it possible to ferry single-seat fighter aircraft – needed as desperately as were the bombers.

At about this stage the Return Ferry Service plans were ready to be put into action to expedite the return of ferry pilots. Liberators were "liberated" from active theatres of war to provide this essential service, and made available to west-bound aircrews, returning them to Montréal in hours instead of days.

The first RFS flight on May 4$^{th}$, 1941 brought seven aircrew members back, and made postal history in the process. Several letters postmarked May 4 left the United Kingdom and arrived the same day, bearing the same date postmark, in Gander, Newfoundland.

A substantial passenger, freight and air mail operation mushroomed from these Outbound and Return Ferry flights: a full-scale global airline had now become an integral part of wartime communications and supply lines touching every corner of the British Commonwealth, and in co-operation with the United States Army Air Force, Pan Am Air Ferries, girdling the planet.

The rapid growth begged a restructuring. CPASD gave way to ATFERO which in turn became the Royal Air Force Ferry Command. The Americans were done with neutrality and pitched in whole-heartedly. But, because ATFERO was a civilian authority, this precluded American military personnel from flying delivery aircraft under ATFERO command to any of the North American dispatch points.

## The Ferry Command roster – mid-1941 and 1943

However, be it from Montréal or Bermuda, ferry pilots, usually civilians from Canada, the United States or a Commonwealth country - would then take over and fly the planes overseas.

The total pilot roster – all 415 of them as of midnight July 14$^{th}$, 1941, when the CPASD contract terminated – included:

207 civilian pilots
118 RAF pilots
36 Air Transport Auxiliary pilots (who ferried aircraft from Prestwick within the United Kingdom)
33 BOAC pilots
18 RCAF pilots
3 Royal New Zealand Air Force pilots

Of these, 59 per cent of the civilian pilots were American, 10 per cent Canadian and the balance from other countries.

Crews completed the great Dorval base during the summer and autumn of 1941. By October 4$^{th}$, 1941, operational headquarters had moved onto the base from downtown Montréal. That base was then known as Dorval Airport, but is now the Pierre Elliot Trudeau International Airport, often shortened to the Montréal-Trudeau Airport.

Dorval had now become the nerve centre of the ferry service, under Air Chief Marshall Sir Frederick Bowhill, who had been Director of Coastal Command in the Battle of the Atlantic.

When he arrived in Dorval, he could count on more than 100 fully-trained crews at his disposal.

By 1943, Ferry Command effectively conducted its business with 2,000 civilian employees and 1,000 military personnel – a two-to-one ratio of civilians over military, showing just how strong the civilian support to the Allied Armed Forces actually was. For every pilot, there was a need for at least three other aircrew to fly the larger aircraft, and a swell of ground services which had to be provided each aircrew and aircraft on the delivery schedule.

Most of the Ferry Command civilians provided all the essential ground support crews for all aspects of a dynamic and giant international air service, from payroll, accounts payable, expense accounts, supplies of all sorts and kinds, equipment provisioning, equipment, aircraft flight testing, ground support, technical, medical, logistics, housing accommodations, cafeterias, in-flight meals, ground transportation. You name it, Ferry Command had it.

### Ferry Command was becoming the very model upon which today's civilian airlines are based

Also that summer, Eric Fry, of the Dominion Geodetic Survey Branch, discovered an ideal spot for a new airport from which aircraft could take the Arctic Circle route – a large sandy plateau 100 feet (30 m) above a swampy patch of forest: it became the new home of Goose Bay, Labrador. Supply boats arrived in September. Runways were ready to receive aircraft in November, and the first ones arrived on December 9th, 1941.

In January 1942, Liberators began making regular take offs from Goose Bay, which became one of the busiest airports in the world during the war.

Mounting pressures forced the Allies to shift their focus to the Mediterranean and Africa throughout the remainder of 1941 and 1942. Desert conflicts absorbed vast amounts of air power and the chief need in Africa included such bombers as Marylands, Baltimores, Bostons, and later, Mitchells.

Ferry Command would, could, and did, deliver the goods.

## 8. Ferry Command in Flight

### ...and with his first flight, another airborne scare

When he joined in ATFERO 1942, Sheldon held a quasi-military rank which by the end of the war had been upgraded to the military equivalent of a Squadron Leader.

Not only did he get his quasi-military rank on joining Ferry Command, he also got his first "boot" on his first delivery of a Lockheed Ventura bomber – when high over the North Atlantic.

Ferry crews, of necessity, were short-handed. An experienced pilot usually went overseas with a mechanic, experienced in twin-engine machines, along with an RAF Sergeant radio operator and another RAF Sergeant navigator, but without a First Officer, or co-pilot. More often than not, crews consisted largely of civilian radio operators, civilian navigators and, in the Lancaster bombers, a fifth crew member was added, a civilian co-pilot.

There were not enough military air crews available to handle the task at hand: deliver the bombers which were coming off the huge American production line at a rapid clip.

For the most part air crews delivering multi-engine bombers consisted of no more than four men, and no less than two – often civilians, especially during the early stages of Ferry Command. Between 1941 and 1942 the British Commonwealth Air Training Plan kicked into high gear and began training hundreds of thousands of air crews, and the Americans had finally begun churning out military air crews as well.

The radio operator, checked out on handling flaps and landing gear, usually occupied the co-pilot's position from which rudder and flying controls had been removed.

Larger than the Lockheed Lodestar, the Ventura had two Pratt and Whitney R2800 engines, and for the ferry flight, was usually equipped with internal fuel bladders located in the cabin section. Because crew scheduling knew that Sheldon had a lot of experience with the Lodestars, they assigned him his radio operator and navigator.

The original flight plan called for a Gander departure, but bad weather forced him to leave from Montreal, stop at Goose Bay, refuel and fly on to Iceland, then Prestwick.

Once over the Atlantic, the Ventura ate up the miles. Fuel had to be regularly and manually switched from the bladders out to the wing tanks to maintain the proper weight distribution about the plane's centre of gravity. A critical valve-turning sequence had to be followed to permit this transfer.

Crews sometimes forgot to close the correct valves at the end of the procedure and wound up pumping a lot of fuel into the ocean.

His two non-commissioned officers (NCOs) were husky lads, well trained for their jobs and would be fine companions for the long lonely trip.

Another transfer point coming up, and Sheldon called for the valve turning.

Usually the radio operator did this, having the least to do during the long flying hours of radio silence. Sheldon had been trying to make a good track to stay south of the Greenland coast, fighting drifting winds, and keeping his navigator busy with sightings and upgrading position reports for him.

The procedure seemed to be taking too long.

Sheldon leaned back around his seat to see what was going on, as the instrument fuel gauge indicators weren't showing any fuel transfer. The radio operator couldn't get one of the main valves to rotate and finally returned to the cockpit to report his difficulty.

Sheldon instructed the navigator to take up the co-pilot's position and keep his eye on "George", the nickname air crews had given to the aircraft's automatic pilot. Navigators knew enough to change automatic pilot settings and keep an aircraft straight and level at a given altitude. Failure to do this could put the aircraft into a dangerous stall configuration.

He left his command seat and made his way into the dimly lit cabin, down onto the floor, beside the radio operator to study the problem with the non-rotating valve.

The main valve stem had been broken. It had to be opened first before the other valves could be turned, permitting the fuel transfer to take place.

Both worked for a few minutes with a small tool kit, conventional gear on all ferry ships.

The radio operator had snapped the small turning knob, leaving a tiny valve shaft-stub sticking up into the air atop the housing. Sheldon tried to loosen the valve packing, risking a fuel leak if necessary. It had to flow or Sheldon's career and his crew's careers with the ferry service would come to a watery end in the next 30 minutes.

Head-to-head on the cabin floor, arms and legs all over the place, Sheldon and the radio operator tried to turn that stubborn valve stub.

Looking up, Sheldon saw something which scared the hell out of him – "a ruddy big pair of shiny black boots."

Not his, nor the radio operator's. They belonged to the navigator, who should have been watching George in the cockpit.

That's about when Sheldon noticed something unusual about the aircraft. It seemed to be inordinately nose-high. He sensed a deep, un-recoverable stall coming on.

Scrambling to his feet, he raced to the cockpit in time to read the airspeed indicator - dangerously low, as was the artificial horizon. The Ventura pointed to the stars. While leaping for his seat, he grabbed the control column and took corrective action by shoving forward on the column, bringing the Ventura's nose down, de-activating George, and applying more power to the engines.

Agonizingly slowly the nose dipped below the artificial horizon until her airspeed returned to safe limits and Sheldon brought her back to smooth flight.

The navigator, obviously thinking everything would be all right for a few moments, had let George do the flying all by himself and went to see what was happening with the fuel transfer problem.

Obviously, this was a definite no-no.

With the Ventura under control, Sheldon reset the automatic pilot settings, and with a stern warning to the navigator to stay in the co-pilot's seat and never leave it until he, the pilot, returned; Sheldon went aft to tackle the sticky valve.

Within moments, and with the help of a huge pipe wrench, the valve was opened and the fuel began to flow. Sheldon flew on without further incident to Iceland and Prestwick.

### Second delivery flight yields trio of events:
### Setting a personal speed record...
### Avoiding a long-range German Condor bomber...
### Discovering the effectiveness of camouflage

His second delivery flight provided him with three different types of adventure: he set a personal speed record on the way to Prestwick, met his first four-engine German long-range bomber and discovered how effective good camouflage can be.

The B-25 Mitchell made the trip to Prestwick in seven hours and twenty-five minutes, not fast by other speed records which were being posted by other ferry pilots, but good enough for him.

Considering that the average flying time for a Liberator for the same flight stood between nine and twelve hours, he couldn't scoff at his new time in the B-25. 100 mile-an-hour (161 km) plus tail winds helped, but extensive icing conditions en route made the flight seem longer.

Alcohol de-icing on the propellers worked quite well but the props regularly kept throwing off ice chunks, some of which would hit the fuselage. Sheldon wondered just how many bombers would be lost through severe icing conditions. Icing had claimed a few bombers before.

During the very next day, three bombers failed to show up at Prestwick – cause unknown, lost at sea.

Nearing the coast of Ireland, Sheldon saw his first Condor, Germany's largest aircraft, used as a long-range Luftwaffe transport and reconnaissance plane. Like all large Ferry Command Bombers to the United Kingdom, they too were generally unarmed. It had an 80-foot wing span. The Condor came through broken cloud cover in a large valley in the clouds and Sheldon first sighted it coming from about forty-five degrees to his right, at a slightly higher altitude.

Both pilots must have spotted each other at the same time, and both had the same intent: avoid the enemy and don't stir the hornet's nest. Both took instant evasive action, returning to the security of their respective cloud cover.

He never saw the bomber again. Many ferry pilots encountered these Condors; fortunately such sightings resulted in nothing more than memories to be mulled over in later years.

Cloud cover provided a perfect hiding spot. Better than camouflage at hiding something.

But when he flew over Prestwick, Scotland, he was amazed at how good camouflage can really be.

An incoming pilot could only "see" the runway by arriving at an exact altitude on a predetermined heading.

The airport and its runways had been designed and built when the German Luftwaffe were making shipping raids, dropping bombs over the Clyde shipping area. German pilots had been told that they could probably locate and identify Prestwick if they looked hard enough for it, and they all had orders to bomb if they could see it.

Even he was coming in under the best of weather conditions, and looking straight ahead before he began his procedural turns which would line him up with the runway, Sheldon could only make out the Scottish coastline, and stared down at what looked like large coal piles and vast countryside – until he came to the exact point in space where the runway suddenly became visible to an incoming pilot.

### Death comes a-knockin'... gently... disguised as Morpheus

Death nearly came out the winner on a ferry flight for Sheldon, his crew and one VIP passenger during the winter of 1942-43.

This time he was flying a B-17, and had as a special passenger an RCAF officer who had been shot down in the Battle of Britain and had been called to England so that he could receive a decoration at Buckingham Palace.

This bomber was slightly different than its sister ships.

Engineers had modified its high-altitude oxygen systems for crew and passengers. Normal high-pressure systems exploded if their high pressure units were hit by shrapnel or bullets, or by anti-aircraft shells. Engineers designed a low-pressure system, operating with about four hundred pounds-per-square-inch, and pumping oxygen from a series of inter-connected oxygen tanks.

When hit by shrapnel or bullets, the new system had less of a tendency to explode violently as did the higher pressure oxygen systems.

In summer and at lower altitudes, the new system worked well. But this was a winter trip, and Sheldon had the B-17 humming along at well above 30,000 feet (9,144 m) to avoid icing conditions below that altitude.

Sheldon turned to ask his First Officer a question, only to find him slumped over his seat.

To all intents and purposes he appeared to be quite comfortable, probably catching a few winks.

Sheldon continued his visual scan of the cockpit, often referred to in aviation jargon as the front office, to check on his radio operator behind the cockpit. He had his head down, cradled in his arm.

Since he was well out over the ocean, high above the clouds, and everything seemed to be going smoothly, Sheldon figured he'd let both of them sleep gently in the arms of Morpheus, the Roman and Greek god of dreams.

Continuing his sweep, he noticed that the flight engineer, opposite the radio operator, was somewhat more alert, open to small talk. They both chatted for a while, mainly about their VIP passenger, who appeared to be sleeping quite well in a sleeping bag near the only source of heat in the crew compartment aft of the cockpit.

A perfect flight can be a monotonous thing, with the steady drone of the engines and vibrations inducing sleep; cockpit chatter was almost an essential at times to help keep the pilot alert.

The B-17 flew on under the auto-pilot's "watchful eye". Sheldon made a crew check on the plane's internal radio system, asking first for the navigator, whose position was below in the nose of the aircraft.

No answer.

Sheldon hit a switch which should have buzzed in the navigator's compartment.

Still no reply.

Everyone was on oxygen, including the dozing RCAF passenger, whose oxygen feed was plugged into the right, or starboard, supply side. It was the same one feeding Sheldon's and his First Officer's mask. All others were being fed oxygen from the port supply side.

Without warning, Sheldon and the engineer began to experience strange and dizzying sensations. For a few moments, they talked about this unusual happening. As they talked, Sheldon could see flashes pinging on his retinas, making him think he was seeing things, fighting the urge to pass out and go to sleep.

He'd recover and begin to faint again.

On recovering a third nine, he shook his head violently, feelings changing from curiosity and puzzlement to sheer fright.

Suddenly, a new sensation occurred, almost like an out-of-body travel experience, as if he was leaving his physical body with his mind.

Shaking his head, he realized what was going on - he and his crew were slowly being deprived of oxygen.

He and the engineer quickly confirmed that oxygen starvation had to be the problem. The engineer left his board, trailing his long oxygen supply hose behind him, and checked the oxygen flow indicator.

"You're right. Skipper, our oxygen isn't flowing."

Sheldon went into a long, but fast, shallow dive to bring the B-17 down, into thicker and breathable air, and soon levelled out between two well-defined cloud layers at 11,000 feet (3,353 m), where oxygen wasn't needed.

The engineer by then had located the problem: condensation froze at the high altitude, and ice had blocked the flow valve.

Sheldon radioed an emergency.

Field ambulances met the aircraft when it completed its landing roll, to take the crew and his VIP passenger to hospital at Ayr, 10 (16 km) miles south of the airfield, where medical teams began treating them for anoxia.

Few men and women today remember Ferry Command.

Most of Canada's youngsters don't even know it existed, unless their parents are veterans and told them about it, or they learned of it from some other sources, maybe even books like this.

There's not much in print about the organization as a whole, especially from the civilian point of view.

There are many excellent and entertaining books written by pilots who flew in Ferry Command, most of them written from a personal point of view.

Also, there are a number of historical books about Ferry Command written by professional historians – and all with an official military perspective, rather than from a civilian point of view which is presented in these three chapters in this new edition of the original book.

Other sources for information about civilians in Ferry Command have been hard to find despite extensive public and institutional library holdings and even harder-to-locate files about the infrastructure of Ferry Command from files contained in newspaper libraries.

Although much of its operation was shrouded by wartime secrecy, reporters and editors never overlooked a good story when it came from Ferry Command.

Keeping the oxygen starvation incident in mind, which the reporters couldn't have known about, gives cause to wonder about the ironies of war.

One example of such an article (source unknown).

> *Captain Luck... is enjoying the thrilling job of ferrying the big bombers that are blasting the daylights out of the Axis, from North America to Europe and Africa.*
>
> *That's the word brought back from eastern Canada by Public Relations official Leo McKinnon, of C.P. Air Lines, who saw Capt. Luck at the headquarters of the R.A.F. Ferry Command in Montreal recently.*
>
> *The former Edmonton and Calgary pilot who obtained leave from CP Air Lines to join the R.A.F. Ferry Command last May, made eight flights each way above the storm-tossed Atlantic. Four times he flew the North Atlantic route and has made an equal number of flights across the South Atlantic to North Africa.*
>
> *The ex-C.P. Air Lines chief pilot has been at the controls of the giant B-24 Liberators and the swift Martin B-26 Marauders during Atlantic crossings. He was eager to know how things were going around the old home town.*
>
> *Pilot Alex Dame, another former Edmonton flyer, is also flying with the Atlantic Ferry Command. He too is making flights across the North Atlantic.*

What McKinnon (another Yukon Southern colleague) and the reporter didn't fully cover was that Sheldon and other ferry pilots did a lot more than ferry aircraft across "the pond", as the Atlantic was sometimes called.

One just didn't have a valuable, experienced airline pilots in Ferry Command to merely have them ferry bombers.

There were a lot of other types of flying which had to be done across North America – mainly in the field of flight communications, all over the continental United States, much of it for the British Air Ministry Purchasing Commission headquartered in Washington, D. C.

For example, at Christmas 1942, Sheldon was hand-picked to escort Lady Bowhill, wife of the Ferry Command's commanding officer. She and her retinue spent a lot of time doing important public relations for propaganda reasons. It took money to fight a war... a lot of money... money which could only be raised from the American public by high-profile personalities such as Lady Bowhill.

And there was the critical need for regular morale boosts for RAF personnel stationed so far from their homes. She regularly visited Canadian and American bases where RAF personnel were stationed, always winning their hearts with her charm and personality.

Sheldon often flew Lady Bowhill around the continent. At one stage, other ferry pilots jokingly referred to Sheldon as Lady Bowhill's personal pilot.

The RAF Establishment Committee (RAFEC) had set up a series of modification centres in the United States and Caribbean. Sheldon and a few others usually flew RAF personnel to bases such as Washington, D.C.; Nashville, Tennessee, Elizabeth, North Carolina; Bermuda; Nassau; Miami, Florida; Houston and Dallas in Texas; San Diego, California and the odd flight to Tucson, Arizona.

San Diego was the headquarters for the Consolidated PBY flying boat, as well as the Liberator aircraft.

Trips would continue from there into Seattle, Washington, back into Victoria and Vancouver, BC, then into the States to Salt Lake City, Utah, Kansas City, Kansas, and Reno, Nevada before returning to Dorval in Québec.

RAFEC flights were quite different from ferry flights, from a duration and passenger perspective alone, if nothing else. Passengers were mainly military personnel, but included at least one representative each from the House of Lords, and the House of Commons in London, as well as senior representatives from the RAF and the British Army.

The RAFEC called at every point in the world wherever British forces were based. Such trips usually lasted six weeks, and members invariably saw to it that they ended with a shopping stop-over in New York.

This was a far cry from the routine flying days of YSAT / CPAL

On March 11th, 1943, Sir Archibald Sinclair rose in the House of Commons to explain why changes were needed to Ferry Command:

> *All transport aircraft which we now possess, or which we shall produce here, or obtain from America, will be used to meet urgent requirements. With these new aircraft we shall be able*

*to form new transport squadrons. With an increased number of transport squadrons, an organization will be required to control their operations throughout the world. I have, therefore, decided to establish a Royal Air Force Transport Command. To create such a command sooner would have been to put the cart before the horse. It has not been Commanders and staff that we have been short of, but aircraft. Now the Command will come naturally into being through the process of bringing supply and organization into focus. In addition to controlling the operations of the R.A.F. transport squadrons at home, the Command will be responsible for the organization and control of strategic air routes, for all overseas ferrying and for the reinforcement moves of squadrons to and between overseas theatres.*

The organization skirted the globe, with bases flung far and wide, operating at near-peak efficiency.

The bases:

Dorval, QC was the main receiving centre for landplanes from North American factories, head office and the main command training centre.

Boucherville, QC – near Dorval became the marine base for training seaplane crews and dispatching seaplanes, acting as a complement to Dorval for waterborne craft.

Gander, Newfoundland received landplanes from Montreal as a refueling point for flights to Britain, and received seaplanes from Boucherville for the hop to Bermuda.

Goose Bay, in what is now Newfoundland, and Labrador dispatched medium bombers or limited-range aircraft, such as fighters, to American bases in Greenland, or for the 1,550-mile long flight to the British staging post at Reykjavik, Iceland for servicing, refuelling and continuing on the last leg of a delivery flight.

Prestwick, on the west coast of Scotland served as the key European receiving terminal, and the point from which the Return Ferry Service operated.

Elizabeth City, North Carolina, USA served as the transfer point where American seaplanes were handed over to British crews, and ferried on to Gander or Bermuda.

Bermuda in the Atlantic was the launching point for antisubmarine warfare, and seaplanes from Bermuda monitored ocean convoys, as well as being the dispatch centre for the 3,400-mile long flight to England.

The United States began the South Atlantic span over territory which was then partly British, party American and partly Brazilian. In December, 1942, the RAF and US Army Air Force signed an agreement whereby Ferry Command assumed responsibility for the delivery of RAF aircraft from American plants and fly them to war zones by means of this new span.

Nashville, Tennessee initially received twenty-five aircrews from Dorval to launch it as a new aircraft receiving terminal, with ground administration services and base loaned by the U.S. Air Transport Command.

West Palm Beach, Florida became the key jumping off point for flights heading into the Caribbean and South American legs of the new span.

Trinidad was the first staging post receiving flights from the Caribbean.

Puerto Rico, halfway to Trinidad from the continental U.S., served as an emergency alternate, offered by the Americans.

Para-Belem, Brazil was another staging base near the mouth of the Amazon River.

Natal, Brazil is the most easterly point in the country, and was the last staging post for the 1,400-mile long flight to

Ascension Island in the South Atlantic, several hundred miles to the north of St. Hélène, and the last departure point for Africa.

Pilots flew from Ascension to Accra on the African Gold Coast where a completely separate RAF organization forwarded the aircraft to various African bases. Quite often Sheldon and his colleagues would fly their planes and cargoes on directly to Cairo, in Egypt.

*Atlantic Bridge* authors cited the "uncommon foresight of flying men and Colonial administrators" for the development of the West Africa area staging centre. They "showed unparalleled energy in tropical conditions" since the fall of France in 1940.

"They" included servicemen and civilians.

Between the fall of France and May 1943, over 5,300 aircraft had been ferried by the RAF from the four British West African territories of Nigeria, the Gold Coast, Sierra Leone and Gambia, flying from some forty airfields, flying boat bases and landing grounds.

It cost the British nearly two million pounds to create a reliable Middle East supply route to keep up with the transfer of aircraft from North America.

In February, 1943, Nassau, in the Bahamas - conveniently located an hour's flying time from Miami – came on board, and in less than three months, by May 1943, Transport Command had dispatched a total of I 17 aircraft out of Nassau.

The Azores in the mid-Atlantic served as a strong strategic point and another quasi-ferry service base.

### Accident rate lower than forecast, but deadly... evoking strong suspicions of Nazi sabotage in USA and Canada

Limited though they were in number, accidents did happen, some with tragic results.

The day before Sir Archibald Sinclair stood in the House of Commons in London, England, Sheldon lost a good friend – Alex Dame, the man who had come to his and his passengers' aid when he had to set the Barkley Grow down on a Liard River sandbar.

Alex's death on March 10th, 1943, closed a tragedy-laden chapter in the Dame family, the grim pages of which had begun less than forty days before, on January 25, when his brother Jack lost his wife who died of a heart attack in Nashville, TN.

Less than one month later, on February 22nd, Jack and his two crew members died in a ferry service crash south of Nashville, on a return flight from Miami to Montréal.

At the time of his death on March 10, Alex was only thirty-seven years old. With Ferry Command for the previous eleven months, he had delivered his share of bombers via the bridge spans, and since early 1943, had been assigned as a test pilot in Ferry Command's testing division, headed by Al Lilly.

Alex and his crew lost their lives when their twin-engine bomber crashed on a routine test flight near St. Urbain de Chateauguay, about 20 miles (32 km) southwest of Montréal, and almost directly opposite the Dorval base on the south side of the St. Lawrence River.

The Dame family had made their home in Westmount, QC (then a suburb of Montréal), and cherished among Sheldon's possessions, is a photograph showing Alex, his wife and their child, taken a few days before the crash, which also claimed the lives test observer George C. Denton, of Montréal, and an unidentified RAF aircraftsman.

The news of Alex's death went nation-wide and naturally came to McConachie's attention.

Grant wrote Sheldon on March 31st:

> *I feel the same way you do about the boys that have flown in the northwest and the original lot is gradually dwindling. The loss of Ernie (Kubicck - he'd made it to airline command, and was in the cockpit when CPAL lost its first airliner on a B.C. mountaintop not long before Alex's death) and Alex is felt very deeply by myself and I am sure by you. Though I had several differences of opinion with Alex, I was personally fond of him, but did not feel that he was the type that would make a good airline pilot, but understand with the Ferry Command he did very well indeed.*

McConachie went on to brief Sheldon on events which had taken place with the new airline, and a prediction of what might happen throughout 1943, and later, for CPAL:

> *Our organization is progressing very satisfactorily. We are now operating two trips a day from Edmonton to Whitehorse, one at night and one in the day. We expect to take delivery of three Lodestars next month which will allow us to run from Vancouver to Whitehorse daily instead of just from Vancouver to Fort St. John. This will give us three departures and arrivals each day at Whitehorse. We are also starting on Wednesday to run a daily service from Whitehorse to Fairbanks (Alaska).*
>
> *Many of the junior pilots have been promoted to captaincy and are doing a very good job. Bud Potter is now flying Lodestars on the Yukon, and North Sawle is Chief pilot and doing an excellent job in connection with (Hollick-) Kenyon on the pilot training.*
>
> *Jarvis and Knox from the Prairie Airways are here now and Harvey Johnston is flying a (Boeing) 247 from Whitehorse to Dawson. (Don) Patry is Chief pilot at Vancouver and has Ballantyne and Beckett as captains with him.*
>
> *We are also running Boeings daily down the Mackenzie (River) to Norman Wells and have such old pilots as McNeal, Robinson and Ken Dewar on this work.*
>
> *This coming year we will have flown more miles than T.C.A., insofar as commercial operations are concerned, about the sixth largest in the world – and this is really something, especially when you consider that we have had the organization going for only about a year.*
>
> *Out of Edmonton this coming summer, we will be operating eight Lockheeds, six Boeing 247s and eight Barkley Grows, as we are gradually getting our aircraft standardized in the different districts.*
>
> *We have enlarged our hangar at Edmonton and increased our stewardess staff (some really choice parcels here now).*
>
> *Vic Fox was just in to see me and he had just completed 110 hours and did 22,000 miles (35,406 km) this month, which gives him a cheque of about $940 for one month's work. If the United States' airline basis of pay had been in effect, he would have made $1,100.*

In closing he invited Sheldon to stay in touch with him and let him know how things were going in Ferry Command. Few in Canadian aviation really knew or understood the very close relationship which had matured between these two men.

Sheldon was earning $1,000 a month as a ferry service pilot.

**Despite losses, safety record much, much higher than anticipated… despite repeated evidence of Nazi sabotage to planes**

Ferry / Transport Command racked up a remarkable safety record, with extremely few losses given the thousands and thousands of planes systematically and regularly delivered to active theatres of war all over the planet. Those accidents that did take place were attributed to either successful Nazi sabotage efforts and / or deficiencies within the aircraft themselves, and rarely, if ever, from pilot error.

Sabotage is suspected as having caused a bomber to crash in the heart of downtown Montréal, and brief news reports of the day indicated some men and women had been arrested, suspected of spying.

Newspaper clippings and other sources throughout Canada - mainly the memories of men and women with whom I have spoken since this book first began taking form early in 1979 hint strongly that the Nazis tried their hand at sabotage, right in Dorval itself.

For example, engine-related problems on the B-17s demanded close scrutiny – a few had been lost over the ocean, and no one knew why until pilots began experiencing related engine problems between Montréal and Gander, especially towards the end of the first leg.

Engines would begin to cut out, one at a time, too close to the airport for comfort, and the ferry service had to know why.

Fortunately for all concerned, the problems seemed to occur mainly on nearing Gander, before they refueled the aircraft to resume the delivery trip over the North Atlantic.

Detailed inspections discovered that the long air intakes leading to the carburetors had been loosely stuffed with varying amounts of excelsior, or steel wool.

By the time the planes arrived near Gander, the air had forced the stuffing to compact so much that little or no air was making its way into the carburetor. The compaction would worsen as the air pressure made a tighter and tighter squeeze of the material, and eventually would have plugged the air intake pipes solid.

Undoubtedly whoever stuffed the air intake pipes had high hopes that the engines would lose power over the ocean and crash, without a trace.

Sadly enough, a number of them did just that – vanish, without a word, without a trace.

## Flight and accepting testing provided yeoman service

Ferry Command, before the upgrading to Transport Command, had already established a testing division to detect, among other things, any attempts at sabotage, which was taking place despite a tight security system at Dorval.

The test division also conducted acceptance and performance flight tests on each arriving aircraft, similar to those conducted today whenever a manufacturer delivers a new plane to a customer. In addition, they flight-tested them in conditions anticipated over the oceans, checking out such performance characteristics as handling, fuel flow systems, instrument calibration, engine settings and radio and navigation equipment.

The incidents and accidents were closely investigated under unrelenting pressure for remedial action. Flight planning obviously wasn't at fault, nor were pilot and aircrew proficiency the culprits.

But something threatened to play havoc with the safety record, such as an unusually high number of bone-dry fuel tanks while over the ocean, especially with the Venturas.

Continuous work loads at the manufacturing plants inevitably imposed severe stress conditions, which could have resulted in defective components making their way into aircraft frames, a situation which could not altogether be avoided.

In a bid to push production records even higher, Americans had adopted an "E for Effort" flag, a monthly recognition given to industry workers who outdid previous production records.

All that was entailed in this "bonus" was the flying of a large, attractively coloured banner, with the letter "E" emblazoned on it. Many industry leaders, ranking politicians and military officers wondered if this was a wise move relative to accuracy and quality control, as it soon became a highly competitive thing to see which production crew would win the award next month.

Linked with sabotage, these factors could only cast a pall on what so far had been a phenomenal safety performance.

Al Lilly, previously with the Royal Canadian Mounted Police, headed the testing division.

Civilian aircrews did most of the test flying - pilots were either assigned to Al or he managed to borrow them from somewhere within the group.

Military pilots rarely stayed long enough within the ferry service to be used with any regularity on test flights, which demanded a high degree of continuity in supervision and sustained performance levels by pilots and their crews.

For all the risks they incurred, they did not receive any special favours over other ferry pilots. The best they could claim as a bonus was that they got to go home after a day's work.

If nothing went wrong with their plane, that is.

Some bonus, but it did have its benefits where family men were concerned.

Whenever Sheldon became available in between ferry and communication flights, Al did everything possible to have the necessary orders cut to take advantage of Sheldon's vast experience for his testing division.

One of these flights physically shook Sheldon and his crew to their bones. He'd been checking out two Boston A-20 attack bombers. Planes destined for overseas were provided with extra fuel tanks, installed in different configurations on different aircraft.

Two straps secured those extra internal tanks to the inside of the A-20 fuselage.

He gave the first A-20 a clean bill of health.

Over Montreal, he'd started checking out the systems on the second bomber when all hell seemed to break loose on board.

Certain the A-20 was coming apart at the seams, his crew hastily strapped their parachutes to their backs. Chutes were stock items on all testing and ferry flights, but more often than not during test flights, and even on ferry flights, crew members simply kept their parachutes handy, near their stations.

Before Sheldon gave the order to bail out, all the vibrations mysteriously stopped.

Sheldon couldn't put his finger on what had caused them and began to experiment with different power settings to see if he could duplicate the conditions, and determine if, in fact, they were related to certain speeds and power demands.

Nothing more happened.

Ground inspections revealed the cause of the vibrations: the forward belly tank strap had come loose, allowing the tank to flop around, whopping and smacking into the fuselage, scaring the crew nearly witless. This incident probably fell into the category of human oversight and failure to secure the strap properly before take-off.

Extremely warm weather and a set of manufacturer's specifications compounded a mechanical problem on one of these tests flights. These circumstances generated a lot of confusion, both in the air and on the ground, as Sheldon had to decide between bailing out and saving his life or go for broke, risk his life, but save another aircraft for the war effort.

This one was a Martin Marauder, a B-26. During one such flight one of the tests called for a routine feathering of the engines, one at a time, of course.

The first feathering test failed – the large four-bladed Curtiss Wright electric propeller on the number two (starboard) engine wouldn't de-feather, preventing an engine re-start. The blades remained fixed, facing forward and offering least resistance to the wind. They had to be returned to a normal angle-of-attack position before the engine could be restarted.

Several attempts to de-feather proved futile, and Sheldon gave up on that procedure, reporting the problem to the tower. Temperature factors came into play at this stage. Sheldon could not risk landing the B-26 on the runway in this heat on just one engine.

A B-26 on one engine at lower landing speeds, in high temperatures, was also sluggish in handling - Sheldon couldn't use any final approach flap settings at all under these conditions. This would force the B-26 to arrive over the runway at an excessively high speed.

Sheldon knew that the Dorval runways were too short at that time to handle multi-engine aircraft landing there at high speeds.

He would quickly run out of runway before the airplane stopped rolling.

But Sheldon also knew that he might make it if – and only if – he had a good, long runway in front of him.

Had the air been cold, and denser, it might have been different; hot air doesn't provide nearly the amount of lift which cold air does.

The tower, when notified of the problem, immediately got Al Lilly into the picture, and he and Sheldon discussed the options. Quite a gathering of interested parties made it to the tower that afternoon. Everyone in the tower came to a unanimous conclusion: bail out over an uninhabited area near the airport, and let the plane crash.

He consulted with his crew on the bail-out recommendation. Not only did he hate to see a plane crunch into the ground, but there was always also the risk of hurting someone nearby.

But he hated something also as well: abandoning a perfectly good plane in mid-flight.

Nevertheless, he and his three crew members donned their parachutes, just in case.

If the plane had been on fire, he wouldn't have had any qualms about jumping.

His first plan had been to make a wheels-up, belly landing on the grass adjacent to the runways.

Too risky.

His second strategy: come in from a l-o-n-g way out, straight and low, wheels down, and just as the wheels were to touch the runway, retract the landing gear and hope to damage nothing more than the underside of the fuselage.

Briefing his crew on this second alternative, they decided not to bail out and stick it out with him.

They were going in.

Fate decided to intervene.

During this time, Sheldon hadn't bothered trying to re-start number two engine. Without really knowing why he did so, he tried to de-feather the prop.

It worked, and he gave the engine start control a whack.

Cough.

Sputter.

Vroom.

It stalled.

Suddenly, things returned to normal. And the plane had additional power.

But it was so hot, that even with full flaps down, the B-26 brakes burned by the time that plane rolled to a full stop at the end of the runway. The problem was later shown to be a minor one. The engine re-start system, which included the de feathering mechanism, had overheated, and only did its job when it was allowed to cool sufficiently!

Al Lilly wrote of Sheldon:

> He was one of our best and most experienced pilots, and was called on to fly many of the special VIP flights. I suspect that many others would agree that he was one of a handful of former airline pilots that would be trusted to fly anyone in any plane under difficult wartime conditions. I never knew Sheldon to tend towards exaggeration.

### Smoke spooks four of his eighteen passengers into jumping, two with parachutes... two without

This reputation of playing it straight and cool, as noted by Al, served Sheldon well, especially after a tragic series of circumstances played out while he was airborne on Saturday, May 14th, 1943.

That's the day four of his eighteen passengers left his Ventura, in flight - two without parachutes and two with parachutes.

Every now and then pilots found themselves assigned to milk-runs, sandwiched in between their ocean and trans-continental trips. Sheldon found himself on such a trip that Saturday. He had filed a flight plan for the Ventura from Dorval to Goose Bay to Gander, with a scheduled return with passengers and mixed cargo/air mail.

Heading south from the Labrador mainland airport of Goose Bay, making for Gander on the island of Newfoundland, Sheldon checked his instruments: the Ventura was cruising nicely at 12,000 feet (3,658 m), doing about 230 miles an hour (370 km/hr).

All seemed well, except for a slight odour as if something was burning.

Something was burning.

Out of sight.

He'd soon be crossing the Strait of Belle Isle, not too far ahead, which separates the island of Newfoundland from the Labrador mainland.

The aroma rapidly turned into visible smoke. He cast a questioning glance at co-pilot Tommy Mahann and then to radio operator Johnny Berton. He asked Johnny to check the cabin to see if any of his passengers was, or had been smoking.

Before Johnny could return to the cockpit and make his report, Sheldon located the source of the smoke. It was now billowing upwards, from between the rudder pedals under his feet.

He immediately suspected the cockpit heater, located in the navigator's position below the cockpit, thinking it was overheating. The compartment contained airmail bags for this run, and little else. Had there been a navigator, the problem would not have occurred.

Tommy opened the hatch in the cockpit floor and went into the navigator's compartment to check out the small gas heater, which heated the cockpit through duct work, and found no sign of any flames, though there was a lot of smoke.

While Tommy was below, Johnny had returned to report no one in the passenger cabin had been smoking. Soon Tommy returned to his seat; all three crew members were now mystified.

The northern coastline of Newfoundland slipped by nearly three miles (5 km) below, and soon the bomber was well over the northern reaches of the inland.

Suddenly, a shock wave shuddered through the Ventura.

Sheldon knew exactly what had happened, but not why it happened.

The passenger cabin door had been flung wide open, ripped off the fuselage by the blast of air and hurtled into the 230 mile-an-hour (370 km/hr) slipstream. It had mashed into the fuselage on its way out.

Somebody had opened that door.

Manufacturer's specifications indicated the door could be opened in flight, to permit parachute drops, but not until the airspeed had been reduced to safe operating limits.

This move could have killed everyone on board.

Sheldon ordered Johnny to go back and take a look at what happened.

He returned to the cockpit, bug-eyed, and yelled out:

"For God's sake, Skipper, they're jumping!"

Stunned at this news, Sheldon screamed back: "For Christ's sake! Stop them! Stop them!"

He ordered Johnny to prevent any more unauthorized abandoning of the ship in flight, and immediately reduced power setting while simultaneously pushing the nose of the aircraft down, as fast as he could, hoping that gravity forces would glue his obviously eager-to-leave passengers down onto the cabin floor, and prevent any further bodily motion back there.

In the meantime, he still had the smoke to deal with. Meeting thoughts of fire scudded around his mind: that smoke had to be coming from somewhere. And now the passengers were jumping! Jeezus!

Maybe an engine fire.

He couldn't see any.

But perhaps it was inside one of the engines and not visible yet.

He just didn't know. Nor could he risk hitting the fire extinguishing button for either of the two engines. If it was an engine fire, he could only hope that the faster airflow brought about by the diving action could put it out!

As a precaution, he closed the switch on the cockpit heater, but the smoke still lingered.

So he put the airplane into a dive – hoping that the increased airspeed might blow out the engine fire, then pulled the plane out of the dive, climbing rapidly. When it reached the top of its upward arc, he levelled out the airplane... this action had another desired effect than that of putting out the fire – which Sheldon later learned was *not* in either engine. All of the passengers were now plastered securely to the floor, and he no longer had them to worry about. So he thought.

What had taken place was that, in putting the plane into a high-speed dive, then rapidly pulling up and out to climb, at the top of the climb, as he brought the plane into normal flight, gravity had taken over and the passengers, who for a few moments experienced a no-gravity situation at the top of the arc were pulled right back on to the floor by nothing more complicated than the laws of gravity.

Assured that no one else would jump, most likely through the sheer panic-stricken look in the eyes and faces of the remaining passengers, Johnny returned to the cockpit to make his report.

Finally back on level flight, Sheldon handed the controls over to Tommy and went back to investigate.

He had to try and find out exactly what had happened.

He quickly learned that four of his passengers were gone.

A young corporal who had boarded in Goose Bay told Sheldon that one of the passengers panicked, jumped for the fuselage door when he saw the smoke coming from around the cockpit door, and yelled to the other passengers: "Abandon ship, she's on fire!"

He then jettisoned the cabin door and jumped, without a parachute.

Parachutes had been issued to each passenger before the plane had left Goose Bay.

After Johnny's first check with the passengers, and his return to the cockpit, the passengers could see more smoke coming from up front.

When the young serviceman panicked, some passengers had started strapping themselves into their chute harnesses, while others already had them on,

Three others had stood in line behind the panic-stricken first man.

After he jumped, a second man jumped.

*With* a parachute.

Then there was a rush by other passengers to prevent the others from leaving. In the rush, a third man jumped.

*Without* a parachute.

Then, a fourth, *with* a parachute.

There was nothing more that Sheldon could do but fly the crippled Ventura into Gander.

After landing, a closer look at the tail section revealed that one of two men who jumped had his body severed by the horizontal section of the twin-rudder tail boom.

The two men who jumped without a parachute were never found.

The same inspection identified the problem about the smoke. The gasoline-fired cockpit heater below the cockpit floor had a broken exhaust pipe, and the smoke quickly made its way above, into the cockpit. The mail bags, though not lying on the exhaust pipe, had hidden the exhaust pipe from Tommy's view when he went down to inspect.

Sheldon's action in cutting the power to the heater was a wise one, because, had the smoke persevered, the cockpit crew ran the risk of carbon monoxide poisoning.

The enquiry board asked Sheldon, his crew and passengers if he or his crew had conducted themselves in such as manner as to precipitate a panic among the passengers.

The crew and all of the remaining passengers each gave the same answer: No.

Sheldon said that he had never been able to quite understand what motivated that first young man, a sailor, so precipitously. He likely started to panic, not quite losing control of his reasoning ability, when he saw Johnny come from the cockpit to ask if anyone was smoking, or had been smoking.

As the smoke continued to issue from the cockpit, he must have panicked, and in the unpressurized and noisy cabin likely did not hear or understand Johnny's instructions for all to remain calm. The sailor assumed that the emergency was out of the pilot's control.

Out of compassion for the missing passengers and their families, Sheldon never did enter all of the details into his official written report on the incident. He knew full well just how strong the tendency was to panic under certain emergency conditions, having been there before many times in the bush.

What of the pair who jumped with parachutes?

They made national headlines when they were accidently found and rescued fifty days later, starving and debilitated to a point where a few more days would have brought their death.

Officials at the enquiry thought they might have jumped over the Strait of Belle Isle and made their way to safety near the coastline. They later learned after their rescue that they had actually landed about 20 miles (32 km) from the Straight of Belle Isle – almost 35 miles (nearly 54 km) inland.

The late Jack Hogan was a Newfoundland Ranger when he, as the second man in line, left the aircraft. Something had made him pause at the last second.

He had changed his mind and decided to not jump, but he was pushed from behind by the third man, the second one who had left the airplane without a parachute.

And behind Hogan, came RAF Corporal Eric Butt; this was his first-ever parachute jump.

The families of the missing men were notified in the conventional manner, with an explanation that they had been lost while carrying out military duties in wartime.

Because of the highly unusual and circumspect nature of the hasty evacuation, no explanations were given to the families as to why their sons lost their lives.

If mechanical problems didn't cause enough difficulties, sometimes natural curiosity only made it worse – such as the time a bad engine bearing put Sheldon into a situation where he inadvertently discovered a top-secret base in California.

The flight originated out of Dorval, with a converted Hudson bomber.

The Hudsons were similar to the Lockheed 14 airliners but had larger Wright Cyclone engines. His passengers included Canadian and British officials headed out on a round-robin aircraft production inspection, led by Ralph Bell, who had been appointed by Prime Minister Mackenzie King as Canada's Director of Aircraft Production.

Scheduled stops included Winnipeg, Edmonton and Vancouver in Canada, then south into the United States, with stops in Seattle, Washington, and San Francisco and Los Angeles, California.

Everything stayed routine until San Francisco, which like Los Angeles, is well known for its fog banks – they were more like real fog banks then than the infamous smog funks of today.

The commission spent several days in San Francisco.

On the appointed departure day, his seven passengers were on board by 5:30 a.m.

Sheldon had filed a flight plan calling for a 6 a.m. departure from the Mill airfield in San Francisco.

He had made it as far as the runway, and was number two in the line-up waiting for visibility to improve to take-off limits. He was behind a United Airlines DC-3, also waiting for take-off clearance from the Mill Field tower.

It came and the DC-3 lifted into the thinning fog. As Sheldon taxied onto the active runway, visibility continued to improve. He brought the Hudson up through to clear air and reported his arrival at 2,300 feet (610 m) above sea level.

No sooner had he completed his report to the tower, the right engine seized. It marked the first time he'd seen an engine seize so abruptly. He realized he'd automatically – like a robot – gone through the propeller-feathering procedure and fuel shut-off routine before he was fully conscious of his actions.

The main engine bearing had disintegrated.

Bell sat in the first right-hand passenger seat. An active aviation buff, he was convinced that the engine had seized up too quickly and was generating so much torque that it seemed certain to him that the torque would twist that wing enough to snap it right off – to break it clean away from the fuselage.

It took a little while, but Sheldon diplomatically assured him the wing wasn't about to separate from the fuselage, and that it had not flexed more than normal.

Sheldon duly reported his emergency to the tower, only to be told that as long as he could stay airborne, he should hold to a flight pattern circling about in the southwest quadrant of the radio range

While flying in his assigned holding pattern, Sheldon looked down through a large break in the fog, and sighted a huge, paved area.

Seconds later he saw a very large blimp tethered to a tower. Reporting this to the tower as a superb landing spot, Sheldon was a bit taken aback by the controller's reply – that he had been planning to land at a top-secret restricted area, and he mustn't even consider landing there at all, unless it was an absolute emergency, of course.

The tower also advised him that visibility at Mill field had improved and that if he could remain airborne a bit longer, he could return for a landing. Until further notice, he received approval to circle the immense field below, and proceeded to do just that: circle a top-secret military base for almost an hour, until he got his clearance to return to Mill Field.

He brought the Hudson in without any problem and at the end of its roll-out waited for a tractor to come and tow it away. The tail-dragging Hudson had little taxiing ability on one engine alone, unlike that possessed by a plane equipped with a tricycle landing gear.

### Denying denial of permission to take-off leads to King's Commendation

The flight for which Sheldon received a Commendation from England's King George VI began with a dubious dispatcher in Miami who wouldn't let him get off the ground.

It also happened to be the last trip he'd make for the same RAFEC, late in the winter of 1943-44, not long after the "secret" base "discovery" – only this flight was headed across the South Atlantic span to hop over to Africa and on to England.

The flight began in Dorval but only got as far as Waller Field in Trinidad when the aircraft became unserviceable. Crew assignment alerted Sheldon in Dorval to report for duty and take a specially-converted Liberator, AL-913, which had become one of his favourites from having flown it so often to Trinidad.

Mechanical problems grounded this plane at Dorval, so Sheldon was forced to find another, and received a Douglas C-47, which had been modified to a DC-3 specification, but with a somewhat crowded passenger cabin.

The sixteen seats at the rear of the passenger cabin faced a huge Goodrich rubber fuel bladder which had been installed to give it staying power over the Atlantic.

Since it was a new machine, Sheldon looked forward to the trip to Trinidad and Africa, where he was to pick up his eight very important passengers.

He ran into a reluctant dispatcher in Miami when re-fuelling for the next hop to Trinidad. The American Air Force had taken over dispatching Allied Forces aircraft on the South Atlantic. Accordingly, Sheldon and his navigator had laid out their entire flight plan on the dispatcher's desk.

The big burly dispatcher checked it over carefully, but denied them take-off permission.

Too risky, he said.

Too long a flight for a C-47, considering the extremely adverse headwinds likely to be encountered over the South Atlantic at this time of year.

Plenty of fuel on board, especially with the additional bladder, noted Sheldon.

Nope. Not even with the internal bladder. Not enough.

The USAF had recently incurred a number of losses over the South Atlantic, which they attributed, correctly or incorrectly, to inadequate fuel. This prompted the activation of the Ascension Island base, as it lay about half-way between Natal in Brazil and Africa.

Try as hard as he could, that sergeant wouldn't budge. It didn't matter to him that Sheldon had filed an identical flight plan to the complete satisfaction of the Royal Air Force Transport Command dispatcher in Dorval and, he was here, now, wasn't he?

However, there was a way, if he could prove to the sergeant facing him that there was enough fuel on board.

Show me, said the sergeant.

Quite easily done.

Sheldon simply reverted to an old bush tactic.

Without telling the sergeant his plans, Sheldon and his navigator ambled over to the non-commissioned officer in charge of the fuel dump. If the fuel bladder in front of the passengers wouldn't do, then three additional 45-gallon drums, loaded with fuel, might just satisfy this dispatcher.

A little sweet talking at the dump, and soon, three fuel drums, a manual pump, hose lengths, funnel and spare cloths were loaded into a truck, and secured inside the C-47.

Back to dispatch with the new fuel load, all signed by the dump NCO.

Now would he release the C-47?

Shaking his head slowly in absolute wonderment, the sergeant yielded to superior bush wisdom and approved the flight plan.

Next stop, Trinidad.

Then on to the South American bases, over the South Atlantic, and get to Ascension.

At no time did Sheldon ever need the fuel from those three drums, and he dropped them off at Ascension, telling the NCO in charge of that fuel dump that he was off-loading them for a VIP aircraft which would soon follow his arrival. Sheldon later returned to find the same three full barrels set aside in some unused corner of the dump.

### German fighter pilots "make" Sheldon off the Bay of Biscay

The flight continued to Port Violte, which was then held by the Free French.

Normally the flight would have terminated there for Sheldon, but the RAFEC wanted him to take his passengers on to England. He knew that he had enough fuel on board and if necessary, he could always stop in at Gibraltar to top off the tanks.

His flight plan and course took the C-47 on a route some distance offshore and parallel to the coasts of Portugal and Spain.

Pilots flying this area had been thoroughly briefed on Allied suspicions that the Germans had illegally set up fighter aircraft bases in Spain, violating Spain's supposed neutrality status. A few aircraft had been inexplicably lost at sea along the coastline, and since no one knew for certain they hadn't been shot down, it was better to be informed and be forced to fly further out over the ocean than come too close to the Iberian Peninsula.

He planned to stay well out to sea, and clip along by the outer limits of the Bay of Biscay, the danger area, and make a beeline for Henley Airport, near London.

The VIPs on board included a very senior air force officer, a member of the British cabinet, and other high-ranking military officers and civilian personnel.

Sheldon's navigator on the flight deck was also monitoring radio traffic.

The C-47 droned on, well away from the north Spanish coastline, nearing the Bay of Biscay. His navigator, who worked in Cook's travel agencies before the war, spoke several languages fluently, one of them German. Knowing this ahead of time, Sheldon asked him to stay alert while they flew over this suspect area.

The navigator stiffened in his seat, then jumped out of it.

"Skipper, we've got German fighters close by. They're so close and so certain of who we are that they're not coding their transmissions. They're broadcasting in the clear, and they think they're closing in on us!"

Knowing that a lumbering C-47 couldn't possibly hope to take any kind of evasive action against high speed German fighters, Sheldon quickly saw the only way to escape them – hide in the cloud decks below.

Instinctively, he switched off everything electrical inside the aircraft which he knew wasn't necessary to sustain flight. Warning his passengers about his next few steps, he led the C-47 into a nose dive, heading for the cloud cover as fast as it would gel there. Radio altimeters hadn't been installed in this new plane, so he had to be careful to judge his descent just right. It wouldn't do to avoid enemy fighters just to nosedive into the ocean.

The C-47 broke out underneath the cloud layer, a scant 500 feet (152 m) above the raging, breaking waves below. Nothing more was heard from the German fighters. Sheldon had been warned they might have fairly sophisticated radio detection gear, and for this reason, shut off anything electronic on board the C-47, just in case the enemy detection gear was sensitive enough to home in on his aircraft.

For what seemed an eternity in time, the C-47 flew just above the waves. The patchy cloud cover above was just perfect. Too dark and Sheldon would have had a hard time maintaining a safe distance above the water, too light and the Germans could have found him.

In May 1944, Sheldon became one of the twenty-eight men in Ferry Command to receive an award, or commendation, from his sovereign for exemplary service during the war years.

Royal recognition notwithstanding, there would be no such accolades from his former home office in Canadian Pacific Air Lines.

A month later, a letter from McConachie dulled his prospects for getting his old job back with CPAL.

He'd be welcomed back, all right, but to what position?

Grant's letter:

> ...I was indeed more than pleased to see that you have been commended by the King for your valuable service on the Atlantic operation.

*We are busy as the devil cutting down on our staff here in Edmonton. The old line really built up for a while, but after Mr. Howe's statement, things have been getting tough. The army are taking about eighteen of our pilots, and even with that reduction it may be necessary to let out more.*

*The Canadian Pilots Association has signed an agreement with our company, and it really is a dilly. I think as far as you are concerned, that your seniority will count for the time you have been with Ferry Command up to and for an additional 90 days after the agreement was signed.*

*After that, your seniority will not accrue.*

*I am giving you this information as it appears to me, without studying your particular case very closely.*

*Generally speaking, the agreement docs not allow for seniority to accrue in Air Observer Schools, and the Ferry Command.*

*However, you can rest assured Sheldon, that anything I can do in this regard, I will be only too glad to do.*

*My family are 100% and I sincerely hope yours are the same.*

*I am going to Douglas Island on the invitation of the General Manager of the B.O.A.C. and may have something important to tell you on my return from England. I will give you a call on my way through Montréal. I expect to be leaving here around the 1ˢᵗ of August.*

*With kindest.*

### Gets rep as Churchill's personal... mailman

Not all of the work was done under tension, stress or raw nerve-tingling loads.

Some of it was downright routine. But at times, it took on an exceedingly high-profile nature, such as the time he was called on to fly mail for Sir Winston Churchill during one of the two historic meetings between Churchill and Roosevelt in Québec City.

He and Johnny Berton had been assigned a Hudson for the September, 1944 conference.

The Hudson was on the ramp at the Ancienne Lorette airport – which served Québec – for the duration of the meeting. Sheldon and Johnny were both billeted at the famous Chateau Frontenac, where the conference was being held.

The British Government had taken over the entire complex for the conference, and no one could enter or leave without an escort. During their stay, he and Johnny were always accompanied by a two-man escort, even during nocturnal or daily visits to the city itself, for shopping or a meal.

When it came time to pick up the dispatches from England in Presque Isle, Maine, Sheldon and Johnny would be escorted to their waiting aircraft by military vehicle. Their MPs in Ancienne Lorette stayed with them as they filed their flight plan, did their walk-around aircraft inspection, topped the tanks, and waited until the pilots boarded the plane, and closed the passenger cabin door, sealing it and the mail.

The MPs lingered until they saw the craft taxi out for take-off.

From there, a 55-minute flight took them into Maine, usually arriving at the airport about one o'clock in the morning. If the incoming American transport, a C-54, was early, or on time, there'd be an immediate, on-the-runway transfer of mail bags for the British delegation, and a specially designated mail pouch for Churchill.

Neither Sheldon nor Johnny ever left their plane in Maine, even if the C-54 came in late.

With the mail secured, Sheldon and Johnny flew back to Ancienne Lorette, to be met by their waiting MPs for an escort back to the Chateau.

From this point on, Sheldon became known within the organization as Churchill's personal mailman.

## 9. 231 Telecommunications Squadron, Royal Air Force

What began as a routine communications flight out of Rabat, Morocco and led to an engine fire out of the Azores provoked Sheldon to do something about returning to boat operations in the spring of 1944.

Sheldon had flown Liberator AL-593 to the Azores without incident. Fog had begun to settle in over the airport on take-off, but he managed to squeak out before it socked the airfield right in.

No sooner had 593 broken out of the fog, about 1,000 feet (305 m) above the waves and into a clear, moonlit night, when number two engine caught fire.

Engineer Gale Sweeney initiated emergency procedures to deal with an engine fire, first shutting off the fuel supply to the engine, then cutting the ignition while almost simultaneously tripping the first of two extinguishers in the engine itself.

Nothing happened. The fire wouldn't go out. He tripped the second extinguisher. Still, the fire raged.

AL 593 had cleared the island's rocky beaches, leaving the overland fog behind. Sheldon and the crew knew they couldn't return. One option left if the fire wouldn't go out – ditch.

Eyes darted below looking for a likely forced-landing spot, but there weren't any. Only rocks meeting water.

The entire crew was frightened. An airborne fire is a terrifying experience, especially one the crew can't control, out on a wing. They could only sit, helpless, in what could in the next few seconds become eternity for them.

Suddenly, the fire went out.

Although the fire had lasted only a few minutes, it had felt like hours to the crew.

A few seconds later the feathering system on the dead engine did its job, and Sheldon redistributed power settings to the remaining three engines and continued flying west. What else could he do?

He could have stuck to his original flight plan, going on to Gander for fuel, overnighting and resuming the leg to Montreal the following day. But, he didn't feel like sitting around at Gander when he had three perfectly good functioning engines which could take him directly to Montreal. He knew that if he landed the Liberator at Gander, operations would have him remain with the aircraft until a new engine was flown from Montreal and installed; this held no appeal for him.

Since the tanks were full, there was no reason not to fly directly to Montreal. Navigator Bill Roberts gave him a course correction, and later, announced that a good stiff tail wind was rapidly improving their east-to-west crossing time.

After consulting with Tim Sims, his First Officer, Sheldon decided that when Al 593 neared Nova Scotia, he'd resume radio contact and ask Sydney radio to advise Dorval that he was flying right through.

Sheldon and his crew were badly shaken by the experience. As soon as the rather lengthy debriefing ended, they all decided to accompany flight engineer Ron Williams to his apartment for a couple of snorts. One snort turned into two, and two became a party, with the crew temporarily drowning their memories of the harrowing incident.

Not quite drunk, nor quite sober, Sheldon decided then and there in Ron's apartment that he'd had it with airplanes that only landed on wheels. The time had come to return to flying boats. At least if an engine problem developed out at sea he could land on the water.

One particular individual had to be convinced that Sheldon was just the right pilot for him – Air Commodore Andy Fletcher, a Lethbridge, Alberta, native.

Sheldon had met him during his aviation pioneering days. However, A/C Fletcher was now a senior officer in the Dorval hierarchy. A/C Fletcher completed his education on the Prairies, went to Britain and worked his way up through the ranks of the Royal Air Force.

Sheldon fired up his courage and railed the Air Commodore, who gave him, to his surprise, a decent hearing. A/C Fletcher promised to do what he could for Sheldon after listening to a rather lengthy, almost one-sided, conversation.

Forgetting about the conversation, Sheldon was quite surprised when a crew assignment chief came up to him with a message that A/C Fletcher wanted to contact him, at once.

Sheldon called him right away.

"Luck, are you still interested in flying Coronado boats?"

Sheldon nearly fell over in pleasant shock and disbelief.

Fletcher explained that when Sheldon first called him, there hadn't been any vacancies in the operation, and that he hadn't really expected any. But one of his Australian captains, an experienced boat pilot, decided to transfer back to an Australian operation, creating the new slot.

Late in October 1944, Sheldon headed for the administration office in Dorval, picked up his new travel warrants, checked his gear and headed south. Direct to Elizabeth City, North Carolina, where the United States had a satellite flying boat school for its Pensacola, Florida main training base.

### When 231 first saw light of day

No. 231 Squadron came to life in August 1918, making it through until World War II despite having been disbanded and reformed several times to suit the various needs of the RAF. Disbanded once more on January 15th, 1944, at Redhill, England, it was resurrected on September 8th, 1944, to serve Transport Command.

Its purpose: fly long-range transport aircraft across the Atlantic, and maintain regular schedules to and from Iceland and Prestwick, using Liberators, Dakotas, Hudsons, Skymasters and Coronado flying boats.

No one got on board 231's operational flight roster without a lot of civilian airline experience.

Sheldon met the criteria, as did TCAL's Jack Bradley, Bud Scouten and Eric Bentall, along with a number of pilots from American Airlines, TWA and United.

Its Liberators were extensively modified to suit long-range personnel transport and were outfitted with up to sixteen seats, complete with all the trappings of high office, such as plush rugs. Squadron 231 pilots operated a high-profile, exclusive charter service, which gave the illusion of being a somewhat cushier job than routine ferry flying.

Undoubtedly so, but the demands imposed on 231 pilots were equal to and more than those imposed by active airline operations. Its aircrews had to be tops.

The American Navy offered a number of courses on the PBYs, the twin-engine Mariner Martin and the Coronado flying boats. They would train Sheldon.

Dick Gentry, already placed in the unit by Fletcher, became Sheldon's mentor in flying boat training and upgrading to the Coronados. A retired U.S. Navy hand, Gentry had already taken his refresher course, and also served as Sheldon's check pilot. RAF S/L George Fry assisted in flight training in Elizabeth City, and helped crews in such things as discipline, protocol, accommodations, living habits and other routines which incoming foreign pilots could expect on American bases.

George had been checked out on almost anything which flew from the water, and frequently was Sheldon's co-pilot as Sheldon went through his stiff training regime.

### The Beauharnois, Bermuda and Bathurst

Almost from the day he joined the ferry service, Sheldon had heard about a special flying boat operation which would be established some day. To fly one of these giant machines would have been a dream come true for Sheldon, considered one of the best boatmen in Canadian aviation

All Coronado pilots had to be fully qualified on instrument flight, and have a thorough background on large multi-engine aircraft. Check flights were frequent and often without warning.

The Coronados were immense flying boats, ranking among the world's largest at the time, second in size only to the Pan Am Clipper ships. Three had been assigned to 231 Squadron: *Beauharnois, Bermuda* and *Bathurst*.

The Coronado had a 115-foot (35 m) long wingspan, and when measured from its nose to its twin-boom tail, stretched out at 79 feet (24 m), three inches (7.6 cm).

A six-foot man looked pretty small standing alongside the 27-foot 6 inch (8.15 m) high amphibian aircraft which could take its crew of 10 to a range of 1,490 miles (1,609 km), at a maximum speed of 213 miles an hour (343 km/hr), at 20,000 feet (6,096 m).

The engines gave out enough power to yield an average speed of about 180 miles an hour at between 14,000 (4,267 m) and 15,000 feet (4,572 m). Pilots also considered these same engines its major drawback as they had a high failure potential which created numerous problems.

On long hauls, the Coronado could ferry about 90,000 pounds (40,823 kg), with a crew roster consisting of a pilot, first officer, two flight engineers, and navigation officer. A radio-navigation officer would handle both chores on shorter legs. Depending on the number and standing of passengers, the crew list could also include two stewards for VIP service, one of whom also doubled as a spare engineer.

An electric galley with refrigeration and electric stove supplemented the culinary service which came with the six bed sleeping accommodations.

Sure beat putting a Fokker down on Deadman's Lake!

Seats were removed on freight, cargo and war supplies flights, and the cabin, fourteen steps below the cockpit, became a cavernous cargo bay with an overhead track system for heavy freight. The Coronado could easily handle the largest engine available in World War II.

Sheldon spent day after day practicing take offs and landings in these giant machines, taking full advantage of his previous experience in handling float planes for UAT / YSAT, which included the Ford Tri-Motor, at that time the largest float-equipped plane in Canada.

The Coronado had a deadly characteristic. It's highly stubbed nose gave it, under certain load conditions, a tendency to want to porpoise on the water – to bounce up from the water surface, skip along then try to bury its nose into the water.

A definite no-no.

Pilots and load masters had to be exact in placing their loads, well distributed about the plane's centre of gravity. If the load was too far forward, or aft, the Coronado would tend to porpoise severely, and in such a mode, could self-destruct with fatal consequences for all on board.

His training also included all aspects of taxiing such a large ship, reversing and tacking to either side by judicious use of its engines. Numbers two and three were equipped with reversible pitch Curtiss-Wright electric four-blade propellers, which made it relatively easy to moor and manoeuvre the giant flying boat in tight spaces.

As with other pilots who'd had considerable water flying experience, Sheldon checked out on the Coronados fairly quickly.

### Alert first officer and quick response of the Coronado help save lives

An alert first officer and a good wind, linked with the Coronado's versatility and quick response, helped save everyone's lives on board one day in Trinidad, and prevented a collision with the stern of an American navy vessel.

Sheldon and First Officer Frank Hartley had started a routine ferry run from North America to Africa, and put down at an American navy base near Port of Spain, Trinidad.

Business completed, they prepared for a late afternoon takeoff on the nearly five-mile long harbour which sheltered a tin-roof building at its root. A mined area and an anti-submarine net afforded protection at the mouth of the harbour.

In between the moored vessels lay a long stretch of open water, perfect for flying boats - as long as there was no interfering traffic.

Sheldon had scheduled to arrive at the next stop, Natal, early next morning. On the average this leg could be flown in about fifteen to sixteen hours, once taking him eighteen fighting headwinds. Pilots liked the fact that the Coronado could stay airborne from sunrise to sunset if necessary.

A good wind coming down from the mountain would provide lift for his boat which, with fuel and cargo, grossed about 90,000 pounds (40,833 kg).

On take-off, a Coronado has a habit of coming off the step quite nicely and quickly, helped by retractable wing-tip floats. Once on the step, they were retracted into their nacelles prior to the plane taking to the air.

Sheldon had the plane doing about 60 miles (97 km) an hour; the floats were retracted. She'd be airborne soon.

At this exact moment, the stern of a navy vessel edged out of its moorage, dead ahead. This wouldn't have been so bad had it happened in the larger section of the harbour, but Sheldon had no room to turn left or right. Within seconds the Coronado would hit that stern in a fiery crash.

One or the other had to stop.

He doesn't recall calling for floats down, but a quick sideways look showed him that Frank had already reacted to the emergency and flicked the switch which had begun extending the floats. Concurrently, Sheldon pulled all the way back on his power settings. One thing a Coronado pilot could not do alone: cut back power on four engine throttles, maintain control and lower the floats at the same time.

The floats drop half-way by gravity, and an electric motor drives a long screw which extends them to full position, acting much like outriggers, providing wing-tip support.

While wondering if they'd make it to the water surface in time, Sheldon probably shoved the control column forward to bring the Coronado onto the water – he could not remember.

He rapidly put the two inboard engines into full reverse pitch and applied full power to them. This slowed the Coronado's speed in a hurry, but it also created an enormous howling sound in the harbour.

The Coronado had come down off the step intact, with only the port wing tip scraping the water, causing minor damage to two aileron ribs.

"Hartley was a fine chap and a very competent pilot," says Sheldon.

"I was too busy to see everything and call for everything which had to be done. Some First Officers would have just sat there, not even moved, waiting for instructions from their Captain. They wouldn't have taken independent action, which in this instance was absolutely necessary to avoid an accident."

Hartley's quick-thinking had narrowly averted disaster.

The Coronado stopped a few yards from the horrified looks on the sailor's faces who stood on the stern of the navy ship. Sheldon shrugged, called for and received permission from the harbour movement authority to re-start the engines, then backed some distance from the ship to his earlier moorage.

American personnel began pouring over the Coronado, inspected it, and removed the damaged aileron. They took it to their shops, made repairs overnight, and had it in place for Sheldon to resume his flight the next morning.

Few rode the Coronado unless they were of high civilian standing or top military rank. Sheldon loved that machine and did everything in his power when in control of one to treat it like a queen and a prized possession.

## Coronado goes for a sail alone, without any crew on board – and startles two lovebirds in the process

One fateful night in Nassau, in an ironic twist of fate, the flying boat he loved so much caused a lot of destruction while he slept innocently on board.

On Monday, December 11th, 1944, he'd made the long flight to Africa on Coronado JX 494, and was returning to his base in Bermuda. Sheldon left Trinidad on course, planning for a direct flight to Bermuda. En route he received warning of a gale, and chose Nassau as an alternate, having used it before. He thought Miami would likely be severely congested with all sorts of traffic and guessed that Nassau would be a quieter moorage in which to wait out the storm which was hammering Bermuda.

A heavy swell in Nassau made him execute a rough-water landing. He taxied to the larger and less active of two marine channels, and port authorities directed him to moor 494 at buoy number three. It could secure a vessel as large as the Coronado, which, when not flying, assumed all the characteristics of a cumbersome boat.

Two engineers secured 494 to the buoy with its bridle, leaving it free to weathercock in the wind without hindering nearby vessels.

After such a long trip the crew naturally wanted shore leave, which Sheldon authorized. Nassau offered more in the way of 'civilized' entertainment than what could be found in many African or Brazilian way points.

He chose to remain on board with radio-navigator, Flight Lieutenant McKinley. JX 494's galley was well-stocked, either could select a civilian radio band for good music, each had books on board, and all in all, it should make for an easy, comfortable night.

Severe motion woke Mac in the early hours of the morning. He immediately woke Sheldon: "Skipper, we're adrift! We're adrift!"

Jumping from his bunk to look out the port window, Sheldon confirmed Mac's observation. Lights were flashing by. Be-damned, it was more than just adrift!

Wearing only his shorts, he tore along the companionway, in the dark, flew up the fourteen steps, and went straight to the electrical panel on the flight deck to flick on cabin and cockpit lights.

With Sheldon on one side of the deck and Mac on the other, they looked outside to see where the 494 was going. His first conscious thought on waking was to get to the deck, fire up the inboard engines and bring the Coronado under control, and asked Mac to help him as it took two for this procedure.

In the starboard seat, Mac yelled that the starboard propellers were in the clear as soon as Sheldon flicked on the wing lights.

Things weren't so clear on the port side, however.

A huge sail boat mast stuck up at an angle of about forty-five degrees between number one and two engines. It belonged to the ship to which it was attached, below.

JX 494 had broken free of her mooring buoy and was running amok in the channel, which was also full of expensive yachts, owned by wealthy Americans. One for sure was in some state of disrepair.

Sheldon remembers having said a very bad word. Or two. Or more. The wing lights shone outward, not down, and Sheldon couldn't make out how much damage had taken place on the ship below.

This was, definitely, not good.

He remembered there were other yachts which surely had to be in 494's runaway path.

No point in trying to start the starboard engine alone; he'd just put her into more boats. He'd need both engines to extricate 494 from her awkward position and couldn't start number two because of that mast.

A shudder, a low crunching sound, and the Coronado shook once more. Not wanting to do so, Sheldon looked outside: a few more masts.

Wind gusts estimated at nearly 95 miles an hour, (153 km/hr) averaging about 60 miles an hour (97 km/hr), had rushed up the channel where 494 was moored.

The winds had abated somewhat now, but were relentlessly surging 494 into shallow waters. As the channel bottom rose to meet the surface, so rose the twin-boom tail, looming high above the Coronado.

The tail hit a beach house, shearing a corner from the roof, leaving a large gap into a bedroom below. Wide-eyed in disbelief, two naked bodies leaped from the bed and tore from the house.

Sheldon and Mac knew some hull damage must have taken place. They didn't know about the beach house or the couple, yet, but 494 was nudged into the ground now and would move no more that night. Returning to their sleeping quarters to don a pair of pants each, they next went to the aft cabin door, opened it and looked outside to see what damage 494 had wrought.

At first Sheldon and Mac saw the young couple. She was making a wild fuss about things and the young man was flapping around, still in a state of undress. Then the young woman dropped to her knees, clasped her hands together as if in prayer, and stayed there a while.

Sheldon and Mac jumped the four feet (1.2 m) from the hatch to solid ground. Soon a shore patrol jeep pulled alongside the harbour road. The native MP got out, took one look around, and went directly to the man and women.

He spoke calmly to them, trying to get their version of what had happened.

He returned and heard what Sheldon and Mac had to say. When asked what the young woman had said, the MP grinned and whispered into Sheldon's ear: "They're not married, you know, and she's convinced God did this to her as a warning. She promised to change her life from here on in."

The Coronado had struck the house with the port rudder and fin, making a mess out of the tail assembly and the house. Up front, 494 had acquired a motley collection of oversize barnacles in the form of damaged yachts.

Within two days, the vessels had been removed, 494 freed and taxied to the repair shops to have the tail damage repaired.

By Thursday, December 14, JX 494 took to the air once more, leaving a strange legacy behind: yachts in various degrees of disrepair, one sheared beach house roof and many frazzled nerve endings. Little is known to this day how the problem of making amends to the owners of the damaged yachts was handled, but obviously the problem was settled to everyone's satisfaction.

As commander of 494, Sheldon had to make out a formal report.

When he got to Bermuda, he took a Catalina PBY and flew back with his crew to Montreal, no doubt completing much of the report on the way.

An investigation exonerated him and his crew. They'd made the regulation attachment to the mooring buoy, but a connection between the buoy and its sea floor anchor had snapped, breaking it and 494 loose, free to go where the wind went. That went into his report, as did a number of photographs – no longer in his possession – which showed the extent of the damage on the next-to-final leg of a routine ferry service flight.

### Bahama Navy no longer threat to any Allied shipping

While walking down the corridor to Air Commodore Powell's office in Dorval, Sheldon saw a new, large cartoon posted on the bulletin board.

The wag who drew it did a terrific job, showing a Coronado with JX 494 markings coming down from the air in a manner similar to that of an avenging angel, dragging boats and miscellaneous debris.

Below it, a caption: "Captain Luck and the crew of the Beauharnois destroy the Navy of the Bahamas."

Another afterthought pencilled in, "Bahama Navy no longer threat to Allied shipping."

Wincing as he walked through to the A/C's office, he opened the door, gave formal greetings and presented his written and verbal reports.

Once the session ended, Sheldon rose to walk out of the office.

As he was half-way through the door, the Air Commodore said, "Oh, say Luck..."

Wheeling smartly around, Sheldon replied: "Sir!"

To which the Air commodore quipped:

"In the future when you and your boys are ready to make your next strike, will you kindly notify this office?"

## 10. Pilot of Fortune

Although he wanted to, Sheldon never did make it back to Nassau after that tumultuous day in 1944. By April 1945, he'd been transferred to Boucherville, flying the last summer of the war between Boucherville, QC in Canada and Largs, Scotland.

Released from Royal Air Force, Transport Command in the autumn of 1945 at the ripe age of thirty-three, Sheldon was now a seasoned, accomplished veteran and had earned the respect of his peers and colleagues.

But as with so many thousands of others at war's end, what to do now? For him, the answer was simple: continue flying for a living, but under which corporate flag?

A malaria bug prevented him from joining Trans-Canada Airlines to which he'd been enthusiastically invited. The uncertainties of flight crew futures with Air France – another invitation – made a move to France too risky for him and his family.

As to CPAL, well he had that "protected seniority" problem to deal with.

When he'd been in touch with Punch Dickins in 1942, he'd been promised his seniority protection, and previous position within the company. But, he remembered McConachie's letter stating that the Canadian pilots' association agreement with CPAL did not extend to Ferry Command.

Sheldon returned to the fold, not as Chief pilot, but a senior line pilot. This was a position which despite earlier promises of his being brought in with a higher seniority and position, and it suited him well enough for now.

McConachie still called the shots, but faced a lot of internal pressures. Within a couple of years he'd become CPAL's first and youngest president, and the first "outsider" within the CPR to be posted to such a senior position in a subsidiary. Even though newcomers within the ranks were generally viewed with suspicion, McConachie knew how to handle these problems.

Sheldon faced identical "newcomer" problems after the war as he had faced in 1941 and 1942.

Many within the airline had only heard about Sheldon during the war years, had only known of him by reputation alone and had not known or met him personally. Now they matched a face to the legend, working side-by-side with him in the cockpit.

He had a tough row to hoe to be accepted as the soon-to-become new Chief pilot once again.

Their personal friendship never suffered, but the business relationship between McConachie and Sheldon took a turn for the worse as more and more McConachie was forced to deal with matters of corporate importance which left Sheldon pretty much on his own to cope with his own pile of difficulties.

Perhaps the detractors of Sheldon and McConachie were jealous; perhaps their own at times dogmatic, thundering nature didn't help matters much in their relationship with the newcomers. What counted to the newcomers, in the higher levels of operations management, was that Grant McConachie and Sheldon Luck had been more than bosom buddies before the war, and they assumed that Sheldon certainly must have a lot of pull now that he was back in the company. Many thought he'd exercise his influence with McConachie to grab the Chief pilot's chair once again. All in all, life got harder and harder for Sheldon in this rapidly growing airline.

He mused a lot about these things, fighting mixed up emotions. He and McConachie had stayed in close contact throughout the war years. To help him understand what was happening, Sheldon had to constantly remind himself that McConachie had shared his most intimate plans with him these last three-and-a-half years.

For example, McConachie told him that he, in a way, regretted the fact that CPR had taken over Yukon Southern because he'd negotiated a sweet deal with Croil Hunter's Northwest Airlines. This, claimed McConachie, would have revolutionized air service between the United States, Canada, the far northwest and the Orient.

The only ones who knew of this plan besides Hunter were McConachie, Ted Field, McConachie's uncle, Barney Phillips, and Sheldon: the agreement never saw the light of day.

With Northwest's help, Yukon Southern was really going to fly the Pacific in style. Northwest was to buy out Yukon Southern, operate it as a wholly owned Canadian subsidiary, and put 14 sleeper bunks in the modified DC-3s which would fly the routes. The sleeper service would run from the United

States, through to Regina, Saskatchewan, Edmonton, Alberta, Whitehorse, Yukon, and on to Fairbanks in Alaska.

Later, the DC-3s were to be replaced with the four-engine DC-4s.

During these infrequent World War II meetings and exchanges with McConachie, Sheldon had learned that Northwest's Hunter had visited McConachie shortly before the CPR had bought out Yukon Southern.

McConachie quickly tasted C. D. Howe's displeasure, and knew that Ottawa frowned on international corporate relationships primarily because of the lucrative air mail runs for its own national carrier, TCAL.

By policy, all international air mail runs were to be flown by TCAL. Under the YSAT/Northwest proposal, TCAL inspectors would have joined the YSAT / NA flights on the air mail runs between Edmonton and Fairbanks, and Ottawa simply would not tolerate this arrangement.

His deal with NWA collapsed and McConachie turned to Pan Am early in 1940 for a similar deal. This attempt, at least, is documented in Lamb's history of the CPR:

> ...with very limited resources, (McConachie) had the temerity to announce a service to Siberia in co-operation with Pan American Airways. It failed to materialize, but with the resources of Canadian Pacific behind him, McConachie thought that much ought to be possible...

All these great and grandiose visions might just now come through with CPR's backing, McConachie told Sheldon, but given the new pilots' agreements and newcomers on board, they might have to do so without Sheldon.

Things were getting scritchy within the ranks again, just as they did those last few months before May 1942. The sharing of corporate and confidential information which occurred between Sheldon and Grant in 1945 and 1946 belonged to the past; despite this, Grant kept on imploring Sheldon to be patient, not to rock the boat, that all would be well soon.

He was referring to the day when he would become CPAL's president, but never once stated that objective to Sheldon. He could do more for Sheldon as president than he could when busy clawing his way up the CPR corporate ladder.

Their personal relationship often tended to slip into the corporate world, such as the time Sheldon received the impression from Grant that Sheldon was indeed still chief pilot in his eyes. But the company already had a chief pilot in Edmonton, another chief pilot in Vancouver and North Sawle had been promoted to acting line check pilot.

His good friend North assigned him as check pilot on the Vancouver-

Whitehorse run, and when North moved east with the expanding company, Grant had to ask Sheldon to sit tight for a while.

### Quits CPAL a second time… this time for keeps

Finally, a snow storm, a faulty fuel gauge in a Lodestar and a dressing down by a senior executive prompted Sheldon to quit CPAL a second time, *this* time for good, in the spring of 1946.

The flight which triggered this chain of events left Prince George late one night, with a full passenger load on board. Weather had delayed the flight to shortly before ten o'clock that night, and it was shortly after ten that he was airborne. Sheldon had been at it all day, and was tired. The weather forecasts seemed fine en route, but weren't too good near Vancouver.

He took the flight anyway, since he knew he could receive clearance to fly past Vancouver to the alternate airport of Patricia Bay on Vancouver Island, which serves Victoria. His second alternate lay inland from the coastal range, at Dog Creek, about 50 miles (80 km) due south of 150 Mile House.

Dog Creek was nothing more than a crude facility between Williams Lake and Ashcroft, with buildings and bunks – little better than glorified cabins – for passengers and crew,

As he flew over Dog Creek, also a turning fix and reporting point for direct Vancouver-Prince George flights, the weather began playing its usual dirty, unannounced tricks. At 10,000 feet (3,048 m) he asked co-pilot Stan Emery to request Vancouver company traffic control for clearance to climb to 12,000 feet (3,658 m). The dispatcher listening in on the frequency demanded to know why Sheldon wanted to go higher. Stan reported that they were encountering severe turbulence and light icing.

The weather was playing havoc with the Lodestar and bouncing the crew and passengers around like toys.

The dispatcher ordered Sheldon to return to Dog Creek and land there instead of flying on at higher altitudes to Vancouver or Pat Bay.

The Dog Creek radio operator, also monitoring the frequencies on scheduled flights, called Sheldon when he heard the dispatcher order the Lodestar to land there.

He cautioned him that the runway was clear, but the walkways to the cabins and crew quarters were plugged solid with huge snow drifts. He wouldn't have time to clear the walkways, and heat the cabins for the passengers.

Sheldon didn't like this at all.

While making his protest known both to the Vancouver dispatcher and to the Dog Creek radio operator, he brought the Lodestar around in a 180-degree turn and boogied straight back to Prince George.

The hell with this noise!

No way would he have his passengers walk through snowdrifts and spend a cold and miserable night in unheated cabins, let alone having him, Stan and his cabin attendant, go through the same torture.

This was no way to run a first-class airline! Soon, the Lodestar had landed back in Prince George. Arrangements had been made ahead of time, by radio, for suitable and warm accommodations for both passengers and crew. During the night crews started routine work on the aircraft, checking out the engine and systems and fuel load.

They discovered a real problem: the Lodestar fuel tanks were nearly empty, but the gauge read differently.

Had Sheldon pressed on to either Vancouver or Pat Bay the Lodestar and all aboard would have been reduced to another vital statistic on newspaper obituary pages.

When Sheldon returned early next morning for flight plans and weather briefings, Bill Smith, of the CPAL service crew – later to become general manager of Northern Mountain Air Lines in Prince George – had some disconcerting news for Sheldon about the gauge and tanks.

Smith and his crews had repaired the gauge overnight and topped off the tanks, checking the fuel with wooden dip sticks and a visual inspection of each tank.

Both tried to trace the origin of the problem but couldn't track it down. An error had taken place along the line. The ship had been re-fueled at Fort St. John, and supposedly topped off the night before in Prince George.

CPAL had experienced many problems with fuel gauges on the Lodestars.

Pilots had to rely on reports from service crews who would dip-stick the tanks and report the readouts verbally to the captain, who would stick head outside the starboard cockpit window to listen to ground crew reports.

Whoever filled the Lodestar tanks the night before had to have given Sheldon an erroneous reading.

Sheldon and Bill came to the same conclusion: no written report would be filed on what had taken place, but each would spread the word on the grapevine to exercise extreme caution on accepting dip-stick readings, and apply unrelenting pressure on the company to have those fuel gauge problems remedied.

The flight resumed without further incident that morning.

A few days later, Sheldon found a letter in his dispatch mail slot, from G.A. Thompson, the Vancouver superintendent.

Thompson had been Punch Dickin's boss in Canadian Airways, a stiff competitor during the late 1930s, but now woven into the CPR corporate fabric. Animosity nurtured over the years doesn't stitch well into a new corporate cloth, however, and Sheldon did not need to be psychic to read the troubling waters.

The letter, couched in formal and legalese terms, quoted the CPAL operations manual on legal alternate airports, accused Sheldon of breaching policy, and so on, ad nauseam, ending up with an order for Sheldon to present himself for a formal hearing.

Sheldon immediately called Grant protesting this summary judgment, and again, Grant coaxed Sheldon into taking it easy, to bide his time, because Grant couldn't attend this hearing and be there to smooth the troubled waters.

Obediently Sheldon went to this hearing.

Tempers flared, personalities clashed.

He left disgruntled, certain that he'd been treated unfairly and his judgment questioned.

When he got home, Grant had called ahead and left a message to the effect that somebody was after Sheldon's rear end, that this same person had called to Grant asking for permission to publicly reprimand Sheldon. The caller claimed that Sheldon had purposely violated company rules and should have flown the Lodestar in to Dog Creek that night.

This was just a bit too much for Sheldon, an adventurous, competent and experienced professional. After his globe-circling experiences in WW II, the corporate nit-picking of a sniveling executive wannabe was just too much for Sheldon.

He made up his mind to quit again, and was just waiting for the right set of circumstances, not knowing what they would be nor where they'd come from.

### South America beckons

The call to a new future came from Argentina, by way of London, England, and Washington, D.C. and stemmed from the reputation he'd acquired in Ferry/Transport Command.

At the end of a long return Vancouver-Whitehorse trip, Sheldon had checked into flight operations to find a cablegram from the Argentina Purchasing Commission in Washington, D.C.

Would he be interested in joining the new Argentine flying boat service and help the Argentine airline, La FAMA, set up a new international route structure between Buenos Aires and London?

At double his current CPAL salary.

Would he?

What a question.

Damn right he would.

He immediately wired for more particulars.

When he received them, Sheldon knew where he was going.

On May 22$^{nd}$, 1946, Sheldon left Vancouver for New York City and another first-class international pioneering adventure.

## FAMA

The world's largest family-owned steamship company at the time, Dodero Steamships, began Argentina's new flying boat service.

Commercial aviation in Argentina began as elsewhere as a dream, in July 1919, in Major Shirley Kingsley's eye - he founded the Companio Rio Platense de Aviation (CRPA) in that month.

By January 1920, the company began charter flight operations; within the first six months, the picture looked rosy: CRPA had flown more than 2,000 passengers.

Over the years a number of domestic airlines sprang up throughout the country, some with strong German backing, others with French money and many more with extensive Italian support – a large percentage of Argentineans in aviation were of Italian origin.

FAMA, or Flota Aerea Mercante Argentina – the aerial mercantile fleet of Argentina – first flexed its wings in June 1946.

Not only was this the line which wanted Sheldon, but it was well-connected and well-received in England, promising a great future for a career pilot.

According to the popular international airline magazine, *Air Pictorial:*

> *Although the old Skymaster, and later, the DC-6, formed the backbone of the FAMA fleet, the airline will be remembered in England for its consistent policy of buying British when possible. It bought Vickers Vikings, Avro Yorks, Lancastrians, and even went a long way along the road to ordering the Tudor. This tradition of shopping in Britain was to be repeated in later years when Aerolineas Argentinas became the first airline in Latin America to enter the jet age.*

The British Air Ministry (BAM) had sold three flying boats to Argentina and as part of the sale recommended a number of first-rate pilots to go with them, along with cracker-jack service and support crews.

Somebody in BAM liked Sheldon – he said that he thought that it was "Taffy" Powell – and recommended him as one of those first-rate pilots.

FAMA wanted nothing but the best and recruited, among others, Bruce Middleton – ex-RCAF and TCAL, Bud Scouten, Bob Lows and Slim Jones, whom Sheldon considered to be one of the finest boat pilots that he had ever had the pleasure to meet and work with.

Sheldon flew to FAMA's New York office a few weeks before the company officially came into being by establishing its Buenos Aires-New York service. It had purchased some DC-4s from Pan Am for this run, but wouldn't begin to fly the route until all aircrews were on staff.

Sheldon met another friend from Ferry / Transport Command days, Robert (Bob) Souers, who was senior pilot on the FAMA DC-4s. Bob suggested that Sheldon take his check-out flight on the DC-4 right then and there.

Bob later went on to become chief pilot for Flying Tigers, a freight and cargo airline which earned global fame.

Ronald J. Hall, Senior Director Flight Operations and Systems Chief pilot for Flying Tigers in Los Angeles, CA, said Bob was "without a doubt, the finest chief pilot Flying Tigers ever had, and one of the best chief pilots any company could hope to have."

They were the elite of the aviation world, and FAMA wound up with seventeen of them, along with experienced engineers, mechanics and technicians.

They were the perfect nucleus to train their own fleet operations staff in the coming months and years. FAMA hired Argentineans for administration and all ground support operations.

The Americans in negotiating international agreements and routes with Argentina, had stipulated that all foreign operators who wanted to fly into and out of the United States do so with pilots checked out to American instrument flight rule standards, in addition to meeting their own country's license requirements.

Piece of cake for Sheldon.

Anyone with his level of experience had little or no difficulty converting to the DC-4s.

FAMA had not originally planned on starting a new international flying boat operation from scratch.

Pan Am had done most of the extensive ground work, and FAMA picked up discontinued ground services from Pan Am. It also acquired former Pan Am facilities in Rio de Janeiro and Natal, and in Lisbon, Spain, and Bathurst, as well as on the extreme western coast of Africa, known then as British Gambia.

For startup flights to England, the company bought three Sunderland flying boats, flew them to Maryland where they were converted to Sandringham configurations, re-equipped with American engines and outfitted with seats for 42 passengers in a deluxe cabin layout.

One of these boats had been assigned to Sheldon during his few weeks in the United States before he headed south.

Within a few weeks Sheldon had locked up first position on the Buenos Aires-London flight, and soon after that Dr. Colin Jenel, third man from the top at FAMA, invited him to become chief instructor for the airline.

Sheldon viewed the operation as routine, not so different from what he used to do in UAT / YSAT days. Once he got there he noted a number of differences between Argentina and Canada.

Argentina was a different country with a radically different and difficult political-cultural system than what he'd become accustomed to in Canada. It also has a lot of geography similar to northwestern Canada, but with a much more pleasant climate.

From his point of view, this operation was just an elaborate and well-paying extension of what he'd been doing since he first joined UAT in 1936, but in a much nicer climate.

### Fierce national pride presented image problems. Solution - hide those *foreign* aircrews elsewhere

Sheldon soon found the thorns in his new bed of roses: to cite but two of them - a natural but fierce Argentinean pride and language barriers.

Friction soon set in between the foreign air crews and the Argentinean air crews they were training. The Argentinean nationals had naturally wanted a crack at flying these fabulous new machines themselves as command pilots, and not be seen or perceived as being mere co-pilots of these magnificent aircraft.

To calm Argentina's prestige and help improve its public image abroad, it was important that Argentinean aircrews could be seen by the public and by the media as being in command of these magnificent ships of the air as they arrived in, and took-off from foreign lands.

Foreign crews were prohibited from boarding FAMA aircraft while wearing their FAMA uniforms, anywhere.

Foreign aircrews had to board their aircraft dressed in civvies.

FAMA officials stressed that this illusion of Argentinean control of modern large airliners be seen everywhere FAMA flew; that it was especially important for Argentina's image abroad; and that it be perceived as a resourceful nation able to train such proficient and competent professionals as its own aircrews.

FAMA insisted that two Argentine pilots, each resplendent in full Captain and First Officer uniforms, be seen by passengers and onlookers, especially in New York City and in London, England, as entering the cockpit, obviously in complete command of their sleek aircraft.

The foreign crews were to remain unobtrusively out of the public view on the ground, while the Argentine crews taxied the planes away from the boarding and deplaning ramps to the vicinity of the runways.

Far from probing eyes, foreign crews then took over the flight and resumed training their Argentine aircrews.

Since Sheldon and many of his friends didn't put too much stock in judging a man's abilities by the uniform he wore, this Argentinean need for a good public image didn't bother them too much.

What cut to the quick was being ordered to take a back seat in this matter.

After all, they had quite some pride also, being among the handpicked to help establish international standards within FAMA.

**Languages differences may be amusing but could also be deadly on long flights… and wandering bulls and runways do not mix well**

The language barriers presented difficulties which were often amusing, but sometimes potentially deadly.

Nor did they help smooth ruffled feathers in cockpit communications between foreign and national crews-in-training.

The following incident serves to illustrate the frustrating and sometimes frightening experiences which at times confronted Sheldon and his friends on long international flights.

Thick fog had greeted Sheldon as he flew over Bathurst one morning. All he could see below were the tops of the masts of the larger ships in harbour. He couldn't put the plane down where it usually landed.

The coast line over which they'd flown earlier was clear, but the plane was too low on fuel to return. He could only continue making circuits over the harbour and hope the fog cleared before his tanks dried up.

As he circled the fog showed signs of thinning. Radio reports from the ground told him it was clearing enough in some locations, but not at the usual landing spot. Fine from the ground, but still not good enough from the air, and he was running out of time. Soon he'd have no choice but take their word for it and try to follow their directions.

A quick look at the fuel gauge told him it was time to trust those in the harbour. They gave him approximate headings, and briefed him on the number and sizes of vessels to the right and left of his new approach path.

The four-mile wide harbour permitted him to do something he'd never do on a routine final approach: come in low and level from a long way off, similar in many respects to what he'd had to do in blind practice approaches in the Coronados.

Only difference between 1944 and 1946: now he'd be coming in on fumes and the engine manufacturer's reputation.

Starting the tricky descent, he noticed his first officer pick up the microphone, and mutter something into it.

Sheldon's Spanish wasn't good enough for him to understand, and his attention was focused on the next few miles.

Moments later the steward appeared on the flight deck, bearing a tray on which sat a glass of water and two aspirins.

For the first officer.

This was no time for a God-damned Aspirin, he remembered thinking to himself!

Sheldon flung out his right arm and sent the tray flying across the large cockpit.

His first officer obviously had no idea nor was he remotely aware of the hazards involved in this approach.

So much for the language barriers in training foreign crews.

Yet this first officer was no mere boy.

He'd been in the Argentine naval air service for about eighteen years before joining FAMA. However, Sheldon later learned that he'd only accumulated about eight hundred hours of flying time in those two decades, and most of them on German-built float planes.

Sheldon instantly regretted his spontaneous and thoughtless act, knowing he'd reacted savagely and unfairly to someone who was totally ignorant of the impending disaster facing them.

Despite these little adversities, many events and incidents did result in lasting memories and acquaintances which later matured into good friendships.

A distraught bull on an Argentine runway resulted in one of those lasting memories.

On a beautiful day, he'd taken two nationals on familiarization flights aboard a DC-3.

Company policy, which Sheldon helped formulate, upgraded newcomers to the DC-4 co-pilot's seat by checking them out closely in both the left (command) seat and right (co-pilot), seat on the DC-3s.

His young charges that day were doing quite well in qualifying as first officer on the DC-4s.

After a couple of go-rounds at the original Buenos Aires airport, Sheldon suggested that they let him out for lunch while they continued on their own, checking each other out on touchdowns and take offs.

He'd been with them long enough, riding the jump seat, and letting each take a number of turns in the co-pilot's seat. DC-3 captains they may have been, but in the DC-4s, they'd be doing all their work in the right, or co-pilot's seat and that's where Sheldon wanted them to practice.

They were competent enough to make their own circuits for now and Sheldon had to turn them loose sooner or later. Since he was hungry, this was as good a time as any.

Airport traffic was light.

Aviation authorities had leased a large section of ranch while the new airport was being built some miles away. No permanent buildings dotted this farm-field airport, save for a few wooden structures and a control tower.

Sheldon instructed the pilots to taxi to the far end of the runway and let him off there; he'd walk to the terminal, at the other side of the field.

As instructed, they let him off, and Sheldon stood there, watching the DC-3 taxi and take to the air. He began to stroll at a leisurely pace, almost like home.

In the distance he made out two men on a tractor/compactor unit grooming another runway. Above, fleecy clouds trundled lazily by, almost worth lying on the grass and counting them.

Behind Sheldon, a rip-snorting bull.

Sheldon had eyes for only what he saw.

The bull had eyes fixed on Sheldon.

Maybe the DC-3 engines frightened or terrorized it. Maybe he felt nobody else had any right to his turf. That the bull himself didn't belong there, but had escaped from the ranch bordering the field, didn't bother the bull at all.

Sheldon's sixth sense must have been on overtime.

He turned and made up his mind fast that this was the ugliest and meanest looking bull he'd ever seen in his life. It stood there, snorting, and pawing the grass, not 30 feet (9 m) away.

Too damn close!

His farm days telegraphed a message from long ago: move. Run, don't walk.

Both began their run at the same time. Sheldon headed for the tractor which he had dismissed from his mind a few moments before. Once again a bit of farm wisdom popped to the surface. He could do something the bull couldn't: stop and turn on a dime.

He did. Again and again, zigzagging his way to the tractor, whose driver by now had seen Sheldon's problem.

He made two more quick sidesteps. Both men reached down from the tractor and pulled him up by his arms.

Then a whump – the bull hit the tractor side just as Sheldon made it onto the tractor.

The bull roared by.

Seemingly furious at having missed, it swung around in front of the tractor, aimed for the radiator and charged full-tilt.

Wham!

He buried his horns into the front end of the machine, destroying the grill and relocating the fan closer to the cylinder head. Steam billowed from the engine as the bull pulled away, probably with a stunning headache, grill parts hanging from his horns dangling like Christmas decorations.

Cut, hurt and bleeding profusely, the bull bellowed, lowered its head and resumed its attack on the tractor. Each time it hit the tractor, the entire unit shook, including the three scared men on board. That bull even managed to shove the tractor sideways to its original location.

His limited knowledge of Spanish led him to believe the two Argentineans were praying to a Lady. However, he believed the situation called for a more direct appeal, straight to the Chief Himself, in plain English.

All of this messing around with a tractor caught the attention of the Pan Am base manager and crew at the terminal. He jumped into the company jeep and came to the rescue of Sheldon and his two rescuers.

The bull took off after the men and the jeep, making straight for the terminal's aircraft service area.

Another monster stood there, much bigger than the bull. A Pan Am DC-6, with two of its engines ticking over, being readied for its night flight to New York.

### DC-6 props threaten to chop the bull

Distracted by this larger target, the bull slowed and ambled under the belly of the aircraft. Suddenly, it turned and veered left, undecided, and went right into the narrow space between the turning propellers of engines number one and two.

It went through that tiny space unscathed, much to the relief of all. The base manager wasn't sure how he could explain to head office that a bull had damaged a propeller. Undaunted by its near miss at being converted into bull burger, the bull picked up speed and tackled a ten-foot high chain link fence, scattering everyone who had gathered behind it to witness the remarkable scenario which had been unfolding during the last half hour. Spectators took to nearby trees, fearing the fence would yield to the bull's now diminishing charges.

Sheldon returned to the safety of the shop area in time to see two cowboys from the ranch approach the bull on horseback, boleros spinning noisily in the air above their heads.

He could almost hear the sounds – whirl, swish, and thwunk.

The bull slowed immediately.

They led him back, much subdued, to the ranch where he belonged.

The poor beast had hurt himself so much that vets had no choice but to put him to sleep.

Through it all, Sheldon's two students, oblivious to the interesting activities below, had continued their landings and take offs on the distant runway.

His expertise with aircraft, relationship with all crews, and success in training nationals earned him a solid reputation among FAMA executives. So much so that they relieved him of all training chores, and assigned him to the United States, with a covering letter to the Douglas Aircraft Company in Santa Monica California. It reads, in part:

> *This is to introduce Captain Sheldon Luck, who is one of our Commander Captains on our aircraft, as also Chief Instructor for our training crews.*

> *Captain Luck has undertaken the task of finding the proper schools for our men in the United States and to supervise the training of same. We should be very grateful for any help you may be able to give him in the latter part of the men's training, in your plants at Santa Monica, especially where the familiarization of the DC-6 is concerned.*
>
> *Captain Luck is hereby authorized by us to keep in constant touch with you on the DC-6 program in such a way that he might act as liaison officer between both companies for any problems which may come up in the course of construction of our (new) aircraft.*

While on this new assignment, a promotion in effect, Sheldon ran across his friend North Sawle, and learned that CPAL had issued a superb training manual on the DC-6. He asked North if he could get a copy for his Argentinean crews. At North's recommendation, Sheldon called Grant in Montreal, and asked him for a copy.

They renewed their friendship with this telephone call and Grant agreed to let Sheldon have a copy of the manual. Grant closed by asking Sheldon to visit him in Montreal before going back to Argentina.

A good idea, thought Sheldon, and soon did just that. After a pleasant reunion, he walked away with the training manual.

Sheldon covered a large part of the United States in the early spring of 1947 helping FAMA set up its training programs for the new DC-6s being made by Douglas. He settled on American Airline's Ardmore, Oklahoma, school as the training site. American Airlines had bought the base from the American Army after the war, and it was ideal for FAMA's twenty-two DC-6 pilots, since AA equipped it with two DC-6 simulators.

However, later in the spring of 1947, political control had changed hands drastically in Argentina. His New York FAMA office friends warned him that returning to Argentina would be too risky for him.

### Political uncertainties in Argentina
### prompt Sheldon to return to Canada

Sheldon chose to return home – to the family farm in Langley, B.C., to Isabel and to the children.

He and Isabel had bought an eighty-acre ranch and Sheldon decided it was high time to take a leave of absence from flying for a living. He'd become a rancher/farmer.

A few lean years stared commercial aviation in the face – at least until another war got the economy moving again, this time Korea, when the massive airlift requirements for men, resources and supplies would trigger a new round of aviation activity in Canada and the United States.

And especially for Canadian Pacific Air Lines.

During that dry period, from the summer of 1947 to 1950, Sheldon succeeded in packing in a fair amount of freelance flying despite the downturn in the economy and in commercial aviation in general.

Three enterprising businessmen who knew Sheldon well saw a chance to profit from war surplus assets, and wanted to develop a supply base at Haines, about a 100 miles (161 km) west of Whitehorse and readily accessible to Skagway and Port Chilkoot at the north end of the Lynn Canal in Alaska.

Their intent: lease part of Port Chilkoot, tie in with a steamship company to the port, then fly the freight north about a 100 miles (161 km) to Haines, and then into Whitehorse at rates which they predicted would be cheaper, and faster, than by White Pass and Yukon Railway which ran from Skagway, Alaska, in to Whitehorse, Yukon Territory.

They reasoned that with Sheldon as their pilot they could extend their services into Dawson, Aklavik (now Inuvik), Great Bear Lake, and Sawmill Bay: why there was no limit to the profits they could reap!

With the acquisition of some surplus C-47s and later, DC-3s, how could they lose?

Easy as taking candy from a baby.

However, the trio, George Simmons, Northern Airways, T.C. Richards, owner of the Whitehorse Inn, and Vancouver insurance man J.B. Slessor, couldn't get Ottawa to support their plan.

George in the meantime wouldn't give up.

He retained his main office where it always had been, in Carcross, opened an office at the Whitehorse Inn, and kicked in a Fairchild 71 to handle freight. Sheldon did manage to make an occasional flight for the group, and helped Richards make a number of special arrangements and charter flights with Cy Becker in Edmonton.

In the meantime Sheldon also flew for Frank O'Sullivan, one of the contractors engaged in bringing out abandoned pipeline supplies left over from the Canol project.

This was another epic undertaking, similar in scope and objective to the Bomber Road which saw airfields built throughout the interior of B.C. and the Alaska Highway.

Then there was the Canol project which involved building a 600-mile long pipeline between Norman Wells in the Northwest Territories, and Whitehorse. A re-built American refinery in Whitehorse processed the NWY oil – discovered in the 1920s – which was trans-shipped to service American based planes in Alaska.

Frank, a Lethbridge native, had asked Sheldon to quit the trio and join him in his development plans, promising to throw in a Lodestar to sweeten the pot.

An interesting departure from the original plan, but it too stalled and Sheldon stayed on Frank's payroll for a while.

Grant popped up once again, this time in Whitehorse. He and Sheldon threw open mental hangar doors to rehash the good old days and tried to and probe each other's minds about what they were doing now, and what plans, if any, they might have for tomorrow.

As before, the subject of Sheldon's returning to the fold surfaced - much more remote than at any time before, with a new warning from Grant that the company had changed considerably since May 1946.

A new airline agreement was in force, but Grant hinted quite strongly that once back on salary, Sheldon would rise quickly within the ranks.

Sheldon really thought it over carefully, and did not at all like the idea of returning to the bottom again. Better the devil he didn't know elsewhere than the devil he knew within CPAL.

Little wonder Sheldon was stunned by a June 1st, 1949 article which appeared in what was considered Canada's national magazine, *Maclean's*.

It ridiculed his relationship with Grant and belittled him as a professional.

Written by Frank Hamilton, the three-page article went into some depth on both McConachie and the company, and zeroed in on his smooth-talking abilities to handle and overcome staff disagreements.

Grant had moved to Montreal in 1946 and in 1947, he had become president of Canadian Pacific Air Lines.

What readers learned of the relationship between Grant and Sheldon:

> ...Like most prominent businessmen McConachie has enemies, but his are far from outspoken. Charlie (Punch) Dickins was vice president of CPA in 1946. He was reportedly slated for the presidency and was also backed by a powerful block of CPR executives, but McConachie got the job. Dickins quit, became manager of the de Havilland Aircraft Co. Today he refuses to talk about McConachie.
>
> McConachie uses his charm and a one-of-the-boys attitude to keep his airline running smoothly. Nearly all CPA's older (in service) employees call him 'Grant' because they've known him all their working lives. He has a certain personal magnetism that attracts key men to him. Practically all the top pilots and mechanics he met in his early days now work for him —even his

first mechanic, Bill Sutherland, who is now his aircraft inspection chief.

### The Boss is a trouble-shooter

> But McConachie expects unswerving loyalty. If he doesn't get it he can be tough. His oldest buddy, Sheldon Luck, once called the luckiest pilot in the world, is now a British Columbia farmer because he fell out with McConachie. At the end of the war, chief pilot of CPA, Luck was offered a flying job in South America at twice his Canadian salary. McConachie didn't want him to go. Luck went but in a few months the deal fell through. When he tried to rejoin CPA McConachie coldly told him that he would have to start at the bottom of the ladder again as a copilot. Luck chose farming instead. ...

Obviously, Hamilton never had a chance to confer with Sheldon, and must have interviewed Grant when he wasn't in a good frame of mind about Sheldon.

The pain of the article, said Sheldon, had just about faded.

Unfair and unsubstantiated, maybe, but who can blame Hamilton if he too was mesmerized by Grant's smooth-talkin' ways and charismatic charm, and chose not to look up any other sources to confirm what he might or might not have been told by Grant about Sheldon.

He wasn't alone: many others within the company knew Grant and Sheldon had gone through many torturous sessions and had had their ups and downs, like anybody else.

### CPAL considerably larger than TCAL

Like Dickins, Sheldon probably didn't want to talk about Grant either in those days. By now what had begun as a merger of YSAT with CAL and eight other companies had grown to international stature: CPAL's new trans-Pacific routes added 15,824 miles (24,140 km) of overseas airways to its 9,770 domestic miles (14,484 km).

CPAL had 52 aircraft against TCAL's 47.

TCAL had 7,912 domestic miles (11,265 km) and 8,275 overseas miles (12,875 km), but five times the amount of business thanks to the protectionist policies of the Canadian government.

It's too sad that Hamilton couldn't have pointed out one fact, which stood alone, without the need of ever having to consult with Sheldon. There was no doubt that Sheldon admitted to being unhappy with the company in May

1942, and again in 1946, but he did what any honourable man would do under the circumstances: stop bitching and resign.

The Lucks and McConachies were never really far apart from each other, even when they weren't in the same business together. Take the case of Grant's Uncle Harry.

Ron Keith, in his biography of Grant, described Uncle Harry on Page 44:

> *Uncle Harry's activities had always fascinated Grant, and he had looked forward to the happy renegade's visits to the household. These visits had occurred whenever the summer circuit of country fairs passed through Edmonton. For Uncle Harry had a keen eye for a fast buck and a slow yokel, and he ran a midway concession of dubious fairness at an enormous profit.*
>
> *...Uncle Harry was a memorable sight. His bald cherubic features dignified with silver-rimmed spectacles could have identified him as a kindly professor or a family doctor...*

Grant had wanted to take off to join the Chinese Air Force and fight the Japanese.

Uncle Harry thought this was too much for a young sprightly lad such as Grant and lured him into the aviation business in Canada instead with $2,500. Grant took a train from Vancouver – he'd been staying at Uncle Harry's hotel room - and went right to Winnipeg to purchase his first blue Fokker aircraft.

China lost a potentially great mercenary and Canada gained an international aviation giant.

Uncle Harry and Sheldon had been great friends since their first meeting in the mid-1930s.

Uncle Harry kissed the ground one day after being a passenger on a Yukon Southern flight which Sheldon had flown from Vancouver to Prince George. The Barkley Grow had developed asymmetric flap problems, forcing Sheldon to make a sweaty-palm landing at the old Prince George airfield, where Highway 97 crosses the Yellowhead Highway today.

*Asymmetric flaps can flip a plane upside down during the landing approach, as one flap is up, the other is down; an uncommon problem which puts an immediate fear of God into a pilot when it takes place.*

The harrowing landing scared everybody on board, including Sheldon.

Once he knew his feet were firmly planted on the ground, Uncle Harry bent down and kissed it.

And his respect for Sheldon's flying ability grew that day by leaps and bounds.

Now with another adventure just around the corner, Uncle Harry wanted Sheldon to fly for him – despite the fact that Uncle Harry hated flying.

If Grant McConachie was a first-class dreamer who could whip up visions of grandeur, his Uncle Harry was outstanding as a man who could come up with a workable scheme in nothing flat, and support it with backers.

While Sheldon had been with FAMA, Uncle Harry went out and bought himself a Beech 18 aircraft. It would be the ferry aircraft for his exclusive rich man's retreat and lodge at the north end of Stuart Lake in the mid-central reaches of British Columbia, about 500 miles (804 km) north of Vancouver.

He'd already started extensive land development at the site, but the Beech 18 proved too rich for his limited resources and he traded it in for a Cessna 195 on floats.

After listening carefully to his plan, both Isabel and Sheldon thought it had merit. Uncle Harry also dropped some pretty impressive corporate names as backers and potential clients, and Sheldon figured times were lean, so take the offer.

He would become a director in the company on a small share basis, and draw a monthly stipend for looking after the Cessna and flying it, and be construction superintendent while Uncle Harry drummed up financial support and sought new members for the club/lodge.

Soon after signing an agreement, Sheldon left home again, flew to Calgary to pick up the Cessna, where he met another ex-YSAT pilot, Bobby Hunter. Bobby left YSAT to work for, in succession, Manix Construction, the Department of Transport and finally the Alberta Government Air Service. Both enjoyed the reunion immensely and Bobby gave Sheldon his check flight on the five-seat plane.

Uncle Harry made arrangements ahead of time, and had Sheldon fly it to CPAL in Vancouver where crews put it on floats.

The club/lodge never quite made the grade. Sheldon flew that Cessna all over the map for Uncle Harry throughout the summer of 1950, bringing in a number of fishing parties, but that was about it. Membership fees started at $3,000 a hit, along with an annual $1,000 repeating fee.

Come autumn 1950, Sheldon heard that spectacular things would soon take place in the far north, and left Uncle Harry to pursue these promising new developments.

### Sheldon now becomes a corporate pilot

But before he made it to the far north, Grant would once again be instrumental in landing Sheldon another flying job through to 1951 – Sheldon's first as a corporate pilot, thanks to two engine fires on two TCAL airliners.

Grant and long-time friend, millionaire Frank Lundy, had been sitting together on a TCAL Northstar heading from Vancouver to Ottawa.

Soon after take-off from its first stop in Calgary, an engine fire forced the pilot to return. Re-boarding onto another aircraft, McConachie and Lundy resumed their conversation which had inched its way towards air safety. After the first engine fire, Lundy wanted to go the rest of the way by train.

McConachie persuaded him to fly on with him.

Shortly after take-off, another engine caught fire, and the plane had to return to Calgary - a second time for the two men.

By now Lundy was absolutely certain the only way to get to Ottawa was by train.

McConachie re-persuaded him to continue by plane, which made it safely and without further incident, proving McConachie's point.

During this last stage of the flight, Lundy had gotten his message across: he was definitely afraid of flying. Worse, he never knew what was going on in the cockpit. McConachie realized that as he explained things to Lundy during the flight, Lundy's fears receded in direct proportion to his growing knowledge about aviation and what goes on in the cockpit.

Maybe those pilots, after all, were pretty good guys, Lundy conceded. Always ready with a good idea, figuring a problem was something which only needed an answer to solve. Grant had one for Lundy, knowing Lundy had the money as well.

Why not get his own aircraft?

And his own pilot?

McConachie could supply both: he had a Lodestar, which could be had for a song, figuratively speaking, currently sitting in storage in a Winnipeg hangar, and he knew one of the very best pilots in the business - Sheldon Luck.

Lundy agreed to buy the Lodestar under one condition: that McConachie supply Luck, and another pilot, who had to be from CPAL. McConachie just couldn't ask a young pilot in the organization to risk his hard-earned seniority to satisfy the whims of a millionaire, but a young first officer just might be convinced to take the challenge for the right price from Lundy.

Within a few days, McConachie tracked Sheldon down through Quesnel's CPAL offices. Sheldon had been visiting the Cariboo region, spending time with Isabel's uncle at his gold placer mine operation in the Cariboo Mountains.

The message sent to Sheldon: if he wanted the job flying Lundy around the country, there'd be a ticket waiting at the Williams Lake airport and to get his butt down to Vancouver. Sheldon found it hard to say no, and a few days later, was going over the proposal with Grant in Vancouver. Grant sweetened the offer to Sheldon by assigning him a competent and good junior First Officer, Bobby Hammond. He offered Bobby a 90-day protected leave of absence.

Sheldon and Bobby flew to Winnipeg to pick up the Lodestar, CPB, freshly refurbished with Lundy's name running along the top side of the fuselage on both sides. He'd never flown this particular Lodestar for CPAL, but did for Frank Lundy, to his great pleasure and financial reward.

Frank loved a good ball game and Sheldon and Bobby could always look forward to flying, to anywhere a good game was scheduled, be it baseball or football. Frank, his guests and his aircrew visited many famous football and baseball fields throughout North America.

Sheldon enjoyed working for Frank immensely, as did Bobby. He was always a generous employer.

Once, arriving in Toronto, Frank brought everyone to the Royal York Hotel where he maintained a permanent suite. He released Sheldon and Bobby telling them he wouldn't need them for a few days, so they could enjoy Toronto to their hearts' content. As Sheldon and Bobby prepared to retire, the telephone rang.

At eleven o'clock at night.

Frank asked, "Sorry to bother you Sheldon, but can you get me to Edmonton for lunch tomorrow?"

So much for Toronto.

The boss was the boss, and now he'd changed his mind.

"Gee, I don't know Frank. They told me at Malton (airport, now Pearson International) that TCAL had cancelled all but four-engine flights." TCAL had shut down its DC-3 operations because of bad weather conditions between Toronto and Winnipeg.

Frank impressed Sheldon with the importance of tomorrow's luncheon meeting, and Sheldon knew he could fly around the weather - he wasn't limited to formal and precise routes such as TCAL pilots had to fly.

He questioned Frank on what kind of loads he might expect.

Loads?

Just him and his assistant, Mac.

With a light load, they just might have a chance, Sheldon told him. He also knew the Lodestar could handle weather really well.

An evening's sleep now got shot to hell.

Sheldon, Bobby, Frank and Mac were back on the Lodestar for the non-stop flight to Winnipeg, where Sheldon would refuel the Lodestar.

Frank got to Edmonton in time for lunch.

Sheldon and Bobby went to the hotel room for their well-earned sleep, skipping lunch.

No sooner had he fallen asleep, so it felt, than he heard a knocking on the door.

Asking who was there, Sheldon heard a two-word answer.

"It's Frank."

Struggling out of bed, shaking cobwebs from his head, Sheldon staggered to the door, ignoring the light switch completely.

"Yes, Frank?"

"You tired?"

Affirmative nod.

"Yes, pretty tired. What do you want?"

"Well, I figured you might be tired and 1 just brought this along thinking it might make you feel a little more rested."

He threw two envelopes onto the desk beside the door, winked at Sheldon, told him to go back to sleep and quietly closed the door.

Bleary-eyed, Sheldon looked at the envelope with his name on it, opened it, and in the dim light, saw what he thought was a $100 cheque.

"Goddamn! He woke me just to give me a cheque for $100?"

He returned to bed, not knowing how fast he fell asleep. When he woke, it was still dark. This time he turned on the lights and took a second look at the cheque. It wasn't for $100, but for $1,000. Bobby got a sizeable cheque as well.

Frank soon learned why he paid Sheldon so well as a corporate pilot.

En route from Vancouver one day, while clearing Cowley at altitude and in cold weather, the right engine pressure gauge light flicked on. The engine didn't quit, and since Sheldon was bringing the Lodestar down to Calgary soon, he simply reduced power to the engine and landed nice and easy.

The light stayed on for the remainder of the flight into Calgary, causing Sheldon to suspect that water had somehow gotten into the fuel tank. He taxied the Lodestar to a maintenance depot for a system check. Crews put the Lodestar into the hangar, covered the wings with a heavy tarpaulin, installed heaters and drained the sumps.

They removed nearly five gallons of water from the fuel tanks.

Refueled for the flight to Edmonton next morning, Sheldon was back on the runway, having filed an IFR plan direct to Edmonton. The Lodestar had just become airborne on the new long runway; gear up, and Sheldon began to climb to his assigned altitude when that same red light flicked on again.

He'd already shoved the throttles to full power demands on take-off and hadn't reduced the settings yet. As he started to do so, number two engine went bang and quit. Under normal conditions he would have merely continued his climb to a higher altitude, notified the control tower and requested an emergency clearance to return to the field on one engine.

However, knowing the red light probably indicated more water in the fuel tanks, he didn't want his second engine to quit on him.

Engines don't burn water.

If it did quit on him, he wanted to be close enough to the runway to be able to glide the short distance down, not to where the nose was pointed, away from the airport.

Within seconds, he had radioed his emergency to the tower, and his fear that the remaining engine would quit on him at any time and had started a

270-degree turn to lineup with another runway.

It hadn't been plowed, and had nearly three inches of snow on its surface, which meant nothing to him, given his years of landing on snow and ice surfaces in the north.

He naturally received his emergency landing clearance.

The instant his tires came in contact with the runway, the remaining engine quit.

He called it one of the luckiest breaks in his career.

Bill Smith, then chief instructor at the Calgary Flying Club, told Sheldon later, in a casual manner, that Frank considered him an expensive pilot, and that the Lodestar was expensive to operate.

Bill told Sheldon that he said to Lundy:

"Now you know why you pay him that kind of money."

Sheldon would never have quit Frank willingly. Bobby had gone back to CPAL for a second 90-day extension on his leave. In the interim Sheldon picked up co-pilots as he needed them. Times rolled by and fortunes changed, with Sheldon at last ferrying the Lodestar to its new owners in Los Angeles.

Now, at last, Sheldon could return to the far north. Those rumours he'd heard before joining Frank began to materialize. Soon after flying Frank's Lodestar to its new owners, Sheldon learned that Tommy Fox of Associated Airways needed another pilot and Sheldon quickly made his way to Yellowknife in the Northwest Territories.

Tommy had taken over the former CPAL base and provided dormitory quarters on the top floor of the hangar. Sheldon's room-mate turned out to be Max Ward, of Wardair fame.

Between November 1951 and March 1952, Sheldon and Max flew for Tommy and got to know each other on a rather amicable basis, a friendship which had lasted over the years; casual and easygoing.

In between flights Sheldon and Max spent a lot of time together. When they remained in the hangar, Sheldon would often see Max working hard on his professional drafting board, designing a home for himself and his wife.

Max had closed operations on his previous company, Polaris, and would on occasion discuss his personal dreams with Sheldon, about owning and operating his own airline one day, and circling the globe with it.

A dream for Max Ward, which, like McConachie's, came true six ways to Sunday with Wardair.

During Sheldon's five-month stay in Yellowknife, he and Max spent many long hours reminiscing and discussing future possibilities.

## Fate shuffles deck for Sheldon and deals him a junior captaincy

Fate shuffled the deck for Sheldon and he left Tommy for yet another airline job, this time with Queen Charlotte Airlines (QCA).

QCA had lost a Canso amphibian (a commercial version of the PBY flying boat) with twenty-nine persons on board on Vancouver Island in the fall of 1951. The company had been operating under a restricted license since. President Jim Spillsbury was looking for experienced pilots to upgrade QCA's IFR division to work up and down the coast from Vancouver. He first got hold of Bill May (the Fay Baker fan dancer pilot), who was running CPAL's test flying division from its Calgary maintenance centre.

Bill told Jim that Sheldon was just the man for the job.

Jim contacted Sheldon in Yellowknife, making him a job offer which was hard for Sheldon to refuse.

Sheldon wrote Tommy a long letter of resignation, explaining all the circumstances, along with his need for more security for himself and his family, still in Langley, BC. He also explained to Tommy about QCA's plans to upgrade to IFR operations, something he had his heart set on.

Tommy took Sheldon's resignation diplomatically, adding that he'd never stand in Sheldon's way. He wrote Sheldon, closing with a reminder that if he ever needed a job again, Sheldon could count on Associated to welcome him back.

Tommy's offer bordered just this side of a prophecy.

Sheldon joined QCA in the spring of 1952 as a temporary captain under the new Canadian Air Lines Pilots' Association agreement, and made more headlines in the process – this time with more air mail firsts, the first being into Kitimat, BC, in the summer of 1952.

Over the next few months Sheldon averaged about eighty-two hours a month in the air, sometimes more. Bill May had left CPAL and joined QCA as its chief pilot and carried out pilot training while Sheldon did on-line check pilot work and upgrading.

A severe winter produced difficult flying conditions prompting Spillsbury to suspend the Kitimat run and reduce the frequency on his airline's other routes. He and Sheldon discussed the problem and Sheldon accepted a lay-off in December.

Spillsbury offered Sheldon $500 a month so that he could remain on the active payroll until March 1953, when QCA could resume its routes with the advent of better spring weather.

Not used to accepting money without working for it, Sheldon refused Spillsbury's offer and spent Christmas 1952 at home, wondering what to do next.

Word spreads fast in the aviation business, and soon Tommy Fox learned of the lay-off through Vern Simmons, his operations manager. The timing was just right: Tommy was planning an addition to his Associated fleet, a Bristol Freighter, and could use Sheldon right about now.

Early in February 1953, Sheldon returned to work for Tommy. It took some time for the Bristol to arrive, so Tommy put Sheldon to work with Art Bell on the company's earlier Bristol, flying a wide variety of charters around, across and above the Arctic Circle.

The job didn't quite develop as Tommy had hoped, and he tried as gently as possible to break the news to Sheldon. But it wouldn't be quite so bad as not having a job, because Tommy already had another lined up for him - on the Atlantic coast of Canada.

Carl Burke's outfit was Maritime Central Airways (MCA). It was a key airline in the ones amalgamated to form the regional carrier that became known as Nordair, and it had leased the Bristols from Associated; Burke could use Sheldon's services in the Maritimes.

In the spring of 1953, Sheldon flew one of the Bristols to MCA, and immediately ran into a bureaucratic snag – he would be permitted, according to a Maritimes' pilots' association agreement in force with MCA, to check out a maximum of up to five pilots, and if he wanted to remain on the payroll, he could do so, but only as a junior captain on the company DC-3s.

Pushing his professional and personal pride into a remote corner of his mind, Sheldon accepted the conditions and flew DC-3s as a junior captain; certainly in seniority only, not in experience.

Then Art Bell arrived with Tommy's second Bristol, changing the scenario for MCA which needed two full crews for their Bristols. MCA pulled Sheldon from the DC-3s and put him to work on the Bristols flying regularly.

One of the company's largest contracts included the Fraser Brace Engineering company job of building radar bases along the Labrador coastline. This involved ferrying men, material and supplies up and down the coast, a prelude to the Distant Early Warning (DEW) line which was two years down the road.

The sites which Sheldon flew into and out of constituted the eastern limits of the McGill and Pine Tree Radar Lines which had been strung out across Canada.

His assignment ended in November 1953, and Sheldon returned to Associated's payroll in Yellowknife.

## Cold war and far northern radar – the DEW Line – beckon Sheldon

In February 1954, QCA received word that Sheldon had returned to northwestern Canada. Things had improved for QCA – it was in the process of expansion, and this time Spillsbury promised Sheldon his tenure would be good until at least January 1955. This meant nearly a solid year's airline work with a pay cheque every two weeks.

Sheldon had become a pilot of fortune, and would fly for money, especially regular money.

He joined Eric Bentall – from 231 Squadron – who had taken over as QCA's operations manager during the summer of 1952, senior to Bill May.

The result – throughout most of 1954, Sheldon enjoyed himself flying Cansos on regularly scheduled flights over some of the most beautiful scenery in the world – Canada's west coast.

Towards the end of the year, Sheldon would meet up with Russ Baker again, and extract a written, contract from him as president of Pacific Western Airlines – believed to be the only one Russ ever signed with a single pilot.

Sheldon learned through highly reliable sources that Pacific Western was going to buy out Queen Charlotte Airlines, despite repeated denials from QCA executives that it would never be sold.

He knew that the sale of QCA was more than pre-ordained – it had in fact been structured without the knowledge of any employee other than Sheldon. He also knew PWA was in line for a major chunk of a multi-million dollar contract to supply the DEW Line construction project.

Russ wanted Sheldon to take over operations on the cold war's Distant Early Warning (DEW) Line out of Hay River, NWT, and accepted Sheldon's counterproposal of putting it in writing by offering a contract giving Sheldon complete operational control of all large aircraft for the duration of the project.

At first reluctant to accept such an apparent plum from a man he suspected was once responsible for having him grounded on an overloading infraction, Sheldon learned that Russ could be as persuasive and charming as Grant had been.

Russ, Sheldon and Dune McLaren polished off two bottles of Queen Anne Scotch while striking the deal which led to Sheldon's contract.

Signatures went on the dotted line on February 15$^{th}$, 1955.

Sheldon had no aspiration to fly a desk or become an airline executive.

He'd been there before and that was enough for him.

Russ Baker had come a long way since he and Sheldon first met on the shores of Stuart Lake in 1937, nearly twenty years earlier.

He incorporated Central British Columbia Airways (CBAC) in 1946, consisting of one aircraft and three employees in Fort St. James.

By 1947, Baker had expanded the CBAC fleet to four planes. In 1948, CBCA opened bases in Williams Lake and Cranbrook, both in BC, and bought two more planes, including what they proudly claimed was de Havilland's first production Beaver, the world-famous bush aircraft.

Three more Beavers joined the roster in 1949. In 1950, the company took over Kamloops Air Service Ltd., adding yet another Beaver and a new base;

then another one in Fort Nelson.

The CBAC fleet grew in leaps and bounds – in 1950 the company purchased three Norsemen and a Travelair to help meet increasing traffic demands for the Aluminum Company of Canada project in Kitimat.

Skeena Air Transport Ltd. came into Russ' corporate holdings in 1951 while the company undertook the million dollar contract to provide air services on the Alcan project.

In 1952 the company moved to Vancouver with a fleet of eighteen planes, absorbing Associated Air Taxi in the move, and changing names: Pacific Western Airlines (PWA). The key to its Yukon operations fell into place in 1954 with the acquisition of Whitehorse Flying Services.

This was a meteoric rise, without a doubt, supporting PWA's claim in its 1955 annual report that it had become the "fastest growing company in the world."

PWA's share of the DEW Line work came under a subcontract to Associated Airways Ltd., until October 1955, when PWA became the prime air services contractor for Western Arctic DEW Line operations.

Sheldon's first flying job involved going to California to pick up the first of two C-46s which PWA had purchased for the contract.

Huge quantities of men, equipment, material and supplies would be moved north and south on this job, as well as extensive lateral air services throughout the High Arctic, from one end of Canada to the other, stopping on the east coast of Baffin Island. PWA's segment included the westernmost locations, Site 9 at Parry Point to Site 24 at Spruce Bay.

It soon became obvious that the company would need many smaller aircraft to handle the lateral movements along the DEW Line – the C-46s couldn't get into many of the smaller sites.

MCA handled the eastern DEW Line supply contract when PWA became the primary air contractor for the western section. CPAL also got a good piece of the pie as well, flying millions of pounds of freight, equipment and personnel to the High Arctic.

Sheldon knew a superb pilot who could help him out, but he wouldn't go after him without Russ doing some legwork first. He was Stan McMillan, who lived in Camrose, Alberta, and, who was reputed to have itchy feet to return to flying.

Russ accepted Sheldon's proposal to go after him first. After all, this was one of the men Sheldon had admired the most during his first few years as a pilot, and he was rather reluctant to go to one of his "heroes" and offer him a job.

Stan would be the ideal man to take over control of all light aircraft movements east and west along the Line.

In due course, Sheldon and Stan got together to discuss details.

Sheldon had also taken control of crew rotation – supplying the DEW

Line kept PWA's 2 C-46s busy night and day, and crews had to be ready at all times. An American, one of the best C-46 pilots Sheldon had ever known, wanted to schedule his own flights and wouldn't accept Sheldon's crew postings. This put Sheldon between a rock and a hard place. No matter how good the guy was as a pilot, he couldn't keep interfering with scheduling of other crews.

When Sheldon had him fired, another PWA executive rehired him without telling Sheldon first. Sheldon only learned about this while he was in Edmonton for a day or so on personal business. When he got word in his hotel room that the American pilot had reported for duty in his absence, Sheldon immediately called Russ to confirm this shocking news.

Rather than become embroiled in another internal bureaucratic mess, Sheldon chose to accept another, unsolicited job offer.

He didn't quit in a huff; he just quit. Russ tried to convince him how badly this competent American pilot was needed, and Sheldon tried to explain how this pilot disrupted crew scheduling to a serious extent, and that this couldn't help but have a multiplier disruptive effect on the morale of other crew members.

Nope, he was needed, insisted Russ.

Maritime Central had gotten word the same day that Sheldon might consider returning east to fly for them once again – as operations manager for DEW Line supply operations working out of Frobisher Bay on Baffin Island, NWT, with his family installed at MCA's DEW Line operational headquarters in the community of Mont Joli, Québec.

He accepted.

The DEW Line project had become one of the world's largest peacetime airlift operations, and MCA had a healthy chunk of the contract to supply from Site 25 east to the easternmost DEW Line radar base at Cape Dwyer on the coast of Baffin Island. DC-3s, C-46s and DC-4s were used by MCA to discharge its contract obligations to the two prime DEW Line builders, Foundation and Western Electric. Other regional carriers had a slice of the pie, including CPAL. Wheeler and Québecair, each with a C-46, and Dorval and Worldair with their single C-46s.

In June 1955, Sheldon went to Fort Churchill, Manitoba, and worked under MCA's operations manager, H.H. (Jonesey) Jones, ferrying supplies from Site 25 to Site 30, Hall Beach in Foxe Basin, and later on through to Baffin Island.

Six weeks later he left Fort Churchill for Mont Joli for a brief period before being immediately posted to Frobisher Bay as operations manager.

### A rarity – lost while airborne

One flight highlights the differences in geography between Canada's eastern and western coasts, and the sheer size of this country. At no time in his career had Sheldon ever been airborne and lost at the same time, except when on the DEW Line eastern project.

Sheldon and George "Brownie" Brown – who retired as a senior L-1011 pilot with Air Canada, had flown a DC-3 from Mont Joli to Frobisher (now Iqaluit), with Sheldon flying most of the way: a direct-line flight of 1,050 air miles (1,609 km) straight north. On arrival, they learned that they would have to turn around and go right back south.

Since George rested on the way up, Sheldon took his turn to catch up on some badly needed sleep on the unscheduled return trip. George, already a competent pilot, took the controls and pointed the DC-3 south over one of the world's most heavily travelled but absolutely un-controlled air routes.

George made one radio contact with the ground after leaving Frobisher Bay on passing Fort Chimo, 400 miles south (644 km) of Frobisher in northern Québec.

Another 650 miles (1,046 km) to go.

It would be a long night alone in the cockpit, with nobody to talk to on the radio.

The long silence on the airwaves was a result of the diurnal effect, induced around sunrise and sunset at certain frequencies, the very ones MCA used on its flights. This effect suppresses the frequencies, resulting in near total silence.

George would have welcomed any radio conversation at this stage. The DC-3 droned on over the tundra at about 9,000 feet (2,743 m) while Sheldon slept peacefully in the empty passenger/cargo cabin.

After a while George wondered when he'd pick up the Mont Joli radio station. The only sound he heard on the long flight down had been a faint letter 'N' on a beacon when he flew by Schefferville, about 250 miles (402 km) south of Fort Chimo.

Cloud cover smothered the entire visible portion of the province. He couldn't see any thing at all below that cloud cover... no land... no water.

Somewhere ahead, God only knew where, Mont Joli waited for them.

George couldn't be far off track, so where was Mont Joli?

About seven hours into the flight, George woke Sheldon.

Although the tanks had been topped off in Frobisher Bay, George worried about running out of fuel if they didn't sight land soon; the tanks were getting low. During the flight, he'd judiciously cross-fed fuel from tank to tank to keep the aircraft in perfect trim and balance. He must have encountered severe head winds to be this far behind in time.

By and by, both reckoned they should be around the vicinity of the 80-mile wide St. Lawrence River, and George asked Sheldon about the possibility of easing down through the cloud cover, finding the river and ditching the

DC-3.

If they could find water, Sheldon agreed they were low enough in fuel to ditch the aircraft.

"Don't worry Brownie, I won't hurt ya," George recalled Sheldon assuring him.

A small break below and Sheldon nosed the plane into it and under the cloud cover. The DC-3 broke out into rain, and both immediately saw what looked like an abandoned airstrip. It was, having been used by Anson aircraft to ferry men and supplies for the Québec North Shore highway which led from Baie Comeau to Sept Isles – known then as Seven Islands.

With inadequate fuel for a second attempt, Sheldon called for full flaps and eased the DC-3 to a safe but quite bumpy landing on the abandoned strip. As the pair opened the cabin door, they saw a Royal Canadian Mounted Police officer standing there beside his car looking at them with a puzzled look on his face.

The policeman told them they had landed near Paninachois on an 1,100-foot (305 m) long grass strip and were but 40 miles 964 km) from Forestville on the north shore of the river. Mont Joli lay across the water only 80 miles (129 km) southwest.

The RCMP constable obliged Sheldon's request for fuel by calling the Paninachois dealer who soon showed up with two drums of high-octane gasoline.

Sheldon and George estimated they'd only had ten gallons left in the tanks when they landed; now they had an estimated one hundred gallons, enough to get them to Mont Joli.

With clearing weather Sheldon was able to work the radio and picked up Mont Joli who now reported skies clear as a bell. They thanked everyone who came out to see them, re-boarded the DC-3 and flew it home, arriving some twenty-five minutes later.

Both marched right over to the Gaspésienne Bar and had a long shot of medicinal spirits before going to their respective families.

One of the more memorable mercy missions Sheldon flew took place in the High Arctic in Davis Strait, between Greenland and Baffin Island.

Cansos, as the Catalina PBY civilian versions were called, weren't on his active roster of current types of aircraft when he was on the DEW Line. But the U.S. Navy found itself in a serious bind: a vessel lay trapped in the ice in Davis Strait and nine crew members were seriously ill and needed to be airlifted to hospital at Frobisher Bay, where after emergency medical care, an aircraft would fly them back to the States.

Icing conditions in the Strait were too severe to dispatch another ship to the rescue of these men.

MCA had a Canso, and after discussing the nature of the mission with Sheldon, they had the Canso flown up from the Maritimes. The company's regular Canso pilot was busy elsewhere, so Sheldon agreed to take the trip.

He left Frobisher Bay with a heavy load of fuel. He'd been warned of the heavy ice pack conditions, and knew he would have to hop between slow moving ice floes a number of times to transfer that many men from the ship to the Canso. He would be unable to stay in one position long enough alongside the vessel for the transfer to be done in one shot – such was the nature of the highly mobile and dangerous pack ice.

Each time the Canso took off, it gobbled large quantities of fuel. Finally, it took three take offs and landings before all nine men and the medics were safely aboard the Canso.

Careful pre-flight planning paid off as Sheldon flew into Frobisher Bay. The condition of the men had improved slightly and a decision had been made to transfer them immediately to a waiting American Air Force DC-6 for a direct flight back to the US.

He recalls it for the sense of adventure this mercy mission gave him and his co-pilot, Ed Sword. Ed retired as a senior Swiss Air captain, and in 1984, wrote Sheldon saying that he felt fortunate that he'd been involved in such a mercy mission.

Even on the DEW Line eastern operation Sheldon made headlines back in Vancouver. This time it was when Vancouver Sun writer Stanley Burke - the Sun's Ottawa bureau man – wrote a feature article on the project and its contractors, including MCA.

He opened his article with the following lead paragraph:

**A Langley farmer is helping run the greatest airlift in the history of aviation**

He went on to describe in great and interesting detail a firsthand look at the scope of the air support for the DEW Line, and the hardships faced by men and their machines in preparing North America's first line of defence against an air attack by Russia from across the North Pole.

In the early autumn of 1957, Sheldon and his family had returned to B.C., ready to tackle the uncertain future.

Time to take a breather and resume farming.

He and Isabel had sold the Langley farm and decided to settle in Fort St. James, on the very spot of land which he'd helplessly stared at when he fell out of his slow-moving Fokker aircraft twenty years before.

It presented quite a break from the demanding routines of flying.

In 1958, he would learn just how demanding the business of running an airline was - Russ Baker had died of a heart attack in mid-November of that year, and Sheldon attended his funeral.

Russ Baker paid a lethal price for a corporate lifetime of punching holes through diplomatic and bureaucratic gauntlets.

Today a propeller monument overlooking Stuart Lake is a silent and fitting tribute to Russ' contributions and achievements in the northwest.

Sheldon had become a serious rancher by the late 1950s, or so it seemed to one and all who knew him, until Bill Smith and Merv Hess learned that he was available.

With Johnny Nielson, Smith and Hess had formed Northern Mountain Airlines (NMA) in Prince George, almost in the geographical heart of British Columbia, some 500 miles (804 km) north and slightly east of Vancouver, almost equi-distant from Calgary, AB and Edmonton, AB.

Business was so good that they needed a spare pilot. Knowing Sheldon was nearby, they naturally sought his help. Nothing serious, you know, just to help us out.

For a bit.

More than willing, Sheldon began flying part-time for them. He'd discovered to his consternation that ranching and farming ate up a whole lot of money in short order. Part-time work as a professional commercial pilot could put a lot of that money back into the depleting bank account.

NMA operated a Beaver, a Taylorcraft and a Cessna 180, and soon Sheldon found himself flying over the familiar territory he loved so much two decades before. Within a year someone else needed a little extra help, if Sheldon wouldn't mind. He was Bill Harrison, of Omenica Airways, in Bums Lake.

## Rancher has licence, will fly... but better yet, he's got wings on his manure spreader

Sheldon had become a freelance pilot with two clients.

A third client poked his head into Sheldon's growing stable of clients: Max Sanderson, of Canadian Exploration, who was a close friend of the owners of BC Yukon Air Services.

They needed a spare, but highly experienced pilot.

Could he find one for them?

They needed one right away, at the height of the hunting season, to service all their charters.

Max visited Sheldon. Was he available, for the customary fee?

Of course! Certainly!

When?

Right now!

That three-section ranch farm in Fort St. James sure did cost a lot of money to maintain, along with a family, when there was no regular revenue coming in.

It felt good to be wanted again.

Curiosity prompted him to ask Max: how did he ever convince BC Yukon to hire him?

Max had a good long talk with owners Hal Comish and Charlie Hamilton. They really were desperate for a good pilot, but he had to be willing, reliable and know the interior of the province almost by heart. He would also have to be absolutely trustworthy as their clients were first-class businessmen and businesswomen.

Max said: "I know a rancher in Fort St. James."

"A rancher?!"

"Don't worry, He's got wings on his manure spreader."

Now it's 1960 and Sheldon has two clients on his list: Northern Mountain, Omenica and now, as he reflected, northbound on a CPAL DC-6 out of Prince George to his newest customer, the third: BC Yukon. Freelance flying from late fall to early spring paid just enough to keep the farm in the black side of the ledger.

Then in the next couple of years, he picked up a fourth client: Newlands Logging, flying its Cessna 172 in between ranching or other client flying charters, and in the process added a Super Cub to his list of aircraft types which he'd flown in his career.

Just as mercy missions were critical to many in the early aviation pioneering days, their value was of no less importance in the 1960s. While freelance flying for BC Yukon, Sheldon was involved in three key mercy missions.

The first took place at the Cassiar Asbestos mining company. An employee had suffered extensive injuries when the huge truck he'd been driving plunged over a steep cliff. The mine superintendent called Sheldon personally at BC Yukon's main office in Watson Lake to make the mercy mission request.

Sheldon took a Beaver on floats to Good Hope Lake, about 250 air miles (402 km) south of Whitehorse, 12 miles (19 km) from the mine site. The injured man had been moved there by stretcher.

Sheldon had a hard time finding good weather breaks over the Cassiar Mountain range, but the flight turned out basically routine to there, and back, into Whitehorse.

He lost sight of the mountains most of the way back to Whitehorse. He made it as far as Ear Lake, the man-made lake created by damming the river above the city, and his landing site.

He was forced to make a night landing on the nearly four-mile long artificial lake, an arduous task in itself for a pilot, who had to "feel" his way through the entire approach and let down. However, he'd been in and out of Whitehorse often enough in the last twenty-five years to successfully complete another mercy mission. The victim was later transferred to Vancouver where he fully recovered from his injuries about a year later.

During a 1963 Labour Day ball game at Watson Lake, a CP Air Lines employee had been injured and lay in a coma. Later that night the doctor tending to him feared brain damage might set in if he wasn't immediately taken to specialists in Edmonton.

Once again, BC Yukon was asked to take the mercy flight. Sheldon checked this one out carefully – just a feeling, nothing more. He discussed it in minute detail with BC Yukon's Hamish and Hamilton.

He didn't feel good about flying this mission right from the start, but couldn't put his finger on the reason why. Not a very professional thing perhaps, but a very human sensation. The company had two Beaver aircraft, designed mainly for daytime VFR operations.

The flight to Fort St. John, where the patient would be transferred to an IFR-equipped aircraft to take him to Edmonton, would be done in darkness.

Sheldon still felt leery. He insisted that BC Yukon request a special clearance from the Department of Transport in Edmonton, and give him written consent before he would agree to take the flight. He really thought that Hamish and Hamilton would be denied permission to fly because the Beavers were not licensed for IFR, which was mandatory for night flying.

**Sheldon's reputation carries the day and helps save another life**

A query came back from the DOT: "Who is the pilot and what is his license?"

When told it would be Sheldon, the reply came back within minutes:

"Mr. Luck is authorized to fly this mission at his own discretion."

Of the two float-equipped Beavers, Sheldon chose IGF because it had extra fuel tanks, giving it more flying hours or longer range, whichever was needed most. Given likely weather problems en route, he wanted an extra margin on his side. Had this been a daylight flight he would have chosen the other Beaver which had a better radio than IGF's.

Also, since neither plane had a back-up radio, Sheldon wanted that extra fuel.

He decided to chuck his feelings aside and went ahead with the flight anyway. It was, after all, a mercy mission. Yet he still knew trouble lay in wait for him up there this night. He didn't think it would be serious enough to risk his or his passenger's lives; the CPAL agent's girl friend would accompany them.

After a smooth take-off from Watson Lake for the 400-mile direct flight, Sheldon pointed the Beaver's nose to Fort St. John.

Before long, cloud build-up obscured many of the light specks far below on the Alaska Highway. It was no longer a question of using those light blips as a visual aid. If he was going to get to Fort St. John, it would have to be well over the top of this cloud deck.

A radio range station at Smith River - about 80 miles (129 km) southeast of Watson Lake – could have helped him make a position check, but it was useless to him as IGF's Automatic Direction Finder (ADF) was unserviceable (not working).

From that point on, he was on top of the deck.

Some 120 miles (193 km) later, he sighted a large break in the clouds and assumed he was a little bit west of Fort Nelson.

He brought IGF down to 8,000 feet (2,438 m), knowing he still had, if he was right about Fort Nelson, 190 miles (307 km) to go before reaching Fort St. John. He hadn't been too far off his estimate as he was flying over Muncho Lake Provincial Park, and knew he was reasonably close to his intended flight track. More cloud forced him to climb higher for clear air, but he couldn't quite make it.

Ice began to form on the windshield.

Fortunately IGF had carburetor heating, and the engine kept on running smoothly. However, IGF's airspeed indicator began acting up, giving erratic readings. This, despite the fact he'd activated the pitot tube heater some time prior (an aircraft's airspeed is indicated by the pitot tube, which under the conditions of this flight, had to be heated to provide reliable information about airspeed).

This added to his difficulties. He tried to call Fort Nelson on the radio, now about 60 miles (97 km) from his track. No reply.

Damn, he thought. He could sure use some of the big, beautiful aircraft he'd flown in the ferry service.

Forging ahead, without any option, he noticed the cloud cover thin to a point where he could bring IGF down to a lower level, flying into warmer air. Ice cleared from the windshield and the warmed-up pitot tube resumed its function as the airspeed indicator resumed conventional readings.

Estimating another hour's flying time before Fort St. John, more breaks appeared in the cloud. Light specks which flickered below could be vehicles or cabins on the Alaska Highway. Then, greater intensity lights came into view - they were burn-off flares from the oil and gas wells in the area.

He knew now where to make his turn for Charlie Lake, and could also make out the lights of the city.

A wind across the lake surface helped him make a good landing, and as he taxied across the water, looking for any place to moor, light had edged its way across the waterfront. He'd been airborne since eleven o'clock, and it was nearly three-thirty in the morning

Someone was supposed to have met him at the dockside.

Communications between Watson Lake and Fort St. John had become fouled up. No ambulance waited for him at the dock-side, as had been arranged prior to his take-off.

In fact, he couldn't make it to dockside right away. He faced a pitch-black lake surface and a crowded dock cluttered with moored aircraft.

Out of sheer frustration, he took IGF to shore, secured it temporarily with the help of the victim's girlfriend, and walked over to the dock to shunt aircraft about alone, making a docking space for the Beaver. He returned to IGF and soon had it tucked into the newly created mooring space.

Still nobody around.

He asked the young lady to stay with her boyfriend and walked off along the road hoping to find a friend's home which he thought was close at hand. Unable to locate it, he wondered what to do next when a man came along and saw Sheldon. He stopped and offered help. The stranger called the ambulance crew and woke the Piper Aztec pilots who were supposed to have been notified and ready for the transfer at the Fort St. John airport.

Another half hour went by before the ambulance arrived, took the agent to the airport and placed him into the Aztec, which then took off for Edmonton.

Having gone with them to see that all went well with the patient, Sheldon saw a CPAL DC-3 squatting on the runway. He learned the crew had been scheduled to return later that day to take the plane to Fort Nelson. CPAL had removed its heavy DC-6s from the Fort Nelson leg because the runway was being repaired. Odd, he thought, that CPAL couldn't have made separate arrangements to have one of its own staff members brought in by that DC-3, which could have flown to Watson Lake – it was licenced and equipped to fly IFR.

Although Sheldon and the CPAL agent who suffered the injury were acquaintances, Sheldon saw him as another man whose life was at stake and required immediate medical attention. To get him to hospital represented a first-class challenge to his professional ability.

Not too long after the Fort St. John flight, he had been called on to take one more mercy mission, please – he ranked it equal in difficulty to the Fort St. John flight, but with an added dimension – he was tired as all get out when he got the call.

Perhaps it is nothing more than coincidence, but it seemed to him that mercy flights had a bad habit of taking place at the end of a long working day. He had just reported in from a tiring day flying over part of the Northwest Territories and was looking forward to an evening off.

A call came in from CN Telecommunications requesting an emergency medical evacuation from where the Alaska Highway crosses the Rancheria River, about 40 miles (64 km) west of Watson Lake, to Whitehorse.

The mission: to meet the parents of a young girl, unconscious from an injury, who would be brought from their camper to the bridge crossing where she could be put on board the plane for the flight into Whitehorse.

He'd never landed on the Rancheria River before, nor could he recall any other pilot who'd landed in that vicinity so he couldn't seek advice. The Rancheria is a fast-flowing mountain stream, but wide enough to accept a landing Beaver, as long as it was against the current.

Another discussion with Hamish and Hamilton.

Only this time they were the ones uneasy about the flight, not Sheldon. They were afraid something would go wrong, endanger Sheldon and the girl, which would reflect badly on the company. Reluctantly they agreed, as long as Sheldon was certain he felt confident enough to make this one more trip.

Weather stayed with him on the inbound flight, offering a clear night with a rising moon. The group promised to light a campfire on shore when they had earlier conferred with Sheldon at the base.

He spotted the campfire, and on landing busied himself with fighting the swift current, slowly but surely edging the plane close to shore. His main concern lay in a possible engine failure – without power the Beaver would have been swept away downstream.

As he neared shore, a couple of men grabbed the left wingtip while someone else held a float and a third secured a line to it.

The girl was brought on board. Everybody there wanted to accompany her, but Sheldon limited the number of passengers to her and her mother. He had to keep the Beaver as lightly loaded as possible for the tricky take-off needed to climb out over the high hills on either side of the river.

Mother and daughter safely aboard, the lines were released and Sheldon tacked the Beaver to the centre of the current, allowing for wing clearance on either side, lifted the float rudders and poured on the power. He flew into the moonlight, keeping the aircraft as straight as possible until he was well over the treetops. Retracting the flaps for more airspeed, he went into a maximum rate of climb and banked towards Whitehorse.

Weather, which looked promising on the way in, packed in as he flew over the Teslin Lake area, not quite halfway to Whitehorse. The Beaver flew in and out of the clouds, and he dared not go lower because of the mountain peaks below.

He recognized a glow of light, through thinning cloud cover, as Whitehorse and breathed a sigh of relief.

However, as in the Fort St. John flight, somebody bungled communications. After a hard landing on the lake, without any vertical visual reference to go by, he brought the Beaver to dockside and found, once again, nobody waiting for him.

Securing the plane, he went to a telephone – it was a direct link to a fuel supply company, where someone answered. Sheldon got a message through to the hospital.

Somebody there had contacted Paul Lucier, an ambulance driver who had been waiting at the Whitehorse airport. A short while later, Lucier drove the girl, her mother and Sheldon to the hospital, where Sheldon was offered a bed for the night, an offer he didn't refuse.

Lucier, a Windsor, Ontario, native, had moved to Whitehorse in 1949, working as a deckhand on the paddle-wheeler, *SS Klondike*, which operated between Whitehorse and Dawson City.

Between 1943 and 1966 he held a number of positions with the Canadian Army and the Department of Public Works, including that of bus driver, mechanic and ambulance driver.

On October 23rd, 1975, he had become the first Senator from the Yukon.

He told me when I interviewed him for his memories of the incident for the first edition of *Walking on Air*, that he recalled waiting for what had seemed to be an unusually long time at the airport for BCYA's Beaver.

## 11. Challenges Continue – from Freelancing to Flying Firefighter

Sheldon flew regularly for four clients until 1964 when yet another opportunity came knocking at the door – putting out forest fires with water bombers.

Now, this was a challenge!

One of his clients was behind this new venture: Bill Harrison, a silent partner in the new firm called Flying Firemen Limited (FFL). The company had purchased two Canso PBY-5A amphibians and converted them to water tankers which could drop hundreds of gallons of water or fire retardant onto forest fires.

FFL president Alex Davidson had known Sheldon from earlier days in Alberta, and had been the first man to bring a Mars Martin water bomber into B.C. to help put out or control forest fires from the air. He had been flying the Mars for a consortium of logging companies and saw the potential in expansion.

Alex wanted to work the southern part of the province from the main FFL base in Victoria, and he and Bill needed someone competent to handle flying boats throughout the north-central interior of the province.

In May 1965, Sheldon's career took a new twist: putting out forest fires from the air, as chief pilot for Flying Firemen.

One month later Grant died of a heart attack at the age of 56, on June 1, in Long Beach, California. Less than five weeks before his death, Grant had written Sheldon a letter asking of him a favour for a McConachie family friend and his boys.

Sheldon granted the favour.

The last time Sheldon had heard from Grant before the favour request had been in January 1964, when he received a Christmas letter in which family friendships were reviewed and business developments briefly highlighted.

Throughout 1965, FFL dumped more than one million gallons (454,610 l) of water onto B.C. forest fires, with pilots putting in more than three hundred hours of flying time in two water bombers.

Ray Williston, at the time B.C.'s Minister of Lands and Forests, saw Flying Firemen as a "group of daring and skilled adventurers whose future is secure."

But their fire-fighting future was secure in that forest fires always break out and always need to be brought under control.

However their financial future didn't look so rosy.

Each converted Canso set the company back $130,000.

By May 11th, 1966, FFL began its second season of this daring, adventurous and dangerous work.

About the only decent way ground fire suppression crews in remote regions can buy time to fight a fire is to bomb it from the air, with water or fire retardant compounds.

The converted PBY-5As were refurbished and modified to include a special belly compartment, equipped with two trap doors, allowing the pilot to skim along a lake surface and in seconds, scoop a thousand gallons of water, taking off again and moments later, dumping the load over a fire.

Flying Firemen's Cansos added a lot of striking power to the provincial fire suppression effort. Often a call would come in to the FFL base in Prince George and the Canso would be airborne in less than fifteen minutes, its tanks filled with whatever fluid or compound called for by the Fire Boss.

In one case, Sheldon averaged a thousand-gallon (3,182 l) drop every five minutes on a fire north of Prince George.

A forest fire wasn't the only way to prove the commercial value of a Canso. A sawmill fire would do.

One broke out in a sawmill along the banks of the Nechako in the industrial region of Prince George, an area known as Isle Pierre. The fire broke out shortly before noon in the log conveyor section leading to the mill's headsaw. The entire ramp was on fire and the mill water pumps couldn't handle the job.

They needed a water bomber.

Sheldon was on standby at the Prince George airport FFL base, and ordered a load of Firetrol – a commercial fire suppressant, pumped into the Canso tanks. With ground radio instructions to guide him, he sized up the fire from the air. The yard was nearly choked with lumber stacks, but he saw one clear path, wide enough for his plane's long wingspread.

The airpath looked like a chute leading straight to the fire.

He made a perfect approach, got the bomber up about 10 feet (3 m) from the ground and bore right in. As he pulled back on the control column, the

Canso responded and climbed. At just the right spot, he released his bomb-bay load.

The first drop tore the conveyor section to shreds, hit the carriage and then the thousand-pound load of Firetrol began doing its work.

Sheldon flew on to Six Mile Lake west of the city and returned for a second pass.

Which put out the fire for good.

After thanking him profusely, mill personnel joked with him, asking which did more damage, the Canso or the fire?

For the original book, I telephoned Frank Tannock, a former B.C. Forest Service fire-fighting official, and asked him for his comments and what he thought about Sheldon. He summed it up nicely by telling me that he recalled:

> ...one of the techniques (of water-bombing fires) he described was his slapshot employed on steep hills...
>
> ...Sheldon will never become an old pilot: he will, in my mind, just fly away.
>
> ...A good friend, and a hell of a man.

Transport Canada frowned on Sheldon's slapshot technique to help put out fires on steep mountain sides, especially for inexperienced pilots.

Even experienced pilots can get sucker-baited by Sheldon's slapshot maneuver. It calls for the pilot to bank his plane so its under-belly is almost level with a steep slope, and very close to it, putting the plane into a steep turn configuration.

Once the pilot releases his tanker's load, the aircraft goes through rapid and dramatic changes in its handling characteristic. If the pilot does not seize immediate control of the aircraft, it can go rapidly out of control in a downward spin, and spiral to the ground on the dipped wing side.

Sheldon did not use this technique unless he knew that it was absolutely called for and he told me that he never willingly tried to teach it to any other pilot. Others may have seen him do it and no doubt it was talked about in many places.

Putting out forest fires from the air took Sheldon all over the province with Alex. Where Flying Firemen went, news reporters weren't far behind. The business is risky and adventurous, a guaranteed headline maker – and once again Sheldon was in the news.

The fire fighting season, which usually runs from May to September, had barely started in 1967 when Vancouver Sun columnist Paul St. Pierre trekked out to Fort St. James to visit Sheldon.

Many people in the aviation business had asked themselves what had become of Sheldon. Was he still flying? Or what? They would soon find out from Paul, who told his readers: "Having raised that question, I shall try to answer it."

He drove from Prince George to Fort St. James only to discover Sheldon had been at the FFL base back in Prince George. Weary, Paul returned to Prince George and finally met Sheldon once again – they'd known each other for some time.

Describing him as "a big grey quiet man, one of the more knowledgeable survivors of that team of early bush pilots," he listened as Sheldon fascinated him with descriptions of putting out forest fires.

This was precision flying, requiring good judgment in picking out lakes with long approach paths and easy ways out.

"Over the fire, it's more difficult," he told Paul, who passed this on to his readers.

"Sometimes you've got to be no more than 25 feet (8 m) or at the most 50 feet (15 m) over the trees. I've seen 1,000 gallons (4,545 l) go over a fire from 200 feet (61 m) and not a drop gets to the fire. It's carried up in steam before it ever hits the ground."

Every now and then Sheldon would get lucky. Instead of getting thumped and thwacked around by a blast of hot air from the raging inferno below, he'd kill the fire stone dead with one pass. Such luck was rare.

When the interview in the Inn of the North hotel concluded, Paul wrote:

> *None of this, of course, answers the question of why Sheldon Luck didn't stick to his resolution of the late 50s when he was determined that he would never fly again, except now and then, for fun. Since he seems to be enjoying himself hugely, why ask? Let us not.*

The year 1968 took an exacting toll on Sheldon, in three gut-wrenching incidents.

The first involved an accident in Calgary, Alberta, which would slowly cripple Isabel for life.

The second involved a fire-bombing accident on Vancouver Island, which claimed the life of a dear friend.

The third hit came during a dead-stick landing on a mirror-flat Mara Lake, south of Sicamous, B.C., almost the half-way point between Calgary, Alberta, and Vancouver, on the Trans-Canada Highway.

On April 29th, 1968, before the fire-fighting season started, Isabel had been visiting family in Calgary and received severe head injuries in a vehicle accident: she never completely recovered.

Her health failed gradually over the years to the point where she died peacefully in a special care hospital in Kamloops, B.C. on June 28th, 1982.

Sheldon tended to her needs as best he could over those years, giving up the precious farm at Fort St. James to raise additional cash to defray horrendously large medical bills. Besides, it was too large a place to operate without Isabel, who before the accident, was intensely involved in the daily routines of the ranch and farm which she loved so much.

Then Alex Davidson and a young co-pilot perished in the fiery crash of a Flying Firemen Canso on Vancouver Island, in full sight of highway motorists.

Sheldon had last seen Alex alive at the Smithers airport, when they had flown in from two different fires. They re-fuelled and were to head back to the same fire when the B.C. Forest Service called Alex to fly south to Victoria where a fire had been giving them serious problems.

Alex took the opportunity to return and check out a young pilot on the Canso and fight the fire at the same time. This water bombing run was visible to hundreds of motorists on the Malahat Highway out of Victoria, when the Canso hit a tree.

Sheldon flew to Victoria to assist in the investigation. He'd barely gotten over the shock of Isabel's accident, and losing Alex, he decided the only thing he could do to retain his sanity and keep his emotions under some control was to work harder than ever.

On one of these flights, he experienced the first emergency dead-stick landing of a flying boat in his career.

He'd been working a fire on the northwest ridge of a mountain at the south end of the ten-mile long Mara Lake in the Shuswap region of the province, about 75 miles (121 km) east of Kamloops. The bird-dog officer in the firespotting aircraft had asked him if he could make one more pass before Sheldon returned to Kamloops for refueling.

He'd flown a number of passes in the previous three hours and asked his co-pilot to check the fuel gauges aft of the cockpit bulkhead. He was told there was enough fuel left for one more pass, but not a second.

The ridge is located about four miles (6 km) north of the southern limit of the lake. Sheldon started down for his final scoop of this session. As he cleared the ridge, the left engine quit.

Seconds later the right one quit.

The Canso tanks were bone dry.

The fuel gauges, easy to misread at their location, have since been moved forward to where both pilot and co-pilot can read them simultaneously.

Sheldon yelled out, "There's no god-dammed gas in this thing!"

Immediately taking stock of his alternatives, he realized there was only one. It was a hot, muggy day, without a breath of air to help him in his approach to the mirror-smooth surface of Mara Lake. Fortunately, there were a lot of miles ahead of him to permit a long, long approach.

Those hours of practice and his experience on floats and flying boats were about to pay off. He remembered one of his good friends, Dick Schiller, had been killed during the war years in Bermuda while trying to execute a deadstick landing on calm ocean waters. All flying boat pilots rely on a careful application of power in the final stages of a calm water landing.

Especially when it's in a Canso.

The Canso has quite a shallow step and needs that last burst of power to overcome the tremendous suction of the water surface on the hull when it makes initial contact with the water. The boat wants to nose in and pilots use this power to negate that tendency.

Sheldon had no such power this time.

He overcame the problem by kissing the water ever-so-gently, and managed to retain control. A boat, ordered by the bird-dog officer when Sheldon reported his fuel-out message, arrived soon after from Sicamous with enough fuel for Sheldon to resume his flight to Kamloops.

Canadair Limited wanted a chance to display its CL-215 amphibious aircraft to the B.C. Forest Service and demonstrate its impressive fire-fighting capabilities in the summer of 1969.

Although enjoying sales world-wide, the company had not yet scored a sale to B.C. Quebec province already owned a large fleet of CL-215s which were doing top-notch service over its enormous forest regions.

The B.C. Forest Service invited Sheldon to test fly the CL-215 and provide a water bombing demonstration. After a check flight with Bruce Lebens, who later joined Wardair as a senior heavy jet pilot, Sheldon flew the Cl-215 to Fort St. John for a four-hour test flight under operational conditions.

The provincial government wanted to see if its performance justified the multi-million dollar price tag.

It met Canadair's specs and publicity, but the price tag was just too rich for the province. Sheldon said it performed beautifully, and agreed with Canadair that it was and is the finest fire-fighting airplane in the world.

Canadair officials invited Sheldon to its sprawling manufacturing plant in suburban St. Laurent – vastly expanded since Bob Noorduyn first produced his Norseman there.

CL-215 sales were far below projections and executives wanted to know why. Too expensive, was the stock answer from B.C.

Sheldon made his report to Canadair test and production test pilots, executives and key engineers, providing astute observations on how it compared to the Canso and Super Canso in fire-fighting. When he ended, a company vice president rose and addressed the gathering:

"Where the hell was this man when we designed this airplane?"

### From bush pilot to jet-props

Late in 1969, Trans-Provincial Airways invited Sheldon to establish an IFR division; they needed a DOT-rated pilot with considerable experience as they planned to use a DC-3 then upgrade their fleet to include turbine-powered Fairchild F-27s.

A number of DOT personnel, and former military pilots were contacted by TPA in their search for the right man. Time and again one name cropped up: Sheldon Luck.

When approached for the job, Sheldon took careful stock of his finances, and Isabel's growing need for more intensive medical care. Their children had their own families: Jamie had settled in New Zealand, Nancy was on the Lower Mainland and the youngest, Grant – named in honour of Grant McConachie – was living in Fort St. James, had his own business, and was a pilot as well.

Sheldon accepted the position, and joined TPA early in 1970, moving himself and Isabel to Terrace to take advantage of the prime medical care facilities available at Alcan's Kitimat medical centre.

In the early 1970s, PWA had farmed out a large segment of its northwestern B.C. route structure to TPA and TPA wanted the F-27s to service these routes, via Smithers, Terrace and Prince Rupert.

Sheldon went to Hughes Airwest in Phoenix, Arizona, to take an upgrading course from piston engines to turbine driven aircraft. He made headlines again, although this time within an internal company publication. He'd been dubbed one of the oldest airline pilots who made the conversion from piston engines to the jet age on a major airline.

Airlines took into consideration conversion costs in upgrading older pilots from pistons to jets. It was often more economical to keep them on the piston planes and pay them jet-prop salaries than have them go on jet-props or jets for the last remaining five years of their employment, when they reached 60 years of age.

Consequently, few pilots over the age of sixty years ever got to that course in Arizona. Sheldon had to work harder than the younger pilots, but enjoyed the experience, all the while enriching his career as a professional pilot.

The F-27 boosted the number of aircraft types Sheldon had flown to 59.

As upgrading continued within TPA, Sheldon received a Telex from the Regional Superintendent Air Regulations, Ministry of Transport, in Vancouver, on August 1, 1974 – when he reached the age of 63:

The telex confirmed him as the:

> ...*company check pilot to carry out proficiency / instrument renewal checks on DC-3 type of aeroplanes only, and line indoctrination checks on DC-3 and F-27 types of aeroplanes only.*

On November 9th, 1974, Sheldon received his own proficiency check from Department of Transport Inspector Al McNutt, on a flight from Terrace to Prince Rupert.

McNutt ticked off every item on the list with an S, for satisfactory, with one exception - he felt Sheldon's circling procedure was just a bit too wide. McNutt's handwritten comments on Captain Luck's proficiency and instrument flying abilities:

> ...*Although Captain Luck's reaction time is slowing, this was a remarkably good ride for a man who has been flying 44 years.*

Throughout his years with TPA Sheldon saw much more development activity take place throughout British Columbia, as much in many cases as he'd seen in the early 1930s and 1940s. As a pilot he had participated in this new development and growth by flying needed supplies for the new Cassiar Highway, the expanding B.C. Railway and other charters for new resource development projects.

After his last flight with TPA in 1975, he felt certain he'd really retire, for good.

### In a hurry to fly home, Sheldon inadvertently triggers a NORAD alarm

Les Kerr, president of Conair Aviation on the Lower Mainland had other ideas. He heard Sheldon was still available, and asked if he would help them out in their fire-fighting operations. Just for this one summer only, please, flying a converted A-26 bomber.

Most of his flights with Conair were routine, until he tripped the North American Air Defense Command (NORAD) alert system with his A-26.

Returning from a fire drop north of Germansen Landing, he decided he wanted to get home fast and took the A-26 up to 14,000 feet (4,267 m).

Baldy Hughes radar base southwest of Prince George immediately reported a "bogey" clipping along at nearly 400 miles an hour (643 km), and no flight plan had been filed anywhere for that quadrant.

What was it?

And who?

The chain of command had this bogey reported to NORAD Headquarters in Colorado, who in turn notified the Canadian Forces Base in Comox on Vancouver Island to be ready to scramble fighters, just in case.

Before Comox decided to scramble its interceptor-fighters screaming after this "bogey", the Comox duty officer, acting on a hunch, called the B.C. Forest Service, which maintains an instant reporting system on all airplanes under contract in fire protection service.

He knew that Conair's A-26s were fighting forest fires in the exact area reported by Baldy Hughes.

In no time at all, the Comox duty officer identified this "bogey" – none other than Sheldon Luck hurrying home.

Unknown to Sheldon, he'd picked up a strong tail wind, which when added to his A-26's normal empty speed of about 365 miles an hour (487 km/hr), had pushed him over the 400 mph figure.

At season's end, Conair held a formal retirement party for Sheldon. Les presented him with a scale model of an A-26 water bomber, inscribed with the registry letters, C-LUCK.

In 1976, Sheldon spent all his time with Isabel and did not fly.

### Just fly for us once more, please, huh?

Al McNutt left the DOT and joined Avalon Aviation, another water bombing company which made extensive use of its Canso water bombers, operating out of Red Deer, Alberta.

Bill Casselman, one of their pilots, was quitting to join Canadair as a jet test pilot on its new Challenger business jet program and Avalon desperately needed a fill-in pilot to round out its contract in Thunder Bay, Ontario.

There was only one good man available on such short notice as far as Al was concerned: Sheldon. Couldn't Sheldon come out to Thunder Bay, and help a friend in need? Temporarily, of course!

This temporary job lasted the entire forest fire-fighting season of 1977.

At first reluctant to leave Isabel, Sheldon consulted with her doctor at the Prince George Regional Hospital. He advised Sheldon to take the job, if for nothing else than his own emotional well-being. Isabel was receiving the best medical care possible and there was nothing more Sheldon could do to help.

Now sixty-six years of age, he accepted Al's offer and drove to Thunder Bay to stomp out more forest fires, the last assignment of his remarkable flying career.

Bill Casselman at first reacted with mild amazement on learning he was being replaced by a white-haired 66-year old water bomber.

He told me he rapidly swallowed his words after his first flight with Sheldon.

At season's end, Sheldon had flown 88 hours. As luck would have it, his professional career which began with a bang and a fire, ended with his putting out a fire!

## 12. Father Dies on Take-off, Son Becomes Instant Solo Pilot

August 4th, 1969: a hot, near-perfect summer day and smack-dab in the middle of the fire-fighting season high in the central interior of the west-coast province of British Columbia, Canada.

Since there was no forest fire in that vast region that day, Sheldon was on standby as a fire fighting pilot at the airport of the central BC interior city of Prince George, some 500 miles (804 km) north of Vancouver.

The deceptive calm of the day would be shattered by a near-panic radio distress call late in the afternoon, a call that would result in the most hair-raising mercy rescue mission of Sheldon's 50-year career in aviation.

On this day, he would get no closer to a large aircraft in distress – nearly 120 miles (193 km) northwest of him – than a loudspeaker in the airport control tower.

In this incident, a frightened and untried air traffic controller prevented Sheldon from talking directly to the totally-inexperienced 20-year old pilot of the large Canso amphibian aircraft which was about to crash nose-first into Trembleur Lake.

Moments before the take-off there had been 13 lives on board.

The pilot had died of a heart attack on take-off.

Now there remained 12 lives on board.

And if something did not happen quickly, and correctly, there would soon be no aircraft flying and no lives left living on board.

A rare type of talk-down rescue mission had begun, one in which Sheldon, three commercial airline pilots, and the air traffic controller were instrumental in helping bring to a successful end less than two nerve-wracking hours later.

The pilot of the Canso had died within seconds of his third, and finally successful, attempt at lifting the Canso up and off of the calm, clear and ice-cold waters of Trembleur Lake, leaving his 20-year old son in the right hand seat at the controls of an aircraft he had barely come to know under his father's tutelage.

This young man had two choices – panic and go down with the plane which it would certainly would have done if not brought under immediate control, or steel his nerves and try to bring the plane under control ... and in the process, make the first solo flight of his life. Usually a solo flight is every young pilot's dream, but for this young man, his solo had mutated into a vivid living nightmare.

As the Canso aircraft throbbed onwards southeast towards Prince George, the SOB head count (SOB = aviation-speak for *Souls on Board*) consisted of 11 adult men and one 14-year old boy, who was tucked into the nose cone of this flying boat as it lifted off the step on Trembleur Lake.

They were about to become death statistics in what had begun as a three-week friendly fishing expedition to the beautiful mountain lakes of BC and threatened to snuff out their lives in seconds.

The cavernous cabin of a Canso made it a natural for conversion by wealthy owners into a highly mobile and sometimes luxurious, motor home with wings. Such was the amphibious Canso assigned with American Registration Number, N70057C and named by its owner, "The Golden Goose", as it prepared for take-off on that hot calm summer afternoon.

The incident began innocently enough for the two men in the cockpit of the privately-owned Canso.

They were 52 year-old senior IBM executive, John Dorr Sr., the owner of the plane, who sat in the left hand, captain's seat and 20 year-old, as yet to solo student pilot, John Dorr Jr., his son, who sat in the right hand co-pilot's seat.

Their check lists complete, they were ready for take-off from the waters of Trembleur Lake, their next destination on their way home to California.

Their 10 fishing companions, who were some of the top business executives in the US, including a 14 year old boy, Evan Ellis, were safely settled in their seats in the roomy passenger cabin behind the cockpit. Their catch and miscellaneous camping equipment was stowed at the back of the aft cabin. The 12 friends had already been in the area for more than a week, fishing, and were planning to visit more lakes before returning home to California.

It had been an absolute dream vacation, so far, for any avid sports fisherman.

They had enjoyed excellent fishing at all the lakes they had visited, the weather had been fantastic and now, moments before take-off they were already spinning the yarns in their heads, probably stretching the truth a little, that they would tell to their envious friends back home about the trip.

A lone bull moose, up to his knees in the cold lake munching contentedly on some water plants, raised his head to watch as the plane swung slowly around to a southerly heading for take-off away from the high ground surrounding the other three sides of the lake. Ahead of the Golden Goose, to the southeast, lay a clear but glassy, nearly 20 mile-long (32 km) stretch of Trembleur Lake waters. Not a breath of wind disturbed the muggy air while above three diverging contrails, etched stark white, crisscrossed the azure sky.

The sudden roar of the engines, as John Sr. reached up with his right hand and set the ceiling-mounted throttles of the big seaplane to full take-off power, sent the moose charging into the woods leaving a trail crushed saplings and even small trees in its wake.

Suddenly sensing something wrong, John Sr. chopped the power, aborting the take-off, leaving only a dying echo to bounce off the surrounding hills.

He hadn't been able to get the Canso onto its shallow, stepped hull, a necessity to break clear of the sucking surface tension of the still water, and take-off.

Unless the plane could get up on the step it would never get enough speed to take off.

It is a problem common to Cansos on glassy-water take offs.

He turned the plane around and quickly taxied back to his original starting point. He hoped to take advantage of the waves he had made on the first take-off run to break the surface tension of the glassy water but by the time he got the plane headed south again his wake had quickly subsided and the lake returned to its original mirror like surface.

Calling on techniques learned from his US Navy experience, he tried coaxing the plane to accelerate up to the magic speed at which it would get up on the step by rocking the wings.

Still it was no go.

There was only one thing left to try. Change the centre of gravity of the ship by moving all the baggage and passengers as far forward as he could get them. He set his passengers to work moving all the camping gear into the forward passenger cabin and even had young Evan sit in the nose compartment ahead and below of the cockpit in the nose wheel well.

From this vantage point Evan had a good view of John Dorr Sr. as he went through the take-off ritual. As the plane began to accelerate on its third try to escape the lake John Sr. felt a slight shift in the ship's response.

Yes this time they were definitely going to make it.

John Dorr Sr. smiled, nodded to his son that they were on the step, eased back on the control column and lifted the reluctant "Golden Goose" to about 15 metres (50 feet) in the air.

John Dorr Senior suddenly slumped unconscious over the controls and died.

Down in the nose compartment, young Evan felt the liberating and exhilarating sensation of flight as the plane surged up free from the lake. He looked up expecting to see the pilot's grin of satisfaction but instead looked horrifyingly into the expressionless, unblinking eyes of the lifeless John Dorr Sr. as he slumped forward over the control column.

Far to the south, in Prince George, Sheldon was staring at the brown-coloured muck that passed for coffee at FFL and was wondering what he should do next. All the routine chores around his water bomber had been done long ago in the morning. His ground crew had headed off to town on some errand or other and would not be back anytime soon. He had released them from stand-by for an hour on the basis that there were no pending fire threats in the area. He on the other hand would be standing-by; there was no relief for his duty.

He was completely unaware of the unfolding drama, with which he would be so directly involved in within the next few minutes, taking place on Trembleur Lake

At that very moment, the flight of "The Golden Goose" threatened to end immediately – at full-throttle take-off speed.

John Sr. was slumped over the controls and no one was flying the plane.

With no one in control, even for a few seconds, during one of two of the most hazardous times of any flight (take offs and landings) it could go out of control in a finger snap.

Should it do that, it would immediately plunge into the cold, icy waters of Trembleur Lake.

His son, John Jr. had taken a few flying lessons on small light planes but had yet to solo. He had sat in the co-pilot's seat of the Canso with his father often and he was well aware of how quickly a pilot must react if anything should go wrong but he had never before been alone at the controls during a take-off.

He immediately sensed that he had to do something and do it fast, to prevent certain death for him and his 10 passengers. John Jr. reacted instinctively when he saw that his father had collapsed over the controls. He quickly took control, struggling to overcome the burdensome weight of his father's body slumped over the controls which was in danger of pitching the plane into a steep nose-down attitude.

He knew, even with his limited experience, that the plane was too close to the water for comfort. He had to prevent it, at all costs and with all his might, from sinking back onto the lake.

John Jr. never felt more alone in his life.

Thankfully his father had drilled into John Jr. and his other three children not to panic in dangerous situations. With great courage and determination, John Jr. thrust aside his immediate horror and concern about what was happening to his much-loved father and as calmly as he could, followed the credo that every pilot learns in his first flying lesson.

No matter what happens, the first and most import thing to do above all other distractions, is "fly the plane!"

He knew that if he could keep the plane more or less with its wings level and keep it in a climb that they would be out of immediate danger.

After that, then what?

Young Dorr shouted loudly - to be heard above the engine noise - for help from his passengers to get his father off the controls while the terrified Evan looked on from his position in the nose. Two of the fishing party on the Canso were doctors and they removed his father from the pilot's seat as quickly and gently as they could and tried to revive him. With his father's immediate needs taken care of John Jr. now anxiously settled down to consider the longer-term consequences.

With agonizing clarity he realized that the outcome of the flight would depend on his ability to land this ugly airplane either on land or water.

He felt sure he was going to need a lot of help and a lot of luck.

How could he know he was going to get exactly that ... and in exactly that order?

A lot of help from Mr. Luck, and not Lady Luck.

John Jr. did not know it at that moment, but the flight would test the strengths and weaknesses of his character along with those of Sheldon Luck, a man a long way away and of whom he had never heard of before today.

What to do next? Who could help him? And how?

Luckily, they were not alone in the air that day.

John Jr. knew enough to immediately radio for help.

And he was heard, loud and clear, by the pilots of three airliners, high above him, two of them quite some distance away.

That traffic – and those who would be involved in the talk-down rescue mission – were: a jetliner, high overhead, coming down via the Arctic Circle route from Europe making for Vancouver; a Canadian Pacific B-737, slightly below the higher jet, which had left Prince George airport and was flying northeast towards Fort St. John; and lower yet, in a different direction, a BC Airlines (BCA) Nord turboprop aircraft coming out of Prince George, westbound, heading for Smithers BC.

John Jr. continued climbing "The Golden Goose" in lazy circles to clear the surrounding mountain tops. Compared to the light training planes he had flown, the controls of this monster were sluggish and heavy. He was wise enough not to make quick control movements and carefully experimented with how the ship responded to his inputs.

Now after having the plane under his control he must get help!!!

His father had left the radio tuned to the Very High Frequency (VHF) international distress frequency of 121.5 MHz and now John Jr. picked up the microphone and calmly called "The Golden Goose's" registration number, "May Day, May Day, May Day, this is November seven zero zero five seven Charlie"

May Day is the call of ships and planes in distress coming from the French phrase, *"m'aidez,"* (help me). Immediately all ears were up on any plane in the area.

At the same time, up in the Prince George airport control tower, Dave Dayton, the duty controller, and an assistant were having a coffee.

Sheldon was on standby at the Flying Firemen Limited Prince George airport water bomber base, a few minutes' walking distance from the control tower.

When John Jr. had hit the airwaves with his shocking news, his message triggered a flurry of calm, controlled activity, and activated all the resources of Canada's Air Traffic Control facilities, the Search and Rescue Headquarters of the Royal Canadian Air Force at Edmonton and the nearby Northern Air Defense, (NORAD) Radar Station at Baldy Hughes.

As soon as he was alerted to the emergency, the traffic controller called the Flying Firemen air tanker base and asked if Sheldon were there, and if he were, would he please immediately come to the tower to help out in an emergency that was now taking place..

Ironically, Sheldon never once got a chance to talk to John Jr. directly.

The two young tower controllers, likely inexperienced in emergencies, were probably nervous, confused and frightened.

Young Dayton said it would be against regulations to let Sheldon talk directly to John Jr.

He was adamant about it, despite every plea Sheldon made.

As far as the senior controller was concerned, this was his tower, his emergency, and he was in charge and would go by the book. Not Sheldon!

Unable to do anything else, Sheldon resigned himself to the worst, hoping for the best. Relaying instructions third-hand was no way to help young Dorr, but it was the only thing he could do. He couldn't leave the tower in a huff to spite the controller and risk 12 lives, and perhaps more if the Canso were to crash into the city.

The senior controller would listen to Sheldon and relay the information to John Jr.

Sheldon acted on information he heard from John Jr. by way of the loudspeaker in the tower.

Sheldon, who became the key man in this drama, did not know that he would be rendered so helpless as to be almost speechless with fury and beyond belief when Dayton refused to let him speak directly with the pilot. He quickly realized, when called to the control tower to assist, that he could do no more than "talk" to this young man at third-hand ... basically, talk down an inexperienced pilot in a desperate attempt to save the lives of all 12 souls who were on board the still-flying aircraft.

The Prince George control tower did not pick up John Jr.'s original May Day call because the Canso was too low, well below the mountain peaks on either side of Trembleur Lake.

The B.C. Airlines pilot, Captain Jack Spurr, who was closest to "The Golden Goose" had to relay the May Day message back to the tower. Once this was clearly established, the pilots of the overhead jetliners, who also heard and relayed the May Day message, listened but remained clear of the frequency once they were acknowledged by Prince George tower.

They immediately went into radio silence, but stood by in the event that they were needed while the Captain Spurr gave instructions to "The Golden Goose" to get it to Prince George

For nearly 30 long harrowing minutes, communications had to be relayed from the tower out to the BCA airliner, and from airliner back down to John Jr. because the Canso was still flying too low for good reception in Prince George.

Once the "Goose" got to within 50 miles (80 km) of Prince George, John Jr. would be able to talk directly to the tower without the need of a relay.

One of the first set of instructions given by Captain Spurr was for young Dorr to take the plane up to a higher altitude and set a course south-easterly for Prince George. Once the plane cleared the mountain tops, the tower controller could pick up his transmissions and talk to John Jr. directly.

Prince George hospital officials, who had been alerted by the tower, emergency crash and fire control crews at the airport, the three airline crews, the tower controller, his assistant, Sheldon, and all the affected aviation agencies in Northern BC were now aware that an airborne drama had begun that would last for nearly an hour-and-a-half.

By the time Sheldon made it to the control tower, he had learned that John Jr. had taken a flying course in California. At least he wasn't dealing with an outright novice, which he had feared at first.

This situation changed when Sheldon learned that save for a few hunting and fishing trips in the Canso with his father, and following through on the co-pilot control column with his father on some landings and take offs, he had no experience whatsoever on anything as large as the Canso.

As a matter of fact, Sheldon knew the aircraft by sight, and knew about the party. A few days earlier, he'd been water bombing a fire north of Trembleur Lake and remembered having seen the Canso moored in front of a shore camp, near a sandy beach on the northwest shore of the lake.

He saw that the party had two tents and had been drying fish on racks in an open birch grove.

This told him a lot about the probable cargo load on board the Canso, in addition to knowing about the passenger load.

Sheldon also had a pretty good idea about the amount of fuel in the plane's tanks. Knowing these things, backed by his own experience with different kinds of loads in flying bush operations over the years, and throughout WW II and in later years operating flying boats out of Argentina and throughout North America, he had a good idea on how the weight might have been distributed, which would be vital for the information that he had to relay to John Jr. to continue the flight into Prince George and make a safe landing.

If he could.

When the Canso appeared over Prince George, Sheldon instructed the controller to tell John Jr. to bring the aircraft to a southerly direction and approach the airport from the south, well removed from any homes, over which the Canso was now flying.

He asked the controller to warn John Jr. to, at all costs, make wide, gently-banked turns onto the final approach to the runway, because Sheldon was certain he couldn't handle that size of aircraft in a steep turn.

Sheldon wanted John Jr. on a long straight-in approach path, coming in at the best possible speed using engine power settings that Sheldon has given to him to arrive over the button, on the threshold of the north-south runway, designated as Runway 33.

The controller, John Jr. and Sheldon kept up a continuous patter of conversation.

Sheldon needed to know a lot of things about the on-board situation in the Canso before thinking out the consequences of any advice that he should give.

He also found it extremely stressing to work under the complication of not being able to talk to John Jr. directly.

John Jr. had relayed such information as engine revolutions per minute (RPM), manifold pressure and other instrument readings for Sheldon. He'd had ample time in the last 75 minutes to experiment carefully and gauge the response of the aircraft to certain control inputs on his part.

John Jr. made a long sweeping turn to the east and then north again to line himself up with the centre line of the runway.

Sheldon gave him airspeed corrections, having determined earlier another critical factor: the Canso airspeed indicator read out in miles-per-hour (MPH). If it would have been in knots and Sheldon had not known this, the approach speeds given by Sheldon would have been too slow and the plane would have crashed before arriving over the runway.

He didn't want to confuse John Jr. any more than he already was.

He'd already made certain that John Jr. had lowered the landing gear, and made certain that he knew that the wheels were down and *locked* in place.

Sheldon's plan: bring the Canso down to the button, and John Jr. would have plenty of room ahead of him. Sheldon estimated, correctly, that the landing gear would be about 10 feet (3 m) over the runway when the Canso crossed the button.

It was no easy feat trying to judge the Canso's height above the runway button from his vantage point some 2,000 feet (609 m) away, and up in the control tower where he watched the plane's movements just before it would touch down on the runway.

It would have been even harder for a novice pilot like John Jr. – given his inexperience in landing any plane alone - to know how high above the runway he was from inside the cockpit, with its limited vertical visibility

The moment that Sheldon had judged the plane to be at the right height above the runway, he had the controller tell John Jr. to immediately pull back on the throttles and reduce power to the engines.

He knew that a tail-heavy Canso would sink, fairly gently, tail-first and the Canso could continue its landing – easy as pie.

Which is exactly what happened.

But, about halfway down the runway, the Canso suddenly swung violently to the right, coming to a stop sitting crossways on the active runway.

At the request of the controller, Sheldon went to the runway to greet the young hero and his passengers. A Flying Firemen engineer went with him to help Sheldon taxi the aircraft from the runway to the ramp used by FFL and the BC Forest Service.

Once on board, Sheldon discovered that John Jr. had faced a new set of problems after the Canso had landed, one which happened without warning.

The hydraulic system to the wheel brakes had leaked.

Each time John Jr. tried to apply the brakes after the landing gear touched down, the broken connection spewed out hydraulic fluid under high pressure, causing the right wheel to suddenly brake while the left one continued to roll, suddenly swinging the plane right.

Sheldon credits the young man with having saved the lives of all those on board.

He took over the controls in a cool-headed manner. He knew enough not to touch those radio controls pre-set by his father prior to take-off, making it instantly possible for him to send out his May Day call on frequencies being routinely monitored by other aircraft.

John Jr. later told Sheldon that had the Canso still been on the water when his father died, he would have closed the throttles, landed straight ahead and then radioed for help on the preset VHF distress frequency of 121.5 MHZ.

But since it was airborne, and nearly 50 feet (15 m) above the water, he decided to continue the flight, knowing he had ample room ahead – enough to climb out and try for Prince George.

He wouldn't have dared to try a water landing this close to the water.

# Epilogue

Sheldon did not stop flying for pleasure, but simply allowed the commercial portion of his license to lapse, satisfied with being a private pilot using his son Grant's Cessna 172.

In January 1984, he chose to not renew his private pilot's license, 54 years and one month from the day of his first solo.

Few outside the aviation community are aware of Canada's Aviation Hall of Fame in Edmonton's Convention Centre. This is a sad reflection of our times.

Despite a strong founding sponsorship from nine corporations and individuals (listed elsewhere) the Hall operates under a spartan publicity and advertising budget.

Air Vice Marshall (Retired) K.M. Guthrie launched a compassionate plea the same night he and Sheldon became a Companion of Icarus in June, 1981.

He stood before friends in the Macdonald Hotel's Rupertsland Room – fronting fellow Companion of Icarus members, their wives, escorts, friends and six young men and women. All were impeccably attired for one of the most prestigious gathering of aviation greats Canada had ever seen in one room.

In a strong voice, heard clearly throughout the room, he said:

Canada must know about its aviation history. The nation must understand the full significance aviation has had and understand the force it continues to exert on its development.

He lamented the lack of public awareness about the importance of aviation to the full growth of Canada as a nation.

The ultimate sadness: his plea fell on converted ears. I was the only writer in the room.

He was right.

Who cares a whit today?

Canadians seem to take aviation as much for granted as they do turning on hot or cold water taps.

The thrill and romance associated with early aviation growth are indeed gone.

Modernization and high technology make aviation work so well that it can be, and, is, taken for granted.

It really is hard to establish a one-on-one personal association with a sleek jumbo jet, which tips the scales at a few hundred thousand pounds or more – a screaming giant groping for air space. Little wonder many view airliners as high-flying posh restaurants with seat belts that clip along at nearly 10 miles (16 km) a minute.

Compared to giant sea cruise liners where a limited number of guests get to dine with the captain, airliner passengers, even those in first class, rarely if ever get to see their flight crews on any kind of a personal basis… other than the captain or first officer taking a seemingly casual walk-through of the passenger cabin during a flight to "check out" the passengers, nod pleasantly here and there, go to the back of the passenger cabin and return to the "front office" to resume his or her flying duties.

*Photo from Sheldon's personal collection taken by a photographer with H.H. Douglas and Company, in Prince George in 1940, when Yukon Southern Air Transport provided regular air service into and out of this central BC city. Passengers loved to have their pictures taken with their pilot (when they could) or at least with their aircraft that either brought them home or were taking them somewhere else.*

Truly, at the time of writing the original book, an era of flight was ending where it became more important to get to the airport in time than to worry about getting your picture taken with the plane or any crew member.

Double-decker airliners were being planned, and with the race to head for space, the science of ballistics was starting to get real respect.

No particular event could exactly mark its passing, but the start of its passing can be traced to the introduction of heavy airliners, known in the trade as "heavies," and Neil Armstrong becoming the first human being to leave a footprint on the surface of the moon.

Both the original 1986 book, *Walking on Air* and this book are my tribute to the end of the era which Sheldon and his colleagues helped create.

Looking back, one can detect five identifiable levels of flight:

Level One: the original pioneers – those who flew between 1909 and 1929
Level Two: those who took up flying from 1930 to 1938
Level Three: pilots from 1939 on, who also graduated to
Level Four: jet and pre-space pilots
Level Five: astronauts, planet landers (the moon in 1969) and space station and space shuttle pilots

Space is without a doubt our next frontier. And given that scientists announced in mid-November 2008 that they can now bend light and make something very small invisible. Therefore, it now seems that space alone is no longer our final frontier (sorry about that, Trekkies!). It really looks like we have time and room to explore new dimensions and re-discover what reality is all about where frontiers are concerned.

Wonder what kind of Sheldon Lucks are awaiting our discovery?

Sheldon is a Level Two pioneer who made it successfully, and with considerable polish, through to Levels Three and Four, stopping short of the pure jet category.

Professional pilots consider him a rarity – a pilot who began as a pilot, and stayed a pilot throughout his entire flying career.

## Canada's Aviation Hall of Fame

Canada's Aviation Hall of Fame came into being in Edmonton, Alberta, in 1973, as a non-profit institution, incorporated as a company under Part II of the Canada Corporations Act. Its nineteen founding subscribers were:

Alcan Canada Products Ltd.

Air Canada

Atco Industries Ltd.

Boeing Commercial Airplane Company

Canadian Pacific Limited

Cominco Ltd.

Comstock International Ltd.

Douglas Aircraft of Canada Ltd.

Eaton's of Canada Limited

Hudson's Bay Company

Imperial Oil Limited

Molson Breweries Limited

Pacific Western Airlines

Reed Shaw Stenhouse Limited

George Richard A. Price

James Richardson & Sons Limited

The Royal Trust Company (Compagnie Trust Royal)

Spar Aerospace Products Ltd.

Woodward Stores Limited

The Hall came into being:

> *To explore and initiate every responsible measure available to elevate, protect and preserve the names and deeds (for the enlightenment of present Canadians and generations yet to come) of those persons both alive and dead, whose contributions to the advancement of Canadian aviation, or acts of supreme gallantry in the arena of aerial combat while a member of Canada's armed forces, have been of superior benefit to the nation.*

In 1981, Sheldon became the 20$^{th}$ new member elected to the Hall since its inception with its original 77 members – two of them women and one a company, Trans-Canada Airlines.

He also received three other honours simultaneously with his induction to the Hall – the first saw him become a Companion of Icarus, the second came from the City of Edmonton and the third from the Government of Yukon Territory.

The City of Edmonton's *Order of Flight* recognized his

> *"...superior contributions as an aviation pioneer to this nation's growth. He shall ever merit the high esteem of the citizens of the great frontier city of Edmonton."*

Ray Munro, the Hall's first president and author of *The Sky's No Limit*, asked the then Yukon Commissioner, James Smith, to produce a special recognition from the Yukon for those inducted into the Hall: thus the *Order of Polaris*, with its medal and scroll. The order is oriented about the North Star – Polaris, a stellar navigational reference point above the northern hemisphere.

Part of the inscription recognizes each recipient for his or her

> *"...outstanding role as a pioneer of aviation in the Canadian north... for courage in negotiating the uncharted wilderness... for dedication and perseverance in developing the Dominion's last frontier."*

In 1982, Max Ward invited Sheldon to attend a ceremony which Wardair held in Québec City, to honour another Hall member, Stan McMillan – naming a DC-10 the *S.R. McMillan*.

Two years later, Sheldon received another accolade – a day in his honour, from radio station CJCI in Prince George, BC. This special *Sheldon Luck Day* came about through the enthusiastic support and drive of Bob Harkins, then features editor at the radio station. Sheldon appeared as Bob's morning talk show guest. He gave a noon-hour speech at the Rotary Club and later that night spoke to a packed house in the new Prince George District Library as guest of the Prince George District Historical Society.

As stated a number of times earlier, Sheldon made many headlines in his career. He's also been referred to in one way or another in at least six other books.

They include:

*Bush Pilot With a Briefcase - the happy-go-lucky story of Grant McConachie*

*Canada's Flying Heritage*

*Ferryman: From Ferry Command to Silver City - Taffy Powell*

*History of the City of Kamloops*

*North from Edmonton Pioneering in Canadian Aviation*

*Walking on Air (original 1986 version)*
is number six, and was for him and his colleagues.

*Pilot of Fortune*
is number seven, my second and last personal tribute to his memory and accomplishments.

If this edition only serves to inspire one boy or one girl, or one man or one woman, to strive for the best and overcome adversity in his or her life, or reach for the moon and bring back stars, then regardless of his or her career choice, it will have served its purpose.

## Sheldon Luck: Resumé

Below is a list of the companies and individuals who made good use of Sheldon's flying skills:

Advance Air Services / Columbia Aviation

United Air Transport / Yukon Southern Air Transport

Canadian Pacific Air Lines

ATFERO

Ferry Command

Transport Command

No. 231 Communications Squadron, RAF

La FAMA, Argentina

Northern Airways

O'Sullivan Construction

Lundy Entreprises

Associated Airways

Queen Charlotte Airlines

Maritime Central Airways

Northern Mountain Airlines

Pacific Western Airlines

BC/Yukon Air Services

Flying Firemen Limited

Trans-Provincial Airways

Conair Avalon

## Sheldon Luck's Ferry Command "Crew Cards"

As Pilot in Command of a RAF Ferry Command aircraft, Sheldon would have been paid $1,000 a flight, a significant amount of money in those days.

Such rewards may seem high, but pilots were given little chance of surviving their trips. The aircraft were unarmed and both the Germans and Japanese were always on the lookout for such planes, their intelligence working full-time to learn what planes were flying where and when, carrying what passengers and what types of cargo. Ferry Command aircraft carried much of the ammunition needed by Montgomery for the North Africa campaign and even transported agents from Camp X, east of Toronto, Ontario to Europe. These courageous men and women were trained to penetrate German lines, often at the cost of their own lives.

Files were kept on Ferry Command pilots and records of every flight were maintained. These light blue cards, known as "Crew Cards," were usually filled out in pencil with details of each flight, including aircraft type, number of stops, etc. Because of the secretive nature of many Ferry Command flights, publication of these "Crew Cards" was restricted for many years after the war.

Sheldon Luck's "Crew Card" file is pictured over the next five pages.

*The front page of Sheldon Luck's file contained personal information which has been redacted for public viewing. Images courtesy the Directorate of History and Heritage.*

*Looking through the cards shows the huge number of hours spent flying and the many different types flown. Even the multi-engine heavies were flown by single pilots and were unarmed.*

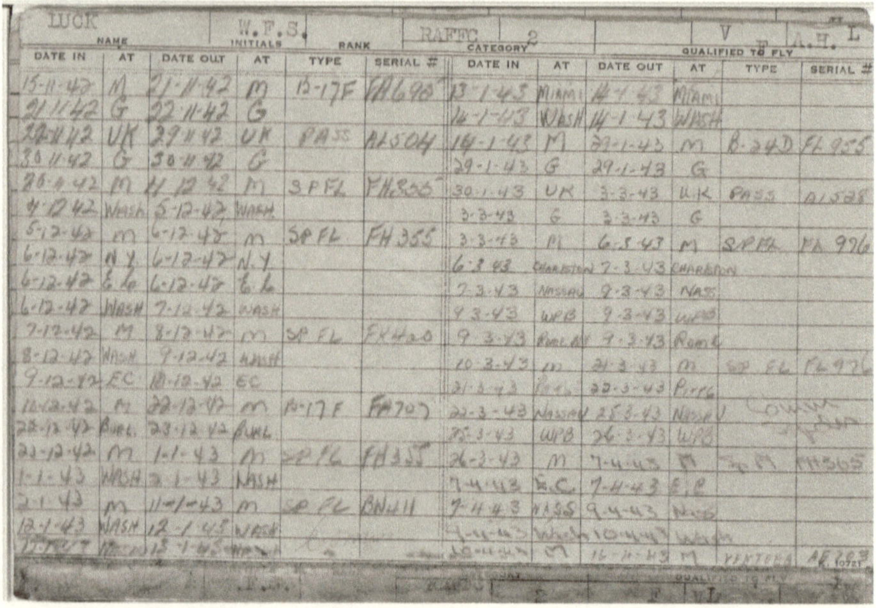

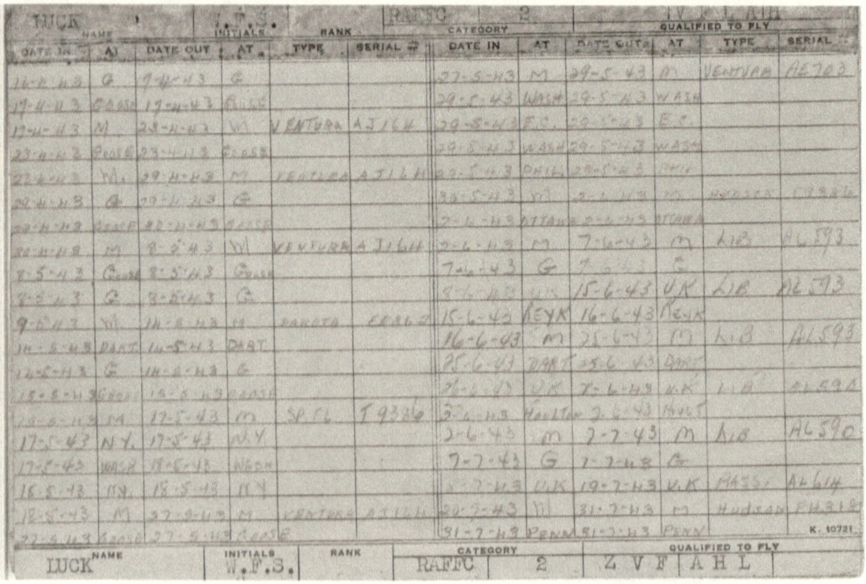

# PILOT OF FORTUNE

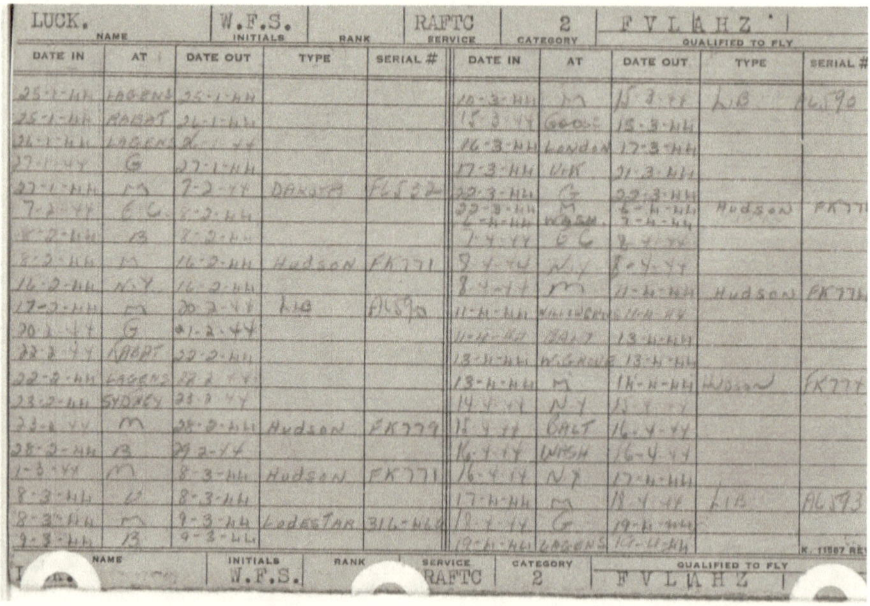

| LUCK. (NAME) | W.F.S. (INITIALS) | (RANK) | RAFTC (SERVICE) | 2 (CATEGORY) | F V L A H Z (QUALIFIED TO FLY) |
|---|---|---|---|---|---|

| DATE IN | AT | DATE OUT | TYPE | SERIAL # | DATE IN | AT | DATE OUT | TYPE | SERIAL # |
|---|---|---|---|---|---|---|---|---|---|
| 25-1-44 | LAGENS | 25-1-44 | | | 10-3-44 | M | 15-3-44 | LIB | AL590 |
| 25-1-44 | RABAT | 26-1-44 | | | 15-3-44 | GOOSE | 15-3-44 | | |
| 26-1-44 | LAGENS | 26-1-44 | | | 16-3-44 | LONDON | 17-3-44 | | |
| 27-1-44 | G | 27-1-44 | | | 17-3-44 | U.K. | 21-3-44 | | |
| 27-1-44 | M | 7-2-44 | DAKOTA | FL532 | 22-3-44 | G | 22-3-44 | | |
| 7-2-44 | E.C. | 8-2-44 | | | 22-3-44<br>6-4-44 | M<br>WASH. | 6-4-44<br>7-4-44 | Hudson | FK77[illegible] |
| 8-2-44 | B | 8-2-44 | | | 7-4-44 | E.C. | 8-4-44 | | |
| 8-2-44 | M | 16-2-44 | Hudson | FK771 | 8-4-44 | N.Y. | 8-4-44 | | |
| 16-2-44 | N.Y. | 16-2-44 | | | 8-4-44 | M | 11-4-44 | Hudson | FK774 |
| 17-2-44 | M | 20-2-44 | LIB | AL590 | 11-4-44 | [illegible] | 11-4-44 | | |
| 20-2-44 | G | 21-2-44 | | | 11-4-44 | BALT | 13-4-44 | | |
| 22-2-44 | RABAT | 22-2-44 | | | 13-4-44 | W. GROVE | 13-4-44 | | |
| 22-2-44 | LAGENS | 22-2-44 | | | 13-4-44 | M | 14-4-44 | Hudson | FK774 |
| 23-2-44 | SYDNEY | 23-2-44 | | | 14-4-44 | N.Y. | 15-4-44 | | |
| 23-2-44 | M | 28-2-44 | Hudson | FK779 | 15-4-44 | BALT | 16-4-44 | | |
| 28-2-44 | B | 29-2-44 | | | 16-4-44 | WASH | 16-4-44 | | |
| 1-3-44 | M | 8-3-44 | Hudson | FK771 | 16-4-44 | N.Y. | 17-4-44 | | |
| 8-3-44 | B | 8-3-44 | | | 17-4-44 | M | 18-4-44 | LIB | AL593 |
| 8-3-44 | M | 9-3-44 | LODESTAR | 316-[illegible] | 18-4-44 | G | 19-4-44 | | |
| 9-3-44 | B | 9-3-44 | | | 19-4-44 | LAGENS | 19-4-44 | | K. 11567 REV. |

| (NAME) | W.F.S. (INITIALS) | (RANK) | RAFTC (SERVICE) | 2 (CATEGORY) | F V L A H Z (QUALIFIED TO FLY) |
|---|---|---|---|---|---|

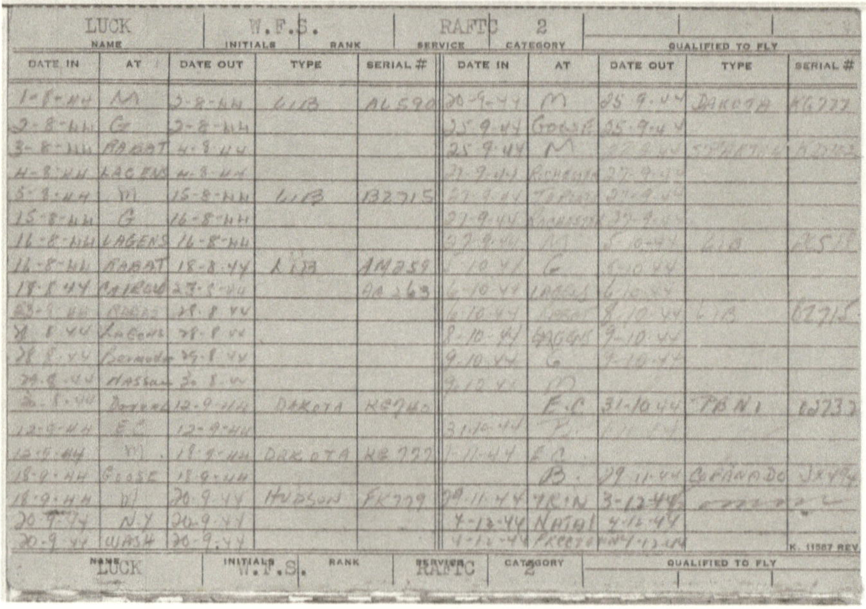

| LUCK (NAME) | W.F.S. (INITIALS) | (RANK) | RAFTC (SERVICE) | 2 (CATEGORY) | (QUALIFIED TO FLY) |
|---|---|---|---|---|---|

| DATE IN | AT | DATE OUT | TYPE | SERIAL # | DATE IN | AT | DATE OUT | TYPE | SERIAL # |
|---|---|---|---|---|---|---|---|---|---|
| 1-8-44 | M | 2-8-44 | LIB | AL590 | 20-9-44 | M | 25-9-44 | DAKOTA | KG777 |
| 2-8-44 | G | 2-8-44 | | | 25-9-44 | GOOSE | 25-9-44 | | |
| 3-8-44 | RABAT | 4-8-44 | | | 25-9-44 | M | [illegible] | [illegible] | [illegible] |
| 4-8-44 | LAGENS | 4-8-44 | | | 27-9-44 | [illegible] | 27-9-44 | | |
| 5-8-44 | M | 15-8-44 | LIB | BZ715 | 27-9-44 | [illegible] | 27-9-44 | | |
| 15-8-44 | G | 16-8-44 | | | 27-9-44 | [illegible] | 27-9-44 | | |
| 16-8-44 | LAGENS | 16-8-44 | | | 27-9-44 | M | 5-10-44 | LIB | AS[illegible] |
| 16-8-44 | RABAT | 18-8-44 | LIB | AM259 | 5-10-44 | G | 6-10-44 | | |
| 18-8-44 | [illegible] | 23-8-44 | | AA263 | 6-10-44 | [illegible] | 6-10-44 | | |
| 23-8-44 | RABAT | 28-8-44 | | | 6-10-44 | [illegible] | 8-10-44 | LIB | BZ715 |
| 28-8-44 | LAGENS | 28-8-44 | | | 8-10-44 | LAGENS | 9-10-44 | | |
| 28-8-44 | Bermuda | 29-8-44 | | | 9-10-44 | G | 9-10-44 | | |
| 29-8-44 | NASSAU | 30-8-44 | | | 9-10-44 | M | | | |
| 30-8-44 | Dorval | 12-9-44 | DAKOTA | [illegible] | | E.C. | 31-10-44 | PBN1 | [illegible] |
| 12-9-44 | E.C. | 12-9-44 | | | 31-10-44 | [illegible] | [illegible] | | |
| 12-9-44 | M | 18-9-44 | DAKOTA | KG777 | 1-11-44 | E.C. | | | |
| 18-9-44 | GOOSE | 18-9-44 | | | | B. | 29-11-44 | CORONADO | JX494 |
| 18-9-44 | M | 20-9-44 | HUDSON | FK779 | 29-11-44 | TRIN | 3-12-44 | [illegible] | |
| 20-9-44 | N.Y. | 20-9-44 | | | 4-12-44 | NATAL | 4-12-44 | | |
| 20-9-44 | WASH | 20-9-44 | | | 4-12-44 | [illegible] | [illegible] | | K. 11567 REV. |

| LUCK (NAME) | W.F.S. (INITIALS) | (RANK) | RAFTC (SERVICE) | 2 (CATEGORY) | (QUALIFIED TO FLY) |
|---|---|---|---|---|---|

## Acknowledgements

Special thanks were extended to the following in the original book, and they continue here in this new and expanded edition:

From Vernon, BC
Bob Veale, a pilot of fortune in his own right, for technical assistance.
Don McDonell, for his editing help.
Ms. Annie Oakley, for her spot checks.

From Welland, ON
Lillian Zdichavsky, for friendship and financial support to keep on trucking.

From Sarnia, ON
Elynda Bourgeois, who generated a four-key index to more than 550 pages of typed manuscript.

From Fort Erie, ON
Ms. Mabel Harber, for her generous support of this project in the late 1980s, through her son, Ken Harbor.

I also extend a special thank you to my former wife, Laura E.C. McLean-Beaudoin, and our three children, Scott, Jay and Bryce, Lake Country, BC, for their support and patience with me over the years, and helping me complete the original book; it took seven years and seven manuscripts before I could complete the first book to my satisfaction and have Sheldon Luck sign and approve the seventh manuscript of his adventurous biography.

Garry Beck, Jr., Niagara Falls, ON, for computer and programming assistance – April 2008.

James McClelland, Emerson, Manitoba, for personal liaison, and Ferry Command research assistance - from June 2008.

Larry McNally, Archivist, Public Archives of Canada, Ottawa, ON, for assistance in tracking and sending more than 250 pages of Beaudoin – Luck Fonds transcript material original that I had prepared from tape-recorded interviews with Sheldon Luck between 1979 and 1986.

The Public Archives of Canada, Ottawa, ON, for assistance in tracking and transmitting to me 31 never-before –published original black-and-white photographs from Sheldon Luck's private collection.

Linda Roote, Niagara College, Welland, ON, for extraordinary consulting services with computers and programming.
K. Parker Wade, Welland, ON, for general editing and reviewing throughout 2008.

Many men and women across Canada have maintained their faith and trust in me, and extended help in so many ways, since I first began this project in February, 1979. They are too numerous to single out and identify in this book, but they all know who they are.

*– Ted Beaudoin*
*September, 2016*

# Select Bibliography

A History of Prince George - author, publisher unknown

Above and Beyond - The Encyclopedia of Aviation and Space Sciences, 1968; New Horizons Publishers Inc., Chicago, IL, Vol. 1 -18

Air Force Magazine; Air Force Publications Limited, Ottawa, Ontario, summer 1981 (Vol. 5, No. 2)

Air International Magazine - Air Transport in Argentina; October 1966

Air Pictorial Magazine; LA FAMA, London, England, date unknown

Airborne from Edmonton: Eugenie Louise Myles, The Ryerson Press, Toronto, 1959

Alberta Report Magazine: Review on hotels in Edmonton (The Macdonald Hotel), August 9, 1982

Atlantic Bridge - The Story of No. 45 Group, written under a freelance contract issued by England's Ministry of Information to John Pudney who wrote it in Bermuda in 1944 (One of only 500 copies printed)

Royal Air Force, Ferry Command 1945 - The Official Account of Royal Air Force Transport Command's Ocean Ferry, 1945 (Prepared for the Air Ministry by the Ministry of Defense, London, His Majesty's Stationery Office)

Bush Pilot With a Briefcase - The happy-go-lucky story of Grant McConachie, Ronald Keith, 1972; Paperjacks (General Publishing), Toronto, Ontario

Car and Driver (Feb. 1978)

Caledonia Days - Prince George Citizen, BC, and the Caledonia Courier (Fort St. James, BC) - Tues., July 28th, 1970

Canadair 204 - Early prototype of the CL-215 water bomber; Canadair Limited, St. Laurent, Quebec, Canadair Service News: various issues on the Cl-215 - 310

Canada's Aviation Hall of Fame - miscellaneous documents and membership roster booklet; Edmonton, AB

Canada's Flying Heritage: Frank H. Ellis, 1954; University of Toronto Press

Canadian Aviation Magazine: 50th Anniversary of flight issue, June 1978, and other issues 1978-84, inclusive, Toronto

Canadian Geographic Magazine - Norseman (p 28) - date unknown

Canadian Pacific Air Lines Limited, April 1st, 1945: pilots' seniority system list, with notes, 1965

Cariboo Yarns - Fred W. Lindsay (date unknown); B.C. Family Herald and Weekly Star: New Airfields Protect North west Canada, Nov. 12th, 1941

CKUA Radio - Radio script, 1947; Edmonton, AB

CP Air News: Vol. 13, No. 5, 1982

Financial Post: April 11th, 1981

Ferryman: From Ferry Command to Silver City - Air Commodore Griffith 'Taffy' Powell, CBE; Airlife Publishing Ltd., England, 1982

History of RAF 231Squadron - Ministry of Defence, England (Air Historica Branch), August 1959

History of RAF 269 Squadron - Web site: Traces of World War 2, RAF -

No. 269 Squadron, 10/05/1940 - 30/06/1940
*http://www.epibreren.com/ww2/raf/269_squadron.html*
History of the Canadian Pacific Railway: W. Kaye Lamb, 1977;
   Macmillan Publishing Co., Inc., New York
ISASI Bulletin: International Society of Air Safety Investigators (date unknown)
I'll Take the High Road - Sholto Watt, 1960; Brunswick Press, Fredericton,
It Seems Like Only Yesterday: Air Canada, the first 50 years -
   Philip Smith; McClelland and Stewart, 1986
KA'NA'TA: The Magazine of CP Air - The Bush Pilots, Ron Keith, Fall 1980
Maclean's Magazine (Nov. 10, 1976)
Next Stop, Hong Kong, by Frank Hamilton, June 1, 1949
Ocean Bridge - The History of RAF Ferry Command, Carl A. Christie with
   Fred Hatch; University of Toronto Press, Toronto and Buffalo, 1997
Pacific Western Airlines: Annual reports, 1955, 1966
Peace River Chronicles - Vera Kelsey - "Red" Powell and the First Airline -
   1919-1942
Preview Flight - Ronald Keith, Jan. 1, 1942
Saturday Evening Post Magazine, January 1942 - Twenty-Four Hours to Asia;
   Mark and Maxine Finley
Sheldon Luck - A Pilot for All Seasons, by Lynne Schuyler, December 1982
Songs of a Sourdough - Robert W. Service (publisher unknown)
The Bedaux Expedition, Alaska Highway News (Sept. 10, 1959)
The CAHS Journal: Canadian Aviation Historical Society;
   The Saga of the Norseman, Fall 1979
The Canadian Aircraft Operator: Vol. 21, No. 13, July 2, 1984
   Canadian Airmen and the First World War
The Lore of Flight - AB Bordbok, Sweden, Maclean's Magazine, 1974
The Magnificent Distances - Early Aviation in British Columbia, 1910 -1940
   Sound Heritage Series, No. 28, 1980 (Provincial Archives Ministry of
   Provincial Secretary and Government Services
The Military History of World War II - Trevor Nevitt Dupuy, Col.,
   U.S. Army, Ret. (Vol. 1 - 18), 1963
The Official History of the Royal Canadian Air Force, Vol. 1, 1980 -
   University of Toronto Press, in co-operation with the Department of
   National Defense, and the Canadian Govern ment Publishing Centre,
   Supply and Services Canada
The Pathless Way - Justin de Goutiere, 1968; Greydonald Graphics Ltd.,
   West Vancouver, B.C.
The Pony Express - RCMP internal publication, Vol. 9, No. 1, Jan. 1984
The Royal Bank of Canada Monthly Newsletter: Vol. 6, No. 3, March 1980
   (Canada in the Air)
The Unforgettable Grant McConachie - Ron Keith, November 1979:
Franklin Watts Inc. News & Views - Aviation in southern Alberta,
   1927-1939, Summer 1982

## Additional Resources

Public Archives of Canada - Sheldon Luck and Ted Beaudoin
Tape recordings and transcripts - (550+ pages) of interviews and notes with and from Captain Sheldon Luck, Ret.; cablegrams, letters (official and personal) magazine and newspaper clippings.
Log book of the late Reid Bennett, Edmonton, Alberta, navigator on board 231 Squadron's Coronado JX 494, involved in the incident in Nassau

*Welland, Ontario, Canada author Ted Beaudoin has earned two national writing award citations in his career as a writer for various North American electronic and print media – ranging from daily and weekly newspapers to commercial and corporate magazines and radio and television. During all these years, he acquired what he claims is an absolute love of, and fascination for, histories – of all kinds, but especially aviation history. Since he knew he could never fly because of vision problems, he decided years ago to dedicate his writing career to all things aviation, with a special focus on aviation and aviation history – private, military, civilian and commercial.*

www.ingramcontent.com/pod-product-compliance
Lightning Source LLC
Chambersburg PA
CBHW021139080526
44588CB00008B/134